Crime & Exclusion

Crime & Social Exclusion

Edited by

Catherine Jones Finer
and
Mike Nellis

BLACKWELL Publishers

First published as a special issue of *Social Policy & Administration*
Vol. 31, No. 5, December 1997.

Blackwell Publishers
108 Cowley Road, Oxford OX4 1JF, UK
and
350 Main Street,
Malden, MA 02148, USA

British Library Cataloguing in Publication Data

Crime and social exclusion.—(Broadening perspectives on social policy)
1. Marginality, Social   2. Crime—Social aspects   3. Crime—Sociological
   aspects
I. Finer, Catherine Jones   II. Nellis, Mike   III. Social policy &
   administration
364.2'56

Library of Congress Cataloging in Publication Data

Crime and social exclusion/edited by Catherine Jones Finer and Mike Nellis.
    p. cm.—(Broadening perspectives on social policy)
Includes bibliographical references and index.
1. Crime.   2. Marginality, Social.   3. Social isolation.   4. Social policy.
5. Social structure.   I. Finer, Catherine Jones.   II. Nellis, Mike.
III. Social policy & administration.   IV. Series.
HV6030.C715   1998
364.2'5—dc21   98–5166
                                                                   CIP

ISBN 0–631–20912–3

Printed in Great Britain by Whitstable Litho, Kent

Contents

Notes on Contributors

John Clammer is Professor in the Department of Comparative Culture, Sophia University, Tokyo.

David Denney is Senior Lecturer in the Department of Social Policy and Social Science, Royal Holloway College, University of London.

David Donnison is Emeritus Professor at the Centre for Housing Research & Urban Studies, University of Glasgow.

Alan France is Research Fellow in Sociology at the Warwick University.

Tim Hope is Lecturer in the Department of Criminology, Keele University.

Catherine Jones Finer is Reader in Comparative Social Policy at the University of Birmingham and Editor of *Social Policy & Administration*.

Alan Murie is Professor of Urban and Regional Studies and Director of the Centre for Urban and Regional Studies, University of Birmingham.

Mike Nellis is Lecturer in the Department of Social Policy and Social Work at the University of Birmingham.

John Pitts is Professor in the Department of Professional Social Studies, University of Luton.

Andrew Rutherford is Professor in the Faculty of Law, University of Southampton.

David Smith is Professor in the Department of Applied Social Science, Lancaster University.

John Stewart is Lecturer in Applied Social Science at Lancaster University.

Paul Wiles is Professor of Criminology at Sheffield University.

Editorial Introduction

This is the first in a series of special issues of *Social Policy & Administration*, intended to stimulate fresh thinking by bringing a wider range of disciplines and approaches to bear on social policy debate. The idea for the series arose from a perception that social policy was in process of reconstruction. The days of the traditional welfare state subject, so wedded to the study of the statutory social services and so committed in the British case to a redistributive rights-based universalistic vision of the fair(er) society, are behind us. Today's social policy is at once more heterogeneous in its approaches and objectives, and more wide-ranging in its concerns. Hence the intention of this series: to broaden the scope of commentary and discussion by inviting a wider range of contributors and, in so doing, to interest a wider audience in the issues raised.

The choice of "Crime and Social Exclusion" for this first venture was based on three considerations. First, there was the obvious topicality of the subject matter. Crime is on the increase. Levels of public *concern* about crime are on the increase. The postmodern society ("late modern" in the terminology of France and Wiles, below) is perceived as being an increasingly dangerous place in which to live. Second, therefore, the control of delinquency by one means or another has become central to the credibility of the new social policy, which is itself more about managing insecurity than guaranteeing security. Third and finally, since the interests of criminology and social policy have been drawing closer together in recent years, in the area of crime linked to social exclusion, this seemed a sound choice for the first of the new series.

While there is clearly much common ground linking various of the papers presented, they fall into three main groups in terms of principal focus. The first three are about safe and unsafe environments; the next three are variously about the "service requirements" of specific groups or categories of young people especially, experiencing social exclusion; the final three offer different kinds of overview of policy developments writ large.

Our first contributor, David Donnison, is no stranger to social policy debate. He has contributed more than most to the expansion of its interests and perspectives. In this case, taking an "awful warning" from America, he counsels against the "lock-em-up" tendency and considers how, at the level of the local community, people might be helped to feel safer with one another. Alan Murie looks specifically at the association of crime with problem council housing estates and warns that attempted solutions in terms of housing management can be no substitute for investment in housing and associated infrastructure regeneration. John Pitts and Tim Hope then take the theme of the problem estate a stage further in their wide-ranging review which includes a comparison of policies pursued on two such estates, one in Britain and one in France.

Heading the next "group" of papers, Alan France and Paul Wiles tackle the much-neglected subject of youth work, comparing the predicaments and needs of socially-excluded young people today with the kinds of youth service provision developed to meet the needs of a generation ago in conditions of postwar full employment. David Denney explores the problems faced by young blacks in their dealings with the criminal justice system, whether as would-be professionals within it or—more typically—as objects on the receiving end, before offering advice as to how a rights-based approach to equal opportunities and anti-racism could hold out better prospects for the future. David Smith and John Stewart then review the evidence on social exclusion in relation to the caseloads of the probation service and suggest how probation practice might and should be adapted so as to reduce rather than add to "exclusionary pressures".

It is quite a leap from the above papers to Andrew Rutherford's grand sweep through history on the subject of "the eliminative ideal", though much of what he has to say strikes a chord with Donnison's observations at the start of this collection. "Elimination" (taking people out of society) is not the same thing as *extermination*, he argues, though the dividing line between them may be blurred. Certainly his comments on the *eliminatory* use of Nazi concentration camps prior to their *exterminatory* function in the Holocaust is one case example readers may find disturbing. After which, and hardly less disturbing in a different sense, comes John Clammer's devastating, awe-inspiring review of how the business of making and maintaining a society is managed in Singapore, the very place Britain's Tony Blair chose to make his first speech about "stakeholdership". Catherine Jones Finer then concludes this collection by commenting on the new social policy in Britain in the light of trends and issues raised in the foregoing papers.

Catherine Jones Finer
Mike Nellis
Editors

July 1997

Creating a Safer Society

David Donnison

Abstract

In some fields of policy Britain tends to follow the Americans. Will crime prove to be one of them? This chapter begins with an exploration of the sources of American influence, and an account of the disastrous course their penal policies have taken. Thereafter attention focuses on the United Kingdom. It is argued that public concern about crime must be taken seriously. Some have called for a "remoralization" of the debate—more "condemnation", less "understanding". But if our aim is to reduce crime, its economic and social context must first be understood; then changed. Delinquency is only one of several responses which people may make to prolonged hardship and frustration; and not necessarily the most destructive. Drawing on experience in many parts of the country, a programme of action to improve people's safety is proposed. Starting with procedures for consulting and involving people—including those who appear to be the source of trouble—a local strategy is outlined to improve opportunities for making an honest living, to stabilize and strengthen communities, to provide better support for the victims of crime and for the most vulnerable families, and better opportunities for ex-offenders. Police and penal services have an important job to do as mobilizers and managers of a society's responses to crime. But, in a country where only 3 per cent of offences lead to a conviction in court, these services cannot do much to prevent it.

Keywords

Safety; Crime; Economic and social policies

Introduction

In places where a lot of people are having a hard time, surveys questioning them about their hopes for the future show that safety for themselves and their families usually comes second only to opportunities for earning a living in a

Address for Correspondence: *David Donnison, Centre for Housing Research and Urban Studies, 25–28 Bute Gardens, Glasgow, G12 8RS.*

decent job. That may not always have been so. National surveys made over a long period show that anxiety about crime has probably increased even more than crime itself. The proportion of people in Britain saying they feel "very worried" about various kinds of crime rose significantly between 1992 and 1994 (Hough 1995). I shall briefly explore the reasons for that important change in public feeling and its implications. It compels anyone who contributes to debate about public affairs to say where they stand on these matters.

Next I shall consider who suffers most anxiety, and what threats to their security people are most worried about. This is a chapter about safety, not only about crime. Different dangers call for different responses.

Turning to crime, which is a source of many of those dangers, I consider its relationship to the conditions in which people live, and the responses which can be made to it at a local scale of action. The whole argument is then very briefly summarized in the concluding section of the chapter.

But, first of all, we should pause to reflect on the extraordinary things happening in the United States, and consider why that country's experience may be important to us.

The Influence of America

Many people have noted that Britain frequently follows in the footsteps of the United States, but this does not happen in every area of the two nations' lives. If we had a better understanding of why this happens in some areas but not in others we would be better able to foresee social trends and respond to them. But I know of no serious analysis of this question. My own thoughts about it can be no more than speculative. But, for those concerned with crime, the question is sufficiently important to justify some speculation.

Sometimes Britain's adoption of North American practices has simply been a part of a worldwide tendency to follow in that continent's footsteps. Advancing technology and its dissemination usually go far to explain this pattern. It is not surprising that useful things like mass-produced automobiles, central heating, television, freezers and e-mail, first established in the United States, should spread to other countries as soon as they can afford them. American economic and technological leadership may then predispose people to accept further American innovations.

But there are many areas of life within the European nations where the American example has been rejected. Sometimes, indeed, innovation flows in the opposite direction. The provision of medical care and the management of health services; policies for the management of land, the control of development and the provision of public transport; social insurance, social assistance and social security in general: these are among the fields in which many Western countries have gone their own way. Their rejection of the American model seems to be due partly to different social structures, and differing traditions about government and the role of the state; or—to put it another way—to the presence of socialist traditions. Britain, during its recent long spell of Conservative government, has probably been more prone than its

4

neighbours to move some way towards the adoption of American patterns in these fields.

Meanwhile, when it comes to popular culture and politics, the American example has often been very influential. All across the Western world, popular music, films and other art forms, and public concern about human rights—the rights of women, ethnic minorities, lesbians and gays, and people with disabilities—have been massively influenced by American practice.

These patterns suggest that the influence of the United States will be strongest when predisposing factors interlock and reinforce each other. Thus when American technological leadership, in communications and the making of music and films, for example, is used to transmit American popular feelings which have a potentially worldwide resonance, about the rights of women, for example, which are in turn supported by economic changes originating in the United States, such as the spread of modern domestic equipment and easier housekeeping routines, for example, then a powerful tide of economic and social trends is likely to flow outwards to other parts of the developed world.

Are American patterns of crime, American attitudes towards it and American policies for dealing with it likely to be transmitted to other countries by interlocking and reinforcing influences of this kind?

Crime: an American Disaster Area

If the growing anxieties, to be seen in many countries, among people who are becoming more worried about their safety helped politicians to mount effective policies for improving matters, that would be no bad thing. But in the United States these anxieties have led to mounting anger against offenders—a veritable demonization of them—and to savagely punitive policies which send growing numbers to prison for very long periods. That has led the Americans into a major disaster: a very expensive policy which is damaging other more valuable programmes, a policy which has unquestionably failed but is now very difficult to reverse. Too many people have staked too much of their credibility on it.

In Britain there are signs that something similar is happening, as figure 1, showing imprisonment rates in different European countries, suggests. So it is very important to note the key facts before we go further down this road.

- No experiment in public policy has ever been so vigorously and completely carried through as the American adoption of tougher penal policies—and particularly their growing use of imprisonment. The numbers of prisoners in Federal and State prisons in the United States rose from 196,000 in 1974, to 1,100,000 in 1995—more than a five-fold increase. Together with those in local prisons, the Americans have now incarcerated more than a million and a half people. This and most of the following points come from Elliott Currie, one of the USA's most distinguished criminologists (Currie 1996).

5

Figure 1

Prison populations: an international comparison

Rate per 100,000 recorded crimes

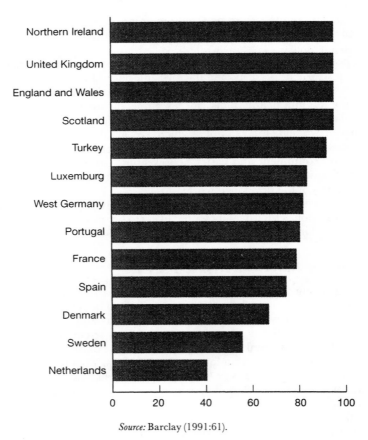

Source: Barclay (1991:61).

- The policy has massive implications for race relations: the increase in the numbers of prisoners has been most rapid among black and Hispanic men and is focused upon places where their communities are most heavily concentrated.
- Federal and State spending on prisons and other "correctional activities" has increased enormously, and most of this money has, in effect, been taken from training schemes, schools, welfare and other services which were among America's most effective crime-prevention programmes.
- "The prison boom has . . . changed what we mean by government. It has made the prison a looming presence in the lives of America's poor . . . " (Currie 1996:7). What has sometimes been called the "war against crime" is also a war of oppression against ethnic minorities. In Baltimore—to take

one example—a majority of young men are black and a majority of those are now in prison, on probation or on parole. Yet the city's homicide rate has increased by 75 per cent since this experiment began—between 1970 and 1994.

- These policies are not intended to work towards closer understanding, integration, reconciliation or mutual respect between offenders and the rest of the community: the traditional objectives of a liberal democratic penal policy. They are intended to punish, to frighten, to deter, and generally to distance and distinguish offenders from others who are regarded as law-abiding citizens. They are archaic.

- These policies have not succeeded in reducing crime. There is no link between trends in crime and high rates of imprisonment in relation to crime. The argument, increasingly heard in Britain, that American experience shows that "prison works" is not true. It is usually based on data for carefully selected cities, time periods and types of offences; and on highly imaginative use of figures for the costs and savings resulting from changes in crime rates. It also neglects the evidence of "victimization" studies, relying instead on dubious official statistics of reported crime rather than the less encouraging experience of representative samples of the population.

Yet there can be no doubt that these policies are popular in the United States, and probably in Britain too. With so much evidence to show that they do not prevent crime there must be other motives at work. They are, in effect, America's main—and very expensive—way of managing unemployment and providing support for the unemployed. The scale of the programme needs to be stressed. Two per cent of American males of working age are now in prison. There are more blacks in jail than in universities, and it costs much more to keep them there. These policies also satisfy the widespread demands of frightened people for revenge. For white people disturbed by the advances made by ethnic minorities over the last 25 years, the fact that these minorities are most likely to be imprisoned may provide further reassurance. Much the same motives are at work in Britain, and some of those who should know better—politicians on both sides, newspaper editors and journalists—are playing to them. When our last prime minister, paving the way for his home secretary to go down this road, said "It is time to understand a little less and to condemn a little more" he was warmly applauded in many quarters.

Why Do We Worry?

So why are people frightened and vengeful? There has indeed been a long-term increase in crime—for many rather obvious reasons. There is far more to steal: television sets and videos in homes which, sixty years ago, had little in them that would have been worth taking; cheque books and credit cards in handbags and pockets which would once have scarcely been worth rifling. Things worth stealing are far more accessible than they used to be: cars left on the street with mobile phones and radios in them; goods displayed, unsupervised, in self-service shops. There are more laws to break, creating new offences associated with car parking, speed limits, insurance contributions, television licences and much else. An increasingly mobile, urban society offers greater privacy and independence, but also more anonymity, less pressure for conventional behaviour, and greater uncertainty about moral standards. The liberation of women from restrictive conventions of the past—their greater freedom to work, to speak to strangers, to go to pubs and on holiday alone—may have deprived them of some of the protection once conferred by seclusion and male inhibitions.

Some of the rising trend in crime figures is due to increased reporting rather than a real growth in crime. People are prepared to protest and to seek the help of the police about many things—theft and burglary, rape and sexual abuse, violence and drunkenness—which used to be concealed, disregarded or dealt with in other ways: not necessarily better ways. The spread of insurance obliges many to report losses, not because they expect redress through the law but in order to make an insurance claim. The rising figures of reported crime may nevertheless alarm people. The fear of crime has increased faster than crime itself, and this has sometimes been attributed to the sensational treatment given to frightening forms of crime by the media. But the media operate in a market. If they devote space to news of this kind, their readers and viewers presumably want them to do so.

Both crime and the fear of it may have increased because we live in an increasingly private society in which we are less likely than our predecessors to get to know our neighbours. We drive to work, to school and to the shops in our cars instead of walking or queuing for the bus; we shop once a week in vast, impersonal supermarkets instead of making more frequent visits to gossip with neighbours in the local corner shop; we shelter behind front doors and garden fences instead of meeting our neighbours on the tenement stairs; and we are more likely to bring beer home in a six pack to drink in front of the television set, less likely to drink with friends in the pub. Traffic hazards and other dangers mean that our children are much less likely than their parents were to be allowed to roam the streets, and we have all become less likely to go to church, to political meetings, to street markets, cinemas, music halls and other public places where we might get to know our fellow citizens, or at least to feel at home in their presence. The characters in television programmes like *Neighbours* become more familiar to us than our real neighbours, and the sense that we are members of some larger civic society fades. The feeling that there is a growing social distance between the average car-driving, house-buying citizen and the people without cars and with no opportunity to buy their own homes is real—and well founded, at least in terms of income differences and the growing tendency of these people to live in separate neighbourhoods.

Paradoxically, the barriers we have erected between us and the rest of the world mean that we feel more exposed to strangers. In country places it may be different, but in the cities where most of us live the people in the street, the supermarket, the next car fuming at the traffic lights and the queues in the social security office are all likely to be completely unknown to us. And strangers are potentially menacing. Fear then becomes cumulative: if others fear us, they are more likely to behave in ways which make us fear them.

The growing numbers of elderly people in the population may also increase anxiety levels because it is older people—and particularly those living in inner city areas—who are most likely to feel unsafe. That is not because they are most likely to be attacked—it is young men in these neighbourhoods who are most likely to become victims of violence—but because they feel most vulnerable. Ethnic minorities, particularly Asians, feel more worried about crime and more unsafe in the streets at night than white people, as figure 2 shows.

Figure 2

Variations in anxiety by ethnic origin

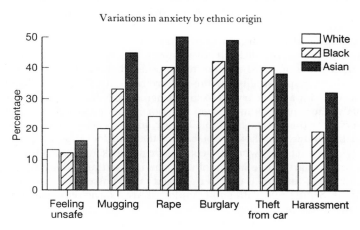

Notes
Weighted data. Source:1994 British Crime Survey.
$N = 11,500$ (core sample)
Chart shows percentages feeling "very worried" except for question on safety, which shows the percentage "very unsafe".
Source: Hough (1995:18).

Findings like these led many to believe that fear of crime is a problem in itself, only loosely related to the real risks involved. Those most afraid of it tend to be worried about a lot of other things too. Perhaps they are just anxious people, needing reassurance rather than protection? But more recent studies tend to discredit this rather paternalistic view. They show that anxiety is fairly closely linked to vulnerability, which is different from risk; they show that a lot of disturbing things happen to women owing to male behaviour which often falls short of recordable crime; and they show that worried people often have a lot to worry about—poverty, insecure jobs, illness in the family and responsibilities for children, as well as living in rather intimidating neighbourhoods. So people's feelings must be taken seriously.

Moral Standards

Before considering how to respond to these anxieties, we should frankly confront John Major's admonition to understand less and condemn more.

9

What should we make of that? Crime is behaviour which damages other people, showing no respect for fellow human beings. So it should of course be condemned and—more important—reduced. But that means we also need to understand it. We cannot choose between the two reactions: they have to advance together.

If my analysis in the previous paragraphs is correct, any response to crime and the fear of it must include an attempt to rebuild a stronger sense of community—greater confidence between citizens of the same town, and the people living in the same street or block of flats. This is the setting which creates and sustains the culture within which moral standards take root and gain strength.

Any initiative of that kind must include action which returns powers to a democratically accountable local government. The systematic transfer of local government functions and powers to nominated, unaccountable, specialist bodies with no responsibility for the welfare of a city as a whole has been a major obstacle for anyone trying to strengthen civic culture and identity.

People's places of work have been a major influence in behaviour. If their employers treat them as expendable labour, to be casually hired and fired as demand fluctuates, we should not expect them to feel much loyalty to the enterprises in which they work. If people have no work at all, then they have no opportunity to participate in one of the principal settings where standards of behaviour have in the past been forged and passed on to succeeding generations. Secure jobs with good employers are a basic requirement for self-respect and crime prevention.

We must deflate the pomposity of so much talk about crime. Moral standards are important, but we are all involved in them. Crime is not "out there", among an "underclass" of menacing strangers. In Britain, one man in three is found guilty of a "standard list offence" before the age of 35, and, if driving offences are added, the great majority of men have been found guilty of offences by then (Barclay *et al.* 1993). For every transaction in the "informal" economy where goods and services are exchanged for cash out of the back pocket, there are customers as well as suppliers. For illicit workers concealing earnings from the social security and tax offices there are usually illicit employers—probably paying low wages and no insurance contributions. Surveys show that most people believe that most people steal things from work—and since making occasional telephone calls on private matters from your employer's phone is theft, that is certainly true of most university teachers, civil servants and other office workers. Most people say they would keep money picked up in the street if there were no danger of being found out. (National Association for the Care and Resettlement of Offenders 1995:8). We all live in a grey world of uncertain virtue.

How we behave in that world depends heavily on the culture in which we live, the opportunities it affords and the pressures it imposes on us. There are always a few individuals who carve out their own destiny without much regard to others' expectations. But for most of us it is harder to keep to the speed limit when every other driver around us is exceeding it, to stay sober in a drunken party, to protest at racist or sexist jokes when everyone else is roaring with laughter at them. When your infant child comes tearfully home saying, "I don't want to go to school any more: there's a boy in the playground who keeps hitting me," how do you respond? Do you say: "Keep away from him, and if he does it again talk to the teacher. I'm sure she'll sort it out"? Or do you say: "If he does it again, roll your fingers up into a hard ball like this, and hit him so hard that he leaves you alone"? Your choice will probably depend on your guesses about the community in which your child has to survive, and about the character of its leaders, the teachers. It is hard to be non-violent in a violent world.

Take a more complex example. I once worked in a housing estate where the flats had underfloor electric heating systems so expensive to use that no mother living on income support payments could keep her child warm and healthily fed and clothed without running into debt. Most of the mothers living in these flats were lone parents living on income support. Some of them, thanks to the help of friends and relatives and to their own remarkable housekeeping skills, cared beautifully for their children and kept within the law. But it is not surprising that the estate had a rather large number of illicitly bypassed electricity meters, a lot of women who were concealing part-time earnings —and part-time men—from social security officials, a thriving market in drugs, and, in the shopping centre, a good deal of shoplifting. All of which is crime. And all of it will tend to increase as the reduction in benefits for lone parents begins to bite. This estate also had a lot of children with bronchial troubles, running ears and other signs of poverty. Since even the families who avoided all these things depended on friends and neighbours who were involved in crime, few people in these streets were prepared to speak to police officers or anyone else in authority. They would lose their friends if they did so. Thus what could be called a criminal subculture developed. It was criminal for sure: but was it as wicked as that kind of jargon suggests? If the alternative to this lifestyle is to see your child underfed or freezing cold, would that be better? For whom?

Morality in this neighbourhood was not being abandoned; it was changing. These were resolute and loyal women, honest in their fashion. Keeping their children healthy and happy became their first obligation, an obligation well understood by their friends and neighbours. If we deplore such a life—as these women certainly did—then we must change the circumstances which create it. If we do nothing, we are not entitled to preach sermons at those involved in it. Nor would there be any point in doing so.

This does not mean that personal choices are impossible or personal example unimportant. They can exert a big influence—particularly when they come from the top. In the United States the Treadway Commission (1987) reporting on financial fraud stated that the "most important factor" reducing fraud is "a visible interest by management and directors in ethical behaviour and strong controls" which will "permeate the organization and limit the risk that fraud will occur" (quoted in National Association for the Care and Resettlement of Offenders 1995:10). The Nolan Committee in Britain had similar things to say about Standards in Public Life.

Towards a Strategy

Before turning to consider action we must clarify aims and purposes. Why write a chapter about safety and crime? Why take so many of the examples used in it from poverty-stricken neighbourhoods? And why say so little about the crimes of richer people? Not because "the perishing and dangerous classes"—as our Victorian forebears used to call the poor—are mainly responsible for crime. But because people having a hard time say they are worried about these things and want something done about them. Because poorer people and ethnic minorities are more often victims of crime and "incivility" of various kinds than richer white people are, and such things happen more often in the neighbourhoods where they live. Because crime and the fear of it play an important part in dividing society by encouraging hostile, uncaring, punitive feelings between groups, neighbourhoods and social classes. And because influential people in this country are already tempted to follow the American lead which excludes and demonizes poorer people, lone parents and ethnic minorities, and diverts resources from the services on which they depend to programmes which oppress and humiliate them.

When, a few years ago, Scotland's Central Regional Council asked their citizens what they most wanted of their local government, greater security came high among the responses. Other authorities which had found the same pattern of opinion had focused at once upon crime; but the Region asked further questions about safety. What were people most worried about? The answers showed a wide variety of fears which varied from place to place. In some a polluting industry was the main source of anxiety. In others it was traffic dangers. "Galloping horses" was the answer given in one village. "You're pulling our leg!" was the Region's first response to this—but no: there was a riding school down the road. Crime and "incivilities"—noise, graffiti, litter and so on—often ranked high, but these problems, too, varied from place to place. A conference was called to discuss the problems of each area, and to mobilize the support of local communities and the help of services best equipped to tackle these problems – public health, traffic management, schools, housing, parks, refuse collection and so on.

I tell this story as a reminder that we must never assume, when people worry about their safety, that we know what the problem is. We must start by listening to them and gaining their help in working out solutions. Listening to the people who are said to be the source of the problem is as important as listening to those who feel themselves to be innocent victims. Another example from this Region may help.

The police were receiving a steadily-growing number of telephone calls from people complaining about disturbances on the street. The callers were typically old people, living in the less popular public housing estates, who complained about young people drinking, shouting, breaking down garden fences, obstructing entry to local shops and generally behaving in intimidating ways. The police responded to all these calls but usually found that no offence was being committed, so they could only tell the youngsters to move on— which set phones ringing from further down the road. When these calls reached 5,000 a year they resolved to look for more constructive responses.

One of these was called the Crosstalk project. First the complainers are invited to a meeting with their local councillor, a local police officer and a community worker from the Chief Executive's Department. The three listen for about half an hour to a torrent of anger: the youngsters are "animals", "disgusting", should be "kicked out". There should be "a policeman on the beat" all the time. Then the official visitors say, each in their own words, that they understand how angry these elderly people must be, but they can offer them no extra police, no new resources . . . the problem is *theirs*. But they may be able to help them to work on it, as others have done in similar places. Another meeting is then arranged. This brings older residents and youngsters together with the same councillor and officials, led by a young actor from a well-known Scottish drama company who has been brought in to help. He plays lively party games with them which compel the old and the young to give up sitting on opposite sides of a circle glowering at each other, get thoroughly mixed up and learn the first names of everyone around the circle. There's a good deal of laughter and everyone gradually relaxes. Then old and young are put together again in small groups of their own age, and told to form "living statues" – clustered figures representing "youth" and "old age", each portraying the other age group. Next they are asked to "turn the volume up" and talk about their stereotypes of the other age group. Questions posed in this way are discussed. "Who thinks cannabis should be legal?" "Why?"

After an hour of this, the councillor and officials, who have been vigorously playing these games along with everyone else, begin talking to the whole group, reminding them that in future the youngsters will still be on the streets and some of them will still get drunk. But they will know the old people and appreciate how intimidating their behaviour can seem to them; and the old people will know the youngsters and appreciate that no one is going to hurt them. " . . . Shall we see how things go?"

These meetings have brought the numbers of phone calls a long way down. The police recognize that they will have to do the same thing again from time to time, but believe this will be a more efficient way of using their time than chasing telephoned complaints. Similar mediation schemes have been developed in many other places, with help from NACRO, SACRO its Scottish counterpart, Crime Concern, the Safe Neighbourhoods Unit and other bodies. The most successful of them call for the training of well-respected local people as mediators, so that when the immediate problems have been resolved the community is left better equipped to tackle such problems in future.

Different tactics will be needed in different places. But the principles of the Crosstalk strategy may still have something to offer. Listen to the people who are frightened. Get to those who make the trouble and listen to them too: unless their behaviour begins to change, the problems can only be shifted from street to street. Bring both groups together in ways which defuse tension and make it easier for them to talk honestly to each other. Where community has broken down, help local people to recreate it. When things go wrong, help them to recognize that the problem is theirs. Others can help them to tackle it, but there is no big daddy in the wings who can stride in and tell everyone to be good boys. Civic leaders wise and brave enough to tell their constituents these things play a crucial part in the story. But it is not every kind of conflict which can be addressed in this way: party games with an actor will not prevent knee-capping in Belfast or battles for drug-dealing territory in Manchester's Moss Side.

We should try to understand what life is like in places where there is a lot of crime, and a lot of poor people who have been excluded from the mainstream of their society. A diffuse kind of anger washes around many of these neighbourhoods—and with good reason. If you doubt that, imagine yourself to be an 18-year-old with no qualifications that count for anything, no prospects of ever getting a decent job, little prospect of being able to support a family or of finding a mate capable of doing so, no prospect of ever driving your own car or motor bike or even your employer's van, unable even to walk to the other end of the housing estate without exposing yourself to the danger of abuse and attack from the youngsters who live beyond the frontiers of your territory. Exclusion is not just a figure of speech.

People cannot go on being angry for long. As individuals and as whole communities they tend to move out of anger in one of three directions, illustrated in figure 3. Many become depressed and eventually sink into

Figure 3

Responses to Prolonged stress

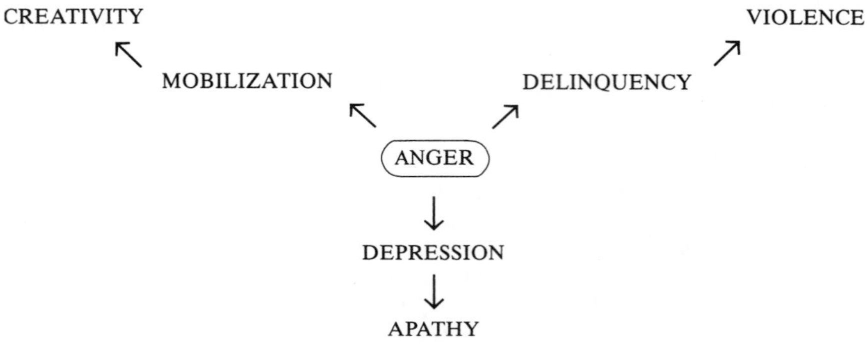

Source: Derived from Carmichael (1991:71).

apathy. Nothing matters much any more. Knock on their doors and invite them to meetings about the future of their estate, invite them to their doctor's surgeries for free screening tests to protect them from life-threatening disease, invite them to the local school pageant—they don't come. They may sink further into dependency on alcohol, into mental breakdown and domestic violence, which tends to rise when incomes fall. They may become very expensive to their city through the costs of illness, family break-up and child neglect. But they do not make trouble for those who manage the city's affairs. They don't turn out for demonstrations and sit-ins or ask rude questions from the back of the hall. And they certainly don't riot.

Others move out of anger into minor delinquency and may eventually go on to more serious crime and violence. They may steal from shops, and break into cars, homes and local workshops; if they become seriously hooked on expensive drugs they may have to work harder at these things to feed their habit; they may begin to deal in drugs and to fight over territory for that purpose. They may find a place in criminal "industries"—money-lending and the policing of repayments to lenders, extortion, pimping and so on. These people cause a lot of trouble to their neighbours, to local enterprises and the authorities responsible for law enforcement, and many of them eventually become residents of our very expensive prisons. But they don't disturb the power structure in any way. Indeed, for politicians who gain a reputation, deserved or not, for being "tough on crime", they may be an electoral asset.

A third group mobilize and organize themselves—and sometimes their communities too—for purposeful action. They may get some training, find jobs and eventually move out to more attractive neighbourhoods. They may, with their neighbours, protest, march, sit-in, nominate candidates for local elections. They may set up tenants' associations, housing co-operatives, drama groups, youth clubs and so on. Some of these people are a thorn in the flesh of those who hold power. They compel them to come to meetings, held at unsocial hours, which go on much too long, and expose them to aggressive questioning and noisy protests. But they may also set going all sorts of creative things which would never have found a place within the conventional bureaucratic system. There are many examples. The Women's College and its offshoots, set up in Castleford by miners' wives after the collapse of the miners' strike, was a celebration of the human capacity to mobilize in the face of disaster. The marvellous mosaic, made by local people, which is spread along two walls in Glasgow's Easterhouse estate is another. The Credit Unions, now being set up at a rate of about one a week in many of the poorest neighbourhoods of Britain provide further examples (Hugill 1996).

These are not the only responses available. In parts of Northern Ireland where people are united by culture and an ideology of revolt, exclusion from the wider society has produced what amounts to a rising which provokes counter-risings in other communities within the same cities. These share some of the characteristics of more creative mobilizations (the political ideology, the mutual support, the community enterprises and Gaelic classes . . .) and some of the characteristics of the delinquent option (extortion, robbery, money-laundering, knee-capping, terror . . .), but they should not be equated with either. Riots elsewhere in the United Kingdom have occasionally had a brief flash of the same purposeful anger—but very brief.

Sometimes it is difficult to decide which of these responses is the dominant one. When tenants in the Hume housing estate threw bags of cockroaches across the counters of the Housing Department which had failed, despite all their protests, to get the vermin out of their flats, some said that was protest and others called it delinquency—depending on which side of the counter they were standing. (This categorization of responses to exclusion is developed from an analysis by Carmichael (1991:71.))

These are some of the conclusions I draw from this analysis. We need to understand individual and collective motives, and the interaction between them. By themselves, neither psychology nor sociology are enough. People do not only respond in negative ways to hardship. They may also respond bravely and creatively. Their capacity to seize creative options depends both on the character of the local community—its traditions, stability, leadership and much else—and on the response they get from people in the power structure. I have been moved by the number of community activists who have, somewhere in their family, a radical tradition to draw on—a father who was an active trade unionist or an uncle who fought in Spain—and I have been concerned that the spread of unemployment, and the decay of trade unions and radical movements mean that these traditions of solidarity and collective action may be dying. Meanwhile, unless they are given continuing advice and support by one or two politicians and officials, community-based projects in deprived areas rarely prosper for long. If civic leaders respond destructively—giving no straight answers, postponing meetings, sending to each one a different official who never has authority to decide anything—they can drive people back into angry cynicism and depression from which it will be harder, next time, to escape. Civic leaders and their officials play vital roles. They need to understand that anger and delinquency are only two responses within a larger array of reactions to exclusion, and not the most destructive ones. People cannot move out of depression and apathy except through anger. Once angry, they may be capable of moving on to more hopeful things. Delinquency is painful for a lot of people, but its perpetrators are at least alive—capable of doing something for themselves—and if people with something more constructive to offer can get alongside them they may move on to more creative things.

Local Action

Faced with crime and frightening behaviour, people tend—individually, collectively and in our Parliament—to call for the police. (It probably goes back to childhood: "Dad, Dad, there's a boy hitting me! Come and help me!") Public debate about crime leads quickly to discussion of policing, courts, prisons and the whole clanking penal apparatus. That debate is often couched in terms of a militaristic kind which distance us from the criminals and make it impossible to consider the causes of their behaviour. Ministers, opposition spokesmen, editors, pundits of every kind, call for "crackdowns" in the "war against crime", more police "in the front line", "toughness" of every kind, to be directed against enemies demonized as "squeegee merchants", "aggressive beggars", "muggers", "animals", "beasts"—a rising scream of hate.

Before engaging in this war dance of vengeance, let us reflect on one figure. Of all the offences committed in the United Kingdom this year, only three in a hundred will lead to a conviction in court (Barclay 1991:31). Figure 4, derived from the British Crime Survey, which starts by seeking the experience of victims of crime, shows how few offences resulted in police cautions or court convictions. The average criminal tends to have a rather poorly developed capacity for planning his future, and great confidence that he will escape the consequences of his actions. At this rate of conviction he will probably be justified—at least for a long time. Police and the whole criminal justice system play very important parts in helping our society to manage crime and its consequences, after it has taken place, but they do very little to prevent it. Those who argue that higher conviction rates would be a more effective deterrent than harsher punishments are right—but only because harsher punishment is so ineffective. We can scarcely expect conviction rates to

Figure 4

What happens to offenders: attrition within the criminal justice system

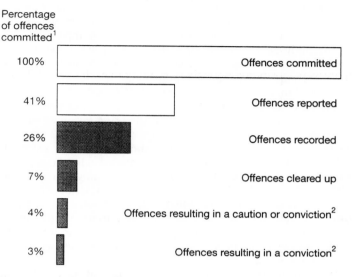

Percentage
of offences
committed[1]

100%	Offences committed
41%	Offences reported
26%	Offences recorded
7%	Offences cleared up
4%	Offences resulting in a caution or conviction[2]
3%	Offences resulting in a conviction[2]

Crime Surveys suggest that about 3 in 100 offences committed resulted in a criminal conviction and 4 in 100 in an offender being convicted or cautioned.

Notes
Criminal damage; theft of a motor vehicle; theft from a motor vehicle; theft in a dwelling; bicycle theft; burglary; wounding; robbery; sexual offences and theft from the person.
Estimates include additional findings of guilt at any court appearance and offences taken into consideration

Source: P. Mayhew et al. (1989), The 1988 British Crime Survey (Home Office Research Study No. 111) and Criminal Statistics, England and Wales, London: HMSO.

double. Even if that impossible feat was achieved, a 6 per cent chance of conviction would not deter many of those undeterred by the present rate. So, to reduce crime, other strategies are needed.

Elsewhere, I have written about the parts which mainstream services of every kind can play in resisting and reducing the social divisions which help to cause many kinds of crime (Donnison 1997). Here I lay out a broad strategy which provides a framework for that discussion. It deals briefly with: (a) the labour market, (b) urban regeneration, (c) policies for family support, (d) opportunities for ex-offenders, and (e) support for potential and actual victims of crime.

The strategy must start with the labour market. Nine out of ten crimes deal with property: burglary, theft, stealing from cars and so on (Criminal Statistics, England and Wales). These crimes have, since 1970, been related to long-term unemployment among young men. The relationship is not a simple matter of cause and effect. High unemployment erodes stability, social order and family life in many communities. Property crimes are also related to changes in consumption: as consumption falls, people are more likely to steal. The quality of jobs matters too: poor-quality jobs are not much better than unemployment as preventers of crime, and there are more of them about when unemployment is high. Before 1970, when there was less long-term unemployment and fewer people without hope for the future, the relationship between crime and unemployment was less clearly marked (for a discussion of the relationship between crime, employment and unemployment, see Downes 1993). Crimes of violence account for only 6 per cent of British crimes. Violent crimes in public places, which are often related to alcohol, increase in more prosperous times, but domestic violence moves in the opposite direction, rising when incomes are falling.

Strategies for improving economic opportunities will exert the most powerful immediate influence on crime rates. People who claim to be working to reduce crime without doing anything about unemployment or the quality of jobs at the lower end of the labour market are, at best, ignorant.

Policies which help to stabilize life and improve services in hard-pressed communities with high crime rates can exert an important influence on safety and crime. The programmes mounted for these purposes under the Single Regeneration Budget and the Scottish Partnership Schemes are an advance on previous schemes of this kind—Educational Priority Areas, Enterprise Zones, Estate Action projects, Housing Action Trusts and so on—because they involve more services and a somewhat more determined attempt has been made to involve local people. But they still focus on a few fairly small patches of the map for limited periods of time. More extensive and lasting programmes will be needed. They should include steps, taking in consultation with local people, to make neighbourhoods safer.

The quality of family life plays a major part in determining how safe our society will be. There is a great deal of evidence to show that family breakdown is related to delinquency, but the relationship is not a simple one: breakdown is apt to be related to unemployment and poverty, which make it harder for parents to cope with crises. Lone parents are far more likely to be poor, but children in families with step-parents often do less well than those in lone parent families. Some of the action to which these findings point—such as the restoration of benefit cuts which have penalized teenagers and helped to bring about an increase in homelessness among them—has to be taken at a national level. But local action will be needed to provide the consistent support for families in difficulty and the good child-care, pre-school education and community services for children and young people which have proved cost-effective in reducing crime.

Police forces can play an important part in preventing crime—not by mounting aggressive crackdowns but by identifying the problems which generate trouble in their area and mobilizing appropriate responses from public, private, voluntary and community-based initiatives.

Probation, prison and other penal services do not have a very encouraging record as preventers of crime. Meanwhile, the parts of the prison experience which do seem to offer hope, such as the education service, are being squeezed out by a system compelled, as numbers increase, to focus on quantity rather than quality. More important still are the opportunities open to prisoners when they have completed their sentences. Training and placement schemes for ex-offenders are difficult to extend while jobs are scarce for so many other people. But they must be given high priority by employers and by any administration, central or local, which is seriously determined to reduce crime. Northern Ireland has the most urgent version of this problem. More than half its large prison population now consists of people sentenced for "political" offences related to the troubles of the last quarter century. Now the peace process has resumed, all of these prisoners will be hoping for release. The opportunities for work and a normal life then open to them will go far to determine how long the process lasts.

This analysis, like most discussion of crime, has dealt mainly with offenders—potential, current and recent. So it is important to remember that the victims of crime need help too. Prompt action may be needed to provide support for victims—but not in the fairly insensitive ways which have been reported after the recent disaster in Dunblane. People suffering shock and injury need comfort offered in ways which help them to retain control of their situation.

Mediation and restitution schemes which bring offender and victim face to face, where each agrees to that, have helped victims by giving them a stronger sense that justice has been done. People who feel particularly vulnerable should be put in touch with support groups or helped to form them where they do not exist. They may include women exposed to domestic violence, children suffering from sexual abuse at home or from bullying at school, people living in old people's homes or in homes for those with learning difficulties. Each need expert help from resolute groups familiar with their situation. Neighbourhood groups living in places particularly vulnerable to crime can be given greater safety and confidence through schemes which seek their help in redesigning buildings and public places, and organizing mutually supportive collective action.

Conclusions

Many people feel that the world has become a more dangerous place than it used to be. Whether that is true or not, the feelings are real enough and political leaders must respond to them in some way if they are to retain credibility. But they will not be trusted for long unless they can respond effectively and honestly. The assumptions that these fears arise only from crime, that criminals are an alien, hostile form of life, not human beings much like everyone else, that they will be deterred from crime by punishment and that imprisonment is the most effective of these punishments—every one of these is mistaken. When offered to us by Ministers and senior spokesmen for the opposition, who are advised by some of the best research groups in the land, these assumptions are also dishonest—for they know very well that they are untrue. Truth—and indeed crime prevention—are not the names of the games they are playing.

This is a hard message for civic leaders. It calls for a wiser understanding of the threats to our security and a capacity sometimes to challenge senior people in their own parties. We must condemn behaviour which shows no respect for other people. But we shall not stop it unless we also try to understand why it happens. Understanding and effective action, theory and practice, have to go together.

That compels us, first, to explore the threats to their safety which most worry people. They vary from place to place and from group to group. The first task of the security services is to mobilize from the community, the private sector and the public services the best response they can collectively muster to these dangers—and that will be a different response in each place.

Turning to crime, which will certainly be one of the sources of danger, our response must start by recognizing that only 3 per cent of the offences committed in Britain this year will lead to a conviction in court. Police, prisons, judges—all the "forces" of law and order—play important parts in every society's procedures for managing crime after it has occurred. They do not—they cannot, by themselves—prevent it. To do that we must:

- recognize that crime, like law-abiding behaviour, arises from the circumstances in which people live, the kinds of community they participate in at home and at work, and the kinds of family life which these communities support;
- involve those most likely to be victims of crime, listen to what they say, and do our best to offer them greater security and better ways of protecting themselves;
- offer potential offenders and their parents a better start in life which helps to set good moral standards and makes it easier for them to live by these standards;
- ensure that everyone can find legitimate ways of making an honest and decent living;
- treat convicted offenders in ways which make it easier, not harder, for them to find a way back into law-abiding lives—particularly by ensuring they have opportunities for work; and
- call upon leading politicians and others who should be among the most respected figures in the land to set standards of behaviour which all can follow.

That is a formidable agenda. But nothing less will make an adequate response to the fears of an increasingly anxious society. If we do not make progress in these directions our leaders are likely to be driven by a combination of factors—rising unemployment, declining wages at the lower end of the labour market, rising crime and growing public anger—down the destructive, dead-end road the Americans have taken.

Notes

This chapter is based on another which appears in Donnison (1997).

Much of the evidence and many of the proposals briefly deployed in this Chapter are set out at greater length in the NACRO Report on *Crime and Social Policy*, and in the

Morgan Report on *Safer Communities: the Local Delivery of Crime Prevention Through the Partnership Approach*, London, Standing Conference on Crime Prevention, Home Office, 1991.

References

Barclay, Gordon (ed.) (1991), *A Digest of Information on the Criminal Justice System*, London: Home Office.

Barclay, G. C., *et al.* (eds) (1993), *Information on the Criminal Justice System in England and Wales*, London: Home Office.

Carmichael, Kay (1991), *Ceremony of Innocence*, London: Macmillan.

Criminal Statistics, England and Wales, London: HMSO (annual).

Currie, Elliott (1996), *Is America Really Winning the War on Crime and Should Britain Follow its Example?*, London: National Association for the Care and Resettlement of Offenders,

Donnison, David (1997), *Policies for a Just Society*, London: Macmillan.

Downes, David (1993), *Employment Opportunities for Offenders*, London: Home Office.

Hough, Michael (1995), *Anxiety About Crime: Findings from the 1994 British Crime Survey*, London: Home Office Research Study 147.

Hugill, Barry (1996), Report in the *Observer*, 11 August, p. 18.

National Association for the Care and Resettlement of Offenders (1995), *Crime and Social Policy*, London: NACRO.

Linking Housing Changes to Crime

Alan Murie

Abstract

Housing figures prominently in debates about crime in Britain. It has become commonplace to comment on the increasing associations between crime and council housing. This paper explores some of the issues which link housing and crime. It argues that it is important to recognize how the social base and geography of housing have changed and to understand processes which lead to an increasing concentration in council housing of those with least choice in the housing market and fewest resources elsewhere. At the same time there is a danger in overstating the associations between crime and council housing and neglecting other associations with housing, and homelessness. In view of the associations between crime and council housing, considerable effort has been expended on developing management and other responses designed to reduce crime. The general view is that a broad approach is required in such initiatives and the limited research evidence does not suggest that housing management action alone is effective in reducing crime. The association which exists between council housing and crime requires a policy response which relates to why the most deprived sections of the community are increasingly concentrated in parts of the housing market and exposed to increased risks, and one which relates to the pattern of opportunities and choices in the housing system and not just to housing management.

Keywords

Crime; Housing; Residualization; Polarization

Introduction

Media and other images of crime in contemporary Britain are generally associated with particular areas of housing. They are in particular associated with large mass council estates and form part of the stereotypes and moral panic associated with council housing. They are also associated with inner-city areas of multiple occupation and with homelessness and hostel accom-

Address for Correspondence: *Alan Murie, Centre for Urban and Regional Studies, University of Birmingham, Edgbaston, Birmingham, B15 2TT.*

modation. These images receive some support from the key statistics on crime. It is apparent that council estates are exposed to the highest risks of property crime, that they are associated with high offender rates and that they, and areas of multi-occupation, are high offence-attracting areas. It is possible that in this the impact of housing policy is wholly benign or that housing estates and housing neighbourhoods are merely the passive receptacles for processes and activities that are determined elsewhere. However, as in relation to other debates about the interaction between housing, neighbourhood and other processes, it is much more likely that housing policy and housing processes themselves contribute to the incidence of crime.

In this paper it is argued that an essential backdrop to understanding crime in contemporary British society is an understanding of the way in which the housing market has developed and changed and operates. Understanding changes in housing is a prerequisite for an adequate understanding of issues related to neighbourhood concentrations of offences and offenders. An understanding of the housing dimension is not sufficient and needs to be integrated with perspectives from elsewhere. However it is an important part of the overall picture.

After a brief review of some of the statistical evidence related to crime and housing areas, the paper focuses upon the emerging pattern of differentiation within the housing market and the changing concentration of deprived groups, especially in council estates. It discusses the arguments that this contributes to a downward spiral in certain neighbourhoods. Finally there is a discussion of the extent to which housing policies and housing management interventions can be developed as a response to the problems observed.

Crime and the Problem Estate

The increasing associations between crime and council housing have generated a number of studies in recent years (Foster and Hope 1993; Department of the Environment 1993; Barke and Turnbull 1992). The most immediate reason for this increased interest is the evidence of the concentration of crime in council estates. The 1988 British Crime Survey showed that households in council tenure faced over twice the risk of burglary of those in owner occupation—92 burglaries or attempted burglaries per thousand households (weighted data) compared with 44 in owner occupation. The greater crime risk faced by council tenants was largely associated with neighbourhoods that were predominantly of council tenure. Council tenants in predominantly non-council areas faced a burglary rate of around the national average but those on predominantly council estates faced much higher levels of crime (Hope and Hough 1988). Even between estates which are predominantly council-owned, there is a considerable variation in crime risk. The British Crime Survey showed that households in council tenure, living in areas of majority council tenure and with the highest levels of poverty, faced a risk of burglary around five times greater than tenants who live in areas where council housing is not the majority and where tenants are better off. At the same time residents of poor council areas were twice as likely to be very worried about becoming victims of burglary in the coming year, as those in better off areas.

23

The residents of council estates which are poor, both in the quality of their environment and dwellings and in terms of their circumstances, are more likely to be victimized by crime than residents of other types of neighbourhood. They are more worried about becoming victims of burglary, and problems such as graffiti, litter and noise from neighbours are much more commonly referred to. Significantly more residents in the "poorer" council areas (52%), believe that most burglaries are committed by fellow residents, than is the case among council tenants living in areas which are not predominantly of council housing (29%). In this context Foster and Hope (1993) also note that research in British cities suggests a strong correlation between the proportion of known offenders in residential areas (the offender rate) and the rates of victimization (the offence rate). The highest rates of both fall within the council sector and offenders living in poorer areas are more likely to offend in areas of similar or lesser social status and particularly in their own area.

Foster and Hope go on to indicate that further analysis of the British Crime Survey shows that overall the victims of most offences are concentrated in relatively few residential areas and particularly that the victims of the more serious offences, such as theft from the person, robbery and burglary are more likely to be found in inner-city areas, including the poorest council estates. In summary, the residents of these areas face a greater risk of being victimized from crime, particularly in the home environment than people living elsewhere, and a disproportionate amount of known victimization occurs there. The conclusion drawn from these analyses is that, both to relieve the burden of crime for these residents, and to reduce the level of victimization overall, there is merit in targeting crime preventative action on the poorest council estates.

These basic propositions about the association between crime and council housing highlight the need to understand what has happened within housing policy and the housing system in order to generate this effect. The situation has not always existed. The affluent working-class neighbourhoods which made up much of council housing in the interwar and postwar years were not associated with crime and social disorganization. Rather, it was the declining inner-city neighbourhoods with deteriorating private rented housing, high levels of turnover and lack of social cohesion that were associated with crime. Problem estates were associated with periods of slum clearance and particular estates developed poor reputations associated with clearance or with dwelling types (see e.g. English 1979; Gill 1977). In these estates there was a cumulative process through which neighbourhoods gained a poor reputation and households which regarded themselves as respectable or were regarded by allocating officers as respectable, preferred not to live there. If they lived there they moved out; if they were offered houses in those estates they refused them. Leaving this aside, the general image of predominantly council areas was of stable neighbourhoods of respectable employed working-class families. The informal and formal processes of social control operating in these communities were often linked to family and kinship networks and workplace relationships. In estates with a dominant local employer, neighbours also often worked together. They were often members of the same trades union, and the disciplines and relationships associated with work spilled over into the organization of neighbourhoods.

The association of crime with council housing is then not inherent in council housing provision and requires some explanation in terms of the changing role of council housing and the differentiation of the council housing sector. However, before exploring this aspect more fully, it is important to offer a cautionary note about the association between council housing and crime. There is a danger that the plethora of statistics which demonstrate this lead to neglect of other dimensions of crime. One example can be used to illustrate this concern. The National Prison Survey of 1991 (Walmsley *et al.* 1992) was designed to fill an important gap in knowledge about prisons and prisoners and to compensate for the shortage of systematic information about the prison population, their childhood circumstances, their schooling, current daily circumstances or about their employment position and living arrangements before they came into prison.

This survey indicates that the prison population is much younger than the general population. It includes a much higher proportion of men and of persons from ethnic minority communities and disproportionately consists of persons from social classes 4 and 5. However the more striking figures for this paper are that 38 per cent of young prisoners under 21 and 23 per cent of adult prisoners said that they had been taken into local authority care at some stage before the age of 16. The comparable figure for the general population is 2 per cent. In a considerable number of cases this was because people had committed a criminal offence. Nevertheless, it suggests that the background to the prison population should not be so simply associated with council housing. Just prior to their imprisonment about a half (49%) of prisoners had been living with their spouse or partner. Twenty-three per cent had been living with their parents or other adult relations and 18 per cent had lived alone. About two thirds (67%) of the prisoners who had not been living with their parents or other adult relatives lived in rented accommodation and about one-sixth lived in accommodation they owned. Five per cent had been in a hostel or other temporary accommodation and 2 per cent had been living on the streets. Of prisoners under 21 who had not been living with their parents or other adult relations, 6 per cent had been living on the streets. Walmsley *et al.* comment (1992:18):

> if the homeless are counted as those who are living in a hostel or temporary accommodation just prior to their imprisonment or were living on the streets, then just 5% of the total prison population were homeless, 8% of remand prisoners and 4% of the sentenced population.

These data point to the importance of insecure housing and homelessness in relation to crime. However, the definition of homelessness produces an inadequate picture of the proportion of the prison population who did not have a permanent residence just prior to their imprisonment. As well as those who were in hostels or living on the streets, 2 per cent had arrived in this country just prior to their imprisonment and another 5 per cent lived in other places which they neither owned nor rented. This will include those already in custody for another offence. In all, some 13 per cent of the prison population, 16 per cent of remand prisoners, 12 per cent of those sentenced, did not have a permanent residence just prior to their imprisonment. Furthermore, many of those who did have owned or rented accommodation were unable or unwilling to return to it on their release. This is a very high figure which suggests that in our enthusiasm to focus upon council housing we should be careful not to neglect the important role that lack of accommodation and access to housing of any kind has in relation to crime. There is a possibility that the importance of homelessness and lack of stable accommodation will be understated in statistics of this kind. Where people's association with their parental home is weak and family relationships are in difficulties, the address notified as the place of residence is still likely to be that of the parent in the absence of any other permanent address. Consequently, people whose place of residence is insecure or temporary and who are on a circuit of homelessness, while retaining some links with the family, will be recorded as living at the family address in the event of any conflict with authority. The significance of lack of independent accommodation and lack of secure permanent accommodation is already apparent in the statistics quoted above, but there is good reason to believe it is understated. At-risk groups of residents are not only concentrated in council estates and we should avoid oversimplifying the position.

The New Geography of Housing

The evidence outlined above indicates that the spatial concentration of crime and victimization owes a considerable amount to the spatial concentration of council housing. What it indicates is that we need to understand the changing geography of housing as well as the extent to which council housing caters disproportionately for at-risk groups including those who are out of employment, are in semi- or unskilled employment and are from other groups with a high risk of being offenders. There is now a considerable housing and housing policy literature which explores these issues. It can be summarized in relation to a number of separate processes. These are discussed in turn below, and relate first of all to residualization and marginalization, secondly to differentiation, thirdly to privatization and finally to processes operating at an estate level.

The process of residualization refers to the long-term trend for council housing to become a less affluent tenure, catering disproportionately for lower income groups, older people, people outside the labour market and for the non-working poor, rather than the affluent working class. This trend has been documented over most of the postwar period (see e.g. Murie 1983; 1997). Successive evidence shows that as the private rented sector in the United Kingdom declined, so the poorest sections of the population which had previously lived in private renting, began to be housed in the council sector. The proportion of households dependent on means-tested assistance shows a steady decline in private renting, associated with the decline of that tenure and a rise in council housing. The owner-occupied sector, although it was expanding at the same time, shows relatively little increase. Family Expenditure Survey data shows the same pattern, with an increasing association between lower income households and council housing. Other data related to lone parents, to unemployment and a range of indicators of relative deprivation demonstrate that the social base for council housing was becoming narrower and associated with more deprived sections of the community.

While these trends are apparent and are documented for a number of decades, it would appear that the process has become more rapid over the last twenty years. This has been associated first of all with increasing social inequality and the widening gap between more affluent and poorer sections of the community, and secondly with active tenure transfers, especially through the sale of council houses. The consequence of this is to shift some of the population of affluent working-class tenants into another tenure, even though they may still live in the same dwellings.

The term residualization is used in the literature with some care. It is not used as a description of a residual or welfare sector in the North American sense but rather to describe a direction of change towards a more residual sector. There is an explicit acknowledgement that the council-housing sector continues to contain more affluent households and a considerable degree of social mix compared with the North American situation. However, this mix is less than was the case in the past, and with demographic and economic trends the concentration of households outside the labour market has become stronger. It is in this context that some commentaries refer to marginalization, rather than residualization (Forrest and Murie 1986). The argument essentially is that council housing has shifted from housing for the working class to housing for the non-working class and those who are marginal to the labour market. In the economy of the 1980s and 1990s this marginal group has had much longer periods outside employment, with much greater benefit dependency, and there is the growth of a generation with very limited experience of employment.

The national and regional, and indeed local, data then show a clear and more distinctive channelling of deprived groups into council housing and affluent groups into owner occupation. This, elsewhere, has been referred to as socio-tenurial polarization and it involves a clear sorting of the population into different tenures much more closely related to their affluence and employment. These different tenures continue to have distinctive geographies. Consequently the geography of housing tenure is much more closely associated with the geography of deprivation. As this pattern becomes established and more apparent, so it generates its own momentum. Households which were content within a socially mixed council-housing sector are less satisfied with remaining in a marginalized tenure. Affluent groups leave council housing more rapidly than in the past and affluent groups are less represented amongst those entering the sector. There is a differential movement in and out of the sector, which compounds and exacerbates the deprived social profile of the tenure.

However, at this point it is important to qualify this picture by referring to differentiation and privatization. Both of these processes highlight the uneven pattern of change across the council sector as a whole. Not all estates were affluent working-class areas and not all estates are changing at the same pace. The literature on dreadful enclosures, dangerous places and delinquent areas demonstrates that there were, in most cities, parts of the council housing stock which were regarded as stigmatized, which had a low reputation and which were avoided by all but those who had no choice. The origins of these reputations are rooted historically and relate to who was originally housed and the reputation of the areas associated with their first inhabitants (see e.g. Damer 1974; Byrne, no date). Gill (1977) has argued that particular characteristics of properties were significant in determining the social composition of areas. In Luke Street, in Crossley, the larger houses within the council sector were predominantly in that area and larger families became concentrated there. This was fundamental to what happened in the area and to its reputation elsewhere.

Local authorities' practice was also a significant influence upon differentiation between estates. The well-recorded practice of housing visitors in grading households as suitable for different grades of property meant a very explicit hierarchy from the least desirable propeties, usually older, less well maintained and sometimes acquired dwellings, to the most desirable properties, usually the new-build houses with gardens. Households whose housekeeping standards were deemed to be poor from observation of the conditions they were living in at the time of application, were graded as only suitable for less desirable properties. These grading practices, as well as more explicit policies to create dump estates (to which households which had poor records of rent payment were moved), policies towards homeless families (where no choice of offer was given) and other discriminatory practices, predictably resulted in concentrations of the most vulnerable and those who had least choice in particular areas. There was an awareness of this amongst both those who lived there and those who did not, and reputations were affected as a result.

So we have a council sector with a range of estates of different reputations being affected by a process of residualization. Very little new council housing has been built since the early 1980s and the tendency has been for the most undesirable estates to achieve the highest turnover levels and for those moving into them to be those with the least choice. So we have created new enclosures with high turnover, transient populations, drawn from the most vulnerable sections of the community in a context of high unemployment and widening social inequality. The new enclosures are less and less like other parts of the city.

It would be wrong to imply that the most desirable and affluent parts of the council sector have completely escaped these changes. However there is reason to believe that they have been significantly insulated from them. They are insulated by a number of factors. Initially because the areas are relatively popular, the properties are relatively good and the neighbourhoods are stable, people are less likely to move out. Turnover is less, the movement in of more deprived households is lower. At the same time the operation of council house sales policies before 1980 and of the Right to Buy since 1980 have offered affluent tenants on the better estates a way of securing their position without moving out of the estate. The evidence about spatial variations in rates of privatization between estates is very clear (see Forrest and Murie 1990). The estates which contain the best-quality, most spacious, traditionally-built houses with gardens tend to be those which were most popular and in highest demand. They have least turnover and higher levels of employment and affluence, and it is these estates which have the highest levels of privatization in the form of the sale of council houses. Consequently these areas now become areas of mixed tenure. The concentration of tenure is lower in these areas and there is a direct link to the data referred to by Hope and Hough (1988).

At one level all that we are seeing is that less popular and attractive deprived council estates are those which remain predominantly in council ownership, and the predominant council ownership variable is in itself an indicator of level of deprivation and attractiveness. The fact that levels of offence and offending are lower in council estates which are not predominantly council is simply an indication they are lower in less deprived and more attractive council estates. The differentiation between different parts of the council sector is rapidly moving towards a polarization between different estates. Part of that polarization is indicated through the process of privatization and part of it is indicated by criminal statistics.

In all of this it is worth reflecting upon the position of the housing manager. The most systematic and effective studies of housing allocation policies (e.g. Henderson and Karn 1987; Phillips 1985), although they are now somewhat dated, provide a convincing picture of the process of allocation and the pressures facing allocating officers and housing managers. These studies suggest a tendency to distinguish between the rough and the respectable, and to channel the respectable households towards stable, non-problematic estates so as not to put these estates at risk. The rough or non-respectable applicants and, disproportionately, those from minority ethnic groups are channelled towards estates with problems, partly because they will not make them any worse and partly because they are the only people likely to accept offers on these estates. Research studies which demonstrate this process go to great pains to argue that what is being worked through is not the individual idiosyncratic prejudices of allocating officers but a systematic process of structured discrimination reflecting the bureaucratic and social pressures which would work on any allocator and which mean that allocators, irrespective of their individual positions, tend to produce the same kinds of allocation patterns. Without some change in the framework within which allocators operate and in the social stereotyping associated with it, there is no reason to believe there will be a significant change of allocation patterns.

Processes on Estates

If the literature outlined above indicates changes in the role and operation of different tenures in the housing system and the implications of this for the geography of deprivation, there is a separate literature which argues that there is a downward spiral which reinforces the disadvantage faced by households on deprived estates.

Households which can only obtain housing in the rented sector are restricted by what that sector can offer in terms of dwellings and living environments. They are often trapped in unsatisfactory environments. The poverty trap further reduces their options, their ability to work their way out of the environments which disadvantage them and their ability to make satisfactory homes in these areas. As certain areas and parts of the market become more strongly associated with poor people and represent poor social environments, those with choice in the housing system are less likely to move to or to stay in such areas. As a result the social and income mix in these areas is further reduced. Households with choice choose to live elsewhere and increasingly the new residents are those without choice. The process of social exclusion involving housing can be summarized as follows:

- Households entering the housing market have differential choices and bargaining power. Those without jobs and with family responsibilities, and those with special needs and outside the labour market graduate towards the rented sectors.
- Those with least choice graduate towards the least desirable dwellings and areas.
- Households living in these areas are dependent on local facilities and low-demand housing areas tend to be poorly served by other services.
- Consequently, those living in deprived areas are less able to build satisfactory homes or avail themselves of opportunities which could increase their incomes and bargaining power, and so enable them to move on.

Taylor (1995) argues that poverty is the root cause of many of the problems faced by residents on deprived estates. She states that many large estates are on the fringes of cities, isolated from economic activity, unlikely to provide a market to viable businesses, either as employers or in the shape of shops, transport and other local facilities. Jobs are scarce, shops are expensive or hard to get to. Public services on these estates are under severe strain because of high levels of demand on shrinking budgets. Long-term unemployment has been shown to lead to ill health, schools with low motivation and under-achievement. There are few facilities or prospects for the higher-than-average numbers of young people. Meanwhile, Care in the Community policies bring more vulnerable people into already stressed communities with few resources to support them.

These problems create huge pressures on family and community life, can lead to tensions between neighbours and together with high population turnover, mean that residents are vulnerable to crime and the fear of crime. The pressures involved interact with each other, to mean that individual problems become more difficult to solve. These pressures result in a spiral of decline and despair. Concentrations of low-income households result from limited access to jobs, incomes and lack of choice in the housing market. They contribute in turn to a lack of political clout, no market to attract quality goods and services, overstretched public services, the stereotypes which reinforce isolation and lack of access to jobs and capital, poor health, low self-esteem and crime.

Taylor emphasizes that this spiral of despair is only one side of the picture, and is concerned to emphasize the considerable strengths in these areas. Nevertheless, the account should be treated with some caution on two grounds. The first of these is how far the spiral of despair does typify estates and neighbourhoods or how far they remain differentiated and varied. The alternative view to the spiral of despair is one which emphasizes the resilience of communities, families and social groups and the minority behaviour which is used to stereotype the characteristics of an estate. The second reservation relates to the equation between council estates and poverty. Limited access to jobs and income and lack of choice in the housing market does not only result in concentrations of poor people on council estates; indeed it may be argued that it is less crucial in these estates. Allocation policies still operate in a way which takes account of factors other than income and employment, and the rights of tenants mean that turnover in better-quality housing is not always high. The concentration of low income households in the private rented sector and even in parts of the home ownership sector may be just as striking. There is a danger that, without balancing the picture of poverty on estates with a picture of poverty elsewhere, there is a tendency to reinforce stereotypes which associate council housing estates generally with low self-esteem and a downward spiral.

Bearing these reservations in mind, Taylor's account is important in moving away from the emphasis in some of the literature on design issues (e.g. Coleman 1985). The processes of determining what happens on council estates, as in other neighbourhoods, are the consequence of a wide range of factors and the interaction between them. Just as the problems on estates are not simply about design, they are not simply about an underclass, single mothers and the absence of male role models. Indeed, Campbell (1993) has argued that the problem in such areas is associated, not with the absence of male role models, but with the wrong male role models.

The processes determining problems on council estates are more complex than any of these approaches suggest. Some households in some estates are living in a state of emergency, exposed to disorder and decline. Rather than forming a self-perpetuating underclass we are talking about communities continuously exposed to severe social and economic deprivation. The crime rates associated with these areas are not the same. In this context Taylor's discussion of a spiral of decline or Ormerod's discussion of social interaction are relevant. Ormerod (1997) argues that the enormous variability in crime rates cannot be explained by differences in factors such as unemployment and suggests a model in which social and economic factors and social interaction are significant. As the proportion of criminals rises, this in itself makes it more likely that the proportion will increase still further and sanctions of social disapproval of the non-criminal part of the population weaken. So the incentive to stop being a criminal is reduced. Ormerod argues that once a critical point is reached, the strength of these feedbacks intensifies and the proportion of criminals rises rapidly and dramatically. These social interaction effects are important within council neighbourhoods and other areas which have changed in the ways described above.

Policy Responses

The increased concern about incidence of crime on council estates has led to a number of policy responses. Alice Coleman's work on the design of estates is not highly regarded in the academic community. It offers an under-contextualized and simplistic view of the impact of design on council estates. Nonetheless, partly as a result of her work, some attention has been given to creating better design, better security and more defensible space on estates. Some of this has focused upon management influences. There has been a wide acceptance that management initiatives will improve living circumstances on estates. The government has actively provided advice on housing and crime prevention. While this advice has tended to emphasize design and maintenance action which can make crime more difficult to commit, it has increasingly referred to management issues. The major study on crime prevention on council estates, by the Safe Neighbourhoods Unit for the Department of the Environment (1993), emphasized the importance of introducing a broad package of measures to prevent crime. It argued that introducing just one type of measure did not appear to lead to successful outcomes and a broad approach including management and social development measures, as well as policy changes, was more likely to prove successful. The more successful schemes included design changes, local management initiatives, physical security measures, police initiatives and social measures, particularly for the young. Inter-agency working and planning and closer involvement with community and residence organizations were also emphasized.

Before and after this research and the advice which built upon it a wide range of initiatives have been promoted. These have not been subject to a great deal of systematic research, and the problems of evaluating the impact of initiatives on areas which are subject to so many change influences remains extremely difficult. In this context it is particularly relevant to look at studies which have endeavoured to carry out such evaluations. Perhaps the most systematic recent example is the study by Foster and Hope (1993), concerned with the impact of the Priority Estates Project. They studied the impact of the Priority Estates Project (PEP) on crime and community life. The Home Office Research and Planning Unit which sponsored this research was concerned to discover whether PEP, which promises to bring about improvements to estates which are also likely to have high crime levels, had a potential for reducing crime. Four means of crime prevention were represented in PEP's approach. These related to design issues, halting the signs of disorder and signifying that the estate is well cared for, investing in the estate to develop a positive view among residents, and increasing community control by residents and housing officials. This is an important and carefully carried out study for the debate about housing and crime. It would not be unfair to argue that in mounting the research the expectation or assumption was that the research would demonstrate that the intensive housing management approach advocated by PEP had a measurable advantageous impact on crime. The study involved a case study of a PEP estate in London and another in Hull, and of a control estate in each city. The control estates were as far as possible similar to the PEP estates.

The conclusions of the study make fascinating reading. They demonstrate the problems in introducing the PEP model, with the London PEP being adversely affected by staff problems which led to disputes and the temporary withdrawal of PEP. Tenants' enthusiasm and co-operation never properly recovered from this. Perhaps more fundamentally, the London and Hull examples demonstrated the limitations of the PEP approach. The gains secured in the PEP estates were not dramatically different from those in the non-PEP estates. In neither case were all the problems resolved. The authors of the report concluded that the PEP model does have a real potential for reducing crime but also acknowledged that there were developments in the other estates which resulted in reductions of crime. More importantly, they concluded:

> on the estates studied during this research all of the successes were only partial—they occurred in either one or the other of the experimental estates, or only for particular areas or groups of residents in each case. This was partly because some groups were easier to reach than others and that the scope of PEP's impact was constrained by underlying and often severe social and economic conditions . . . Within the realms of their remit however there were two obstacles to the wider effectiveness of the PEP model on the estates studied: first, the "quality" of implementation; and second, the instability of residential communities arising from population turnover, social heterogeneity and the "subterranean culture" within estate communities. (Foster and Hope 1993: 83–4).

Put in another way, without denying the beneficial effects of PEP, the focus upon housing management at an estate level does not address the underlying factors leading to the concentration of deprived households on estates and contributing to the downward spiral within these estates. The PEP model is based on an assumption that the fundamental problem on estates was a housing management one, but the research evidence demonstrates that it is not a local housing management problem but one associated with population change and the resources available to populations on estates. Nor is it adequate to argue that the fundamental problem is one of housing allocation policies, implying that some change in such policies would resolve the problem. The Foster and Hope study shows a remarkable awareness of how difficult it was to change the fundamental environment for allocations. Thus:

> Housing officials . . . need to maintain a balanced social mix on estates, while at the same time keeping all dwellings occupied. Being able to do both however may depend upon the ability to match the vacancies arising on the estates with the needs of prospective tenants. Not only did the Hull experimental estate experience a higher turnover but by the end of the study period it was receiving a much greater number of those in desperate housing need than the control estate: the second household survey revealed that 28% of residents had been on the Hull experimental estate for less than three years—compared with 16% on the Hull control estate—of whom 21% had been formerly homeless (the comparable figure for the control estate was 16%). Despite the efforts to improve the experimental estate, about the same proportion of residents as at the outset said they would move if they had the chance . . .

It would seem that the reputation of the experimental estate had worsened over the period with the consequence that the estate was

33

receiving poorer newcomers with other personal and social difficulties.
(1993: 88–9).

Vacancies were occurring differentially across the Hull experimental estate and housing officials were faced with the task of needing to let more flats than houses. Housing officials had the "strongest possible incentive" to maintain occupancy on the estate, yet were faced with a low demand from council sector transfers and an excess of housing unsuitable for children. In practice they had little choice, other than to let the flats to those from amongst the pool of prospective tenants who were in desperate need, whom the council was legally obliged to house, and who were deemed suitable for the available accommodation. These were often the young and poor, and single people coming out of institutions.

> Accommodating them in the tower blocks only further exacerbated the problem since the lifestyle of some of the newcomers served to hasten the departure of even more of the older tenants. In sum a spiral of deterioration was set in train by this allocation process, which appeared to become self-perpetuating. The tragic irony was that the imperative of filling vacant dwellings to maintain the "stability of the estate" may, in the way that things worked have had the opposite effect. (1993: 89).

Foster and Hope commented:

> It is beyond the scope of this study to discover why the pool of prospective council tenants in Hull contained numbers of the young poor, and whether they were disproportionately housed on the experimental estate. Nor can the research suggest a way in which those who make the allocation decisions could stop such a process happening, whilst simultaneously fulfilling all the necessary and desired criteria of public housing allocation. (1993: 89–91)

The implications of this do not seem to have been appreciated by those most closely involved in housing management responses. For example Power (1987: 8) stated that

> Where an estate has been stigmatized over a long period and many vulnerable and dependent households have been concentrated together, it may be necessary to encourage a more varied range of applicants and help widen the offers made to desperate cases for other parts of the housing stock.

Such a conclusion does not face up to the difficulties involved, and does not address the issues about the supply and investment in council housing which in the end are the only way to relieve this situation. Rather than housing management solutions being within reach, or manipulation of housing allocations being likely to change the situation, the most likely future is one of continuing funnelling in of the most deprived to the poorest areas and of further concentration of households with problems in areas with few resources.

Conclusions

The changing role and nature of council housing and changing patterns of crime are related. However, the causal links are not simple and straightforward. The key elements include the changing social composition of neighbourhoods, the loss of social cohesion associated with changing patterns of work, family and kinship links, and the high turnover of population in some estates. Terms such as disorder and decline themselves generate negative views of areas and the responses of people living in such neighbourhoods can be ones of withdrawal from community participation and increasing detachment. Such neighbourhoods are more susceptible to crime. These patterns and processes are important on council estates, although it is essential that we do not stigmatize such estates and neighbourhoods and those living on them by the automatic assumption that such a process occurs. However, the recognition of the nature of these processes should lead us to be doubtful about the capacity of limited management interventions to change the environment and opportunities for those living on such estates. The policy task related to crime and housing, as that related to housing opportunities more generally, involves stepping outside the framework of management and allocations in order to alter the flow of properties becoming available for letting. This can only be done either by new investment in building and acquisition of properties or, at the other end of the spectrum, in active interventions to replace low-demand properties. In both cases we are talking about investment in housing in order to relieve the problems associated with the costs of crime. This goes against the thrust of policy over the last twenty years, where government has actively reduced investment in council housing and used the benefits from its privatization to finance other programmes. What we have is a direct challenge to the funding philosophies of recent years. If management inititives have proved insufficient, new approaches which include investment to break the constraints on choices for households and managers also need to be set in a wider regeneration framework with action to address issues of employment, schools, local services, policing and housing management.

References

Barke, M., and Turnbull, G. M. (1992), *Meadowell: the biography of an estate with problems*, Avebury: Aldershot.

Byrne, D. S. (no date) *Problem Families: A Housing Lumpen-Proletariat*, University of Durham.

Campbell, B. (1993), *Goliath*, London: Methuen.

Coleman, A. (1985), *Utopia on Trial*, London: Hilary Shipman.

Damer, S. (1974), Wine alley: the sociology of a dreadful enclosure, *Sociological Review*, vol. 27, no. 2, May: 221–48.

Department of the Environment (1993), *Crime Prevention on Council Estates*, London: HMSO.

English, J. (1979), Access and deprivation in local authority housing, in Jones, C. (ed.), *Urban deprivation and the inner city*, London: Croom Helm.

Forrest, R., and Murie, A. (1986), Marginalisation and subsidised individualism, *International Journal of Urban and Regional Research*, vol. 10, no. 1: 46–65.

Forrest, R., and Murie, A. (1990), *Selling the Welfare State*, London: Routledge.

Foster, J., and Hope, T. (1993), *Housing, Community and Crime: The Impact of the Priority Estate Project*, Home Office Research Study no. 131, London: HMSO.

Gill, O. (1977), *Luke Street: Housing Policy, Conflict and the Creation of the Delinquent Area*, London: Macmillan.

Henderson, J., and Karn, V. (1987), *Race Class and State Housing*, London: Gower.

Hope, T., and Hough, M. (1988), Area, crime and incivilities: a profile from the British Crime Survey, in Hope, T., and Shaw, M. (eds), *Communities and Crime Reduction*, London: Home Office Research and Planning Unit: 30–44.

Murie, A. (1983), *Housing Inequality and Deprivation*, London: Heinemann.

Murie, A. (1997), *Beyond State Housing*, in Williams, P. (ed.), *New Directions in Housing Policy*, London: Paul Chapman.

Ormerod, P. (1997), Stopping crime spreading, *New Economy*, vol. 4, no. 2: 83–8.

Phillips, D. (1985), *What price equality?* London: GLC.

Power, A. (1987), *The PEP Guide to Local Management Vol. I, The PEP Model*, London: Department of the Environment.

Taylor, M. (1995), *Unleashing the Potential*, York: Joseph Rowntree Foundation.

Walmsley, R., Howard, L., and White, S. (1992), *The National Prison Survey 1991: Main Findings*, London: HMSO.

The Local Politics of Inclusion: The State and Community Safety

John Pitts and Tim Hope

Abstract

While the tendency for low-income groups to become economically marginalized may be a structural feature of the globalizing, post-Fordist economy, the degree to which they are allowed to become socially excluded is arguably a political issue. In many of the polities of the Western world, debate has focused not only on whether the State could or should intervene economically to ameliorate the causes of the "new poverty" but also on how the State should address the increasing rates of "social dislocation"—including youth crime, interpersonal violence, and drug misuse—which have been associated with its emergence. The postwar welfare settlement produced a particular institutional nexus of welfare, justice, punishment and citizenship (Hay 1996; Garland 1985); yet the pressure of increasing social dislocation has also placed great strain on the institutions of the welfare state, particularly at the local level, notwithstanding the ideological commitment of differing governments to continue with the social welfare project.

In this paper, we explore some circumstances in which the politics of the "local state" might mediate—in one way or another—the consequences of economic marginalization. In particular, we draw attention to the role which might be played by local state agencies—as intermediaries between the individual and the national State—in deploying policies which could offset the social exclusion of minorities and youth. By comparing the responses of local agencies to youth crime in two communities in Britain and France we highlight the "vertical" dimension of political relations which links marginalized communities with the wider resources of the State. And while many economies are experiencing similar social dislocations within disadvantaged communities, the vertical dimension may prove crucial in preserving the linkage between their residents and those of the wider, more privileged, society.

Keywords

Social Dislocation; Youth Crime; Britain; France; Local Government; Community Safety

Address for Correspondence: *Professor Tim Hope, Department of Criminology, Keele University, Staffordshire, ST5 5BG.*

Social Dislocation and Community Isolation

Many Western states have been subjected to broadly similar structural pressures in the past two decades which have had a profound effect on their internal distributions of income, wealth and opportunity (McFate 1996). In Britain, the *Joseph Rowntree Foundation Inquiry into Income and Wealth* (JRF 1995) found a considerable growth in economic inequalities since the 1970s—a widening of the gap between rich and poor (Hills 1996). In particular, there has been an increasing polarization of income and wealth at the local level, producing both a greater spatial segregation between better-off and poorer areas (Green 1996), and a growth in concentrated poverty amongst communities within urban areas (Noble and Smith 1996). Generally, two aspects of the resulting "new poverty" seem common: a widespread failure of entry into the primary labour market for low-skilled and otherwise disadvantaged youth—which has consequences for their present and future capacities to sustain independent living, family formation and public participation; and a spatialized concentration of poverty, characterized by the increasing likelihood for the poor to be living in close, residential proximity to those of a similar income level.

Accompanying these trends has been a growth in indices of "social dislocation" (Wilson 1987), including criminal victimization, interpersonal violence, and drug misuse. Between 1981 and 1991 the number of crimes recorded in England and Wales rose from around 3.5 million per annum to almost 6 million—with annual increases of 17 per cent in 1990 and a further 16 per cent in 1991, since when crime rates have stabilized around these all-time record levels. Although the numbers of young people aged between 10 and 17 in the population fell by a quarter during the 1980s—and the decade also saw a dramatic reduction in prosecutions of children aged 10 to 14—recorded crime committed by juveniles rose by 54 per cent (Hagell and Newburn 1994).

Community-level inequalities in crime seem to be mirroring the spatial economic redistribution. Estimates derived from the British Crime Survey[1] suggest that over a half of all survey-recorded property crimes—and over a third of all property crime victims—are likely to be found in just a fifth of the communities of England and Wales. Conversely, the least affected half of the country now experiences only 15 per cent of the crime, spread between a quarter of crime victims (Hope 1997). By the early 1990s, residents of the top decile of high-crime neighbourhoods experienced twice as much property crime and four times as much personal crime as residents in the next worse category. In parallel with the regional restructuring of the British economy during the 1980s, the inequality in crime risk grew amongst local communities, especially those in the less advantaged "Northern" regions of England (Trickett *et al.* 1995a); and local studies at the end of the 1980s registered large increases in crime victimization over a relatively short period (Hope and Foster 1992).

We have argued elsewhere that these patterns of crime mirror the emergent distribution of the new poverty in Britain (Hope 1996, 1997). Residents of high-crime areas in Britain lack economic resources[2] and live in areas where social and rental housing tenures predominate.[3] As the 1980s progressed, the introduction of market mechanisms into the management and distribution of public-sector housing encouraged relatively prosperous elderly and higher-income families to leave public housing—or at least those large estates in the inner city or on its periphery—to be replaced by poorer, younger families.[4] The estates which experienced the greatest changes—and the highest crime rates—saw increasing concentrations of children and teenagers,[5] young single adults,[6] lone parents[7] and the single elderly.[8] Poor, young, Black and Asian families constituted a significant segment of this population in some regions. These neighbourhoods also became a last resort for residents who had previously been homeless, hospitalized or imprisoned, and for refugees from political persecution. And these demographic trends often coincided in the same communities with a lack of access to primary job markets for local youth.[9]

The crime and violence in these neighbourhoods is implosive in that it is committed by, and against, local residents. Research in Merseyside, for instance, found not only that disadvantaged areas had high rates of burglary but also that there was a clear tendency for victims from disadvantaged areas to be offended against from violent crimes nearer their homes than residents from more affluent areas (Hirschfield *et al.* 1997). Its other distinguishing feature is that the young people involved appear not to grow out of it (Graham and Bowling 1995). Hagan (1994) has observed that pre-eminent among the factors which make for higher levels of crime in these neighbourhoods is that young people who, under other circumstances, would have grown out of crime, leaving it behind with other adolescent enthusiasms, become more deeply and more seriously *embedded* in a criminal way of life. This, in turn, means that the composition of adolescent peer groups is older and so, for example, links may be forged between criminal neophytes of 14 and old stagers of 25 (Pitts 1995; Foster and Hope 1993). Thus conflicts which begin in the school quickly spill over into the neighbourhood while the school increasingly becomes a forum for the enactment of neighbourhood conflict.

In sum, the concentration of crime victimization on public housing estates in Britain

> may be due to a failure to prevent the process of criminal embeddedness of local youth—fuelled by low economic opportunity—which escalates their offending activities, with certain vulnerable groups of residents coming to be repeatedly victimized as a consequence, particularly as social controls progressively diminish and the neighbourhood tips into increasing disorderliness. Each element in the process may interact dynamically with the others to account for the sharp growth of crime in particular communities caught in the spiral of deterioration. (Hope 1996: 178)

Explaining the observed correlations between indices of economic inequality and those of social dislocation—especially within local communities—poses difficulty for analysts from both the left and right of the political spectrum, not least perhaps because the issue of inequality, more than any other, has always epitomized such political distinction (Bobbio 1996). For the right, the correlation between the concentrations of crime and poverty can be found primarily in the culture of poverty which is believed to emerge when individuals are made to depend exclusively upon welfare benefits. The concentration of social dislocation in specific neighbourhoods is itself merely a product of the distortions of the housing market introduced by State involvement, which simply concentrates crime-prone individuals together. By contrast, some analysts on the left remain at pains to deny the criminogenic properties of poverty concentration in the belief that a focus on the economic disadvantage of offenders would merely lead to a policy of blaming the poor for their own misfortunes, and would reinforce their social exclusion as a "dangerous class".

Criminological perspectives on the link between economic disadvantage and crime have not fared much better: empirical research has often identified only weak correlations between *individual* economic disadvantage (including unemployment) and crime; while the concept of "social disorganization "—held to promote a condition of anomie or normlessness in communities—has been criticized for ignoring both the specific patterns of organization, adaptation and survival in impoverished communities, and the influence of wider structural inequalities which impinge upon localities (Bursik 1988).

Nevertheless, writing about the "new" American ghettos, Sampson and Wilson (1995) argue that

the most important determinant of the relationship between race and crime is the differential distribution of blacks in communities character-ized by (1) *structural social disorganization* and (2) *cultural social isolation*, both of which stem from the concentration of poverty, family disruption, and residential instability. (1995:44, emphases in the original)

Both forms of (dis)organization are held to impede the ability of local communities to "realize the common values of . . . residents and maintain effective social controls" (Sampson and Wilson 1995: 45). The structural social (dis)organization of communities refers to the prevalence of, and relations amongst, social networks within communities, both informally based on friendship and kinship, and on local organizations and associations. The strength and nature of these relations—comprising a "horizontal" dimension of community relations (Hope 1995a)—provides a community with necessary *social capital* (Coleman 1990) enabling residents to pursue common goals and the collective development of social norms. The concept of cultural social isolation refers to the vertical dimension of community relations (Hope 1995a) and seeks to capture "the lack of contact or of sustained interaction with individuals and institutions that represent mainstream society" (Sampson and Wilson 1995: 51). Not only do residents lacking access to these vertical linkages fail to acquire the *cultural capital* which would facilitate their economic and social advancement—including educational, training and employment opportunities—but the absence of such pathways of opportunity encourages cultural adaptations or "recapitalization"—"an effort to reorganize what resources are available, even if illicit, to reach attainable goals" (Hagan 1994).

If the horizontal dimension of community relations supplies the capacity for community self-determination and control—the traditional focus of community development theory and practice—the vertical dimension serves as a conduit for the "investment" of cultural capital which may be necessary both for increasing individual opportunity and for activating the horizontal dimension of community organization.[10] Yet relatively little attention so far, at least in the criminological literature, has been paid to the effects of "capital disinvestment" (Hagan 1994) in disadvantaged communities—not only how economic disinvestment creates exclusion from mainstream social life but also how cultural disinvestment can undermine or reshape the social capital of communities leading to further recapitalization in illicit and victimizing directions, including the diminution or alteration of collective restraints on "internal" deviance and offending. Thus, if the growth of the new poverty is leading to the social destabilization of newly impoverished neighbourhoods —and additionally undermining residents' capacity for self-determination and regulation—it then becomes a crucial question to ask what role might be played by cultural (dis)investment by the State in mediating or exacerbating the process.

Much of the originating analysis of social dislocation in areas of concentrating poverty has been American—inescapably focusing on the link between race and disadvantage (e.g. Wilson 1987). Yet in his recent research, Wilson (1996) also calls attention to the specifically American approach towards poverty, joblessness and racial discrimination, which has, by tradition, left the ghettos with a relatively weak and sparse *institutional infrastructure*. In particular, while residents of impoverished and dangerous neighbourhoods had strong informal social links with each other, they felt they had

> . . . little informal social control over children in their environment. A primary reason is the absence of a strong organizational capacity or an institutional resource base that would provide an extra layer of social organization. (Wilson 1996: 64)

In this sense, the institutional infrastructure is seen as a resource for families to draw upon, to share the burden of upbringing, and to provide means of guidance, support and control for children. In communities with a sparse infrastructure, the burden of socialization is placed solely and inequitably on individual families, who are equally incapacitated in their ability to take on the tasks expected by society by virtue of the additional burdens of coping with poverty in a stressed and stressful environment (Furstenberg 1993).

In the modern State, the primary means of delivering cultural capital investment has been through agencies providing resources and services to local communities—in education and training, housing, health and other forms of social and recreational service. Yet while the ideological battle since the 1970s has revolved around whether such State investment has served to empower communities or undermine individual initiative and self-restraint, the debate has been conducted, at least in Europe, in the context of a comparatively well-developed institutional infrastructure at the local level. As

Wacquant observes on the basis of his comparison of a black American "ghetto" and a French *banlieue* (housing project),

> the difference between Chicago's South Side and the degraded working-class projects of the Parisian periphery is not simply one of scale, intensity, and depth of deprivation, but more importantly hinges on the different institutional machineries and closure mechanisms that manage and allocate the costs of the ongoing economic restructuring within each of these societies. (Wacquant 1996: 561)

The relative density and extent of agencies and organizations in the French case, compared with the chronic absence and withdrawal of their equivalents in the American case, provided a principal reason why conditions were so much worse in America—not least since the institutions of the welfare state provide a chief means of structuring social order (Esping-Andersen 1990).

The role of the local institutional infrastructure may be seen most clearly in comparison between extremes, particularly in the contrast between the United States and the welfare states of Western Europe. Yet while this polarity points up differences in the *scale and density* of institutions, other differences in the *nature and operation* of the welfare infrastructure—no less crucial in terms of social order—may become apparent through comparisons between European societies. In the next sections, we first compare the differing political responses in Britain and France to the growth of youth crime and disorder during the 1980s and, second, focus on two local communities and their respective institutional-infrastructural response to youth crime.

Youth Justice and Crime Prevention in Britain and France

In 1981 in both Britain and France, approximately 3.5 million offences were recorded by the police. Both countries had witnessed steady increases in recorded crime in general, and recorded youth crime in particular, and both confronted youth riots on the streets of their major cities. However, by the end of the 1980s the number of offences recorded in Britain was approaching 6 million while in France, between 1983 and 1986 there was a decline in recorded offences to around 3 million, where it remained for the rest of the decade (Parti Socialiste Français 1986; De Liege 1991; Home Office 1994). As noted above, while crime appears to have risen fastest in Britain in the poorest neighbourhoods, in France it was in the poorest neighbourhoods that the fall in the crime rate was most marked (King 1989; De Liege 1991).

Britain

We have argued elsewhere that the erratic twists and turns in the politics, policy and practice of youth justice in Britain since 1979 have had little or nothing to do with the changing shape of youth crime, and are better understood as a product of the government's attempts to manage the tensions between its political ideology, economic reality and the desire for re-election (Pitts, forthcoming). The period between 1982 and 1992 witnessed a sustained attempt to contain the burgeoning costs of crime control and the penal system which led to the development, by successive Home Secretaries, of a highly pragmatic strategy of "delinquency management" rooted in a profound scepticism about either the efficacy of imprisonment or the possibility of rehabilitation outside it. Yet the period since 1993 saw the key reforms of the 1991 Criminal Justice Act swiftly abandoned; and between 1992 and 1995 the numbers of juveniles sentenced to custody rose by a third (Home Office 1996).

The aspiration towards social control through "systemic co-ordination" was also pursued through the development of crime prevention policy. The successive publication of Government Circulars (i.e. official advice to police and local agencies), research reports, seminars, organizational changes and demonstration projects throughout the 1980s, the Home Office sought to encourage a *co-ordinated, multi-agency approach* to the prevention of crime in local communities. Although the roots of this approach lie in the mid-1970s (Gladstone 1980), it became incorporated as the orthodoxy for crime prevention delivery during the 1980s, embracing support across the political spectrum (Gilling 1994). Space precludes a detailed history of this policy development, or a discussion of the variety of techniques and agency practices falling within the rubric.[11] Nevertheless, although the general idea that local agencies should collaborate in common cause with residents to tackle problems of crime and disorder in local communities is a popular model across Europe (as is apparent from the discussion below), the particularly British model which has evolved, favoured by Government and the police service, has certain distinctions from other European forms. Three emphases seem worth noting: (1) its crime-specific, problem-solving methodology; (2) a local specificity in the definition of crime problems; and (3) co-ordination activities amongst separate and relatively autonomous agencies.

As regards the last, the call for co-ordination has been made in a context in which relevant local agencies—especially the police, the local judiciary (magistracy), and many of the service agencies of local government—have considerable governmental, operational and policy-making autonomy from each other. From the outset, therefore, the underlying motivation for multi-agency "partnership" in crime prevention was a belief that the resulting fragmented nature of the response to crime would lead to inefficiencies and gaps in the provision of preventive resources. Yet, at the same time, calls for more consistency of direction or the creation of "lead agencies" with core responsibilities—involving either the police or elected local authorities (e.g. Home Office 1991)—have met with vociferous opposition from their respective advocates. As we shall argue below, conflicts of interest—and the pursuit of autonomous goals—endemic in the structure of local agency relations in Britain have not been resolved by the call to partnership.

France

Upon its election in 1981 the Socialist administraton of François Mitterrand faced nation-wide riots in the multiracial *banlieue*. Fearing that they might reach the proportions they had attained in Britain, Mitterrand established the *été jeunes*, a 100,000-strong national summer playscheme, and established a commission of town mayors under the chairmanship of Henri Bonnemaison.

The *Bonnemaison Commission*, which brought together both Gaullist and Socialist mayors to devise a national strategy, produced its report, *Face à la délinquance: prévention, répression, solidarité*, in 1983. The report asserted that if effective action against the causes of crime was to be taken, a policy which was flexible, adapted to local circumstances, and structurally connected with the activities of government departments and local authorities, the judiciary, the voluntary sector and the needs and wishes of citizens, was needed (Bonnemaison 1983).

What set the resulting programme apart from previous initiatives in France and elsewhere (including Britain) was not only the precision with which neighbourhoods and young people were targeted for intervention but also the importance paid to the vertical, political integration of the machinery for delivering community safety (Gallo 1995). At a national level, the National Council for the Prevention of Delinquency, chaired by the prime minister and attended by the majority of town mayors and representatives from the relevant government ministries, was established in June 1983. At Regional level, Councils for the Prevention of Crime chaired by the chief civil servant (the *Commissaire de la République*) with the Chief Judicial Officer (the *Procureur de la République*) as the vice-chair, were established. At local level Communal Councils for the Prevention of Crime, chaired by the town mayors were set up. Communal councils monitored local youth crime patterns, established special working groups to deal with particular problems and targeted central government funds on these problems. Their "arms and legs" were *animateurs sociaux* who worked at face-to-face level with local young people, and latterly adults, to devise local solutions to local problems. To facilitate this process, a national network of Youth Centres, known as *Missions Locales*, was set up in more than 100 towns and cities. In particular, these centres sought to bridge the transition between school and work for the unemployed and the unqualified (aged 16–25) by offering youth training and advice and assistance on matters such as improving literacy, managing financial affairs and finding accommodation. They also encourage young people, particularly the unemployed, to set up and run their own projects (Graham 1993: 135).

Summary

Starting from not dissimilar situations of crime and disorder in the early 1980s, British and French youth justice and community safety policies have developed in markedly different ways (King 1989). In Britain, an emerging "new penology" (Feeley and Simon 1992) has focused primarily on the protection of the public and on the management of the risk associated with particular groups and locales; in France, a national programme of political incorporation and service provision has been instituted. In Britain, the political machinery for implementing prevention has remained undirected and non-centralized, emphasizing co-ordinated partnerships amongst supposedly equal parties; in France, direct, vertical links, organizations, and communication mechanisms were established from the grassroots to the centre of national politics. What impact, then, did these differences have in the respective responses to youth crime in local communities?

A Tale of Two Housing Estates

Between 1993 and 1995 one of the authors (Pitts) was involved in a study of the responses of public professionals, politicians and local residents to youth crime and the violent victimization of children and young people on the "Dickens Estate" in East London and the "Flaubert Estate" in an industrial suburb to the west of Paris (Pearce 1995; Pitts 1995). In many ways, the two estates typified the changing pattern of crime and victimization, and changing professional responses to it, in the two countries in this period. Whereas on the Flaubert Estate there has been a sustained attempt, since 1983, to develop a coherent political and professional response to these problems, on the Dickens Estate the picture was different. During our research, violence—particularly racial violence—on the estate had reached record levels, making it the most violent neighbourhood in a traditionally high-crime London borough. The Flaubert Estate, having topped the French youth-crime league in the early 1980s, now had a level of crime and violence somewhat below the national average. The following vignettes suggest some of the key differences in the responses of public professionals, politicians and local residents to youth crime and disorder on the two estates. It is the argument of this paper that these differences were a product of the two quite different responses to the problem of youth crime and social and economic exclusion by their respective national governments.

Housing

Flaubert: Housing policy aimed to locate the children and relatives of local residents in local accommodation in order to strengthen ties of friendship and kinship, stabilize the neighbourhood and strengthen indigenous sources of social control. This was decided by the locally-elected *Neighbourhood Council* which was established, through negotiations with the mayor's office, as an additional tier of local government in the *quartier* in the late 1980s. All residents of 16 and over, irrespective of immigration status, were allowed to vote for the Neighbourhood Council and around 40 per cent did. Seventy-five per cent of the populaton of the Flaubert Estate were of North African, Central African, Turkish or Portuguese origin, and most had never voted before in any French election. As a result of this policy, however, many apartments were overcrowded, being unsuitable for the many large families on the estate. However new, larger council homes and a new hospital are now being constructed alongside the estate. The Neighbourhood Council had previously initiated a project with the mayor's office in which consecrated rooms were established at the town abattoir where Islamic religious rites could be practised. One of the consequences of these developments had been that requests for transfers off the estate had dwindled while the waiting list for transfers on to the estate had grown significantly.

Dickens: The Housing Department operated a system of housing priority points, determined on the basis of social need. This was a policy which was increasingly difficult to implement in the face of the erosion of good-quality local housing stock occasioned by central government's "right to buy" strategy. This meant that "disruptive" tenants, those who did not pay their rent regularly, the homeless, often young single-parent and Bengali families, and successive waves of refugees were allocated to the unpopular and underused tower blocks on the estate which were notorious for their high crime rate and drug dealing. This had produced a less stable neighbourhood with fewer ties of kinship and friendship. One of the consequences of this has been that the neighbourhood had one of the highest levels of racial attacks in the borough and support for the National Front amongst established white families was strong.[12]

Employment

Flaubert: Local employment policy aimed to offer local jobs in the public and voluntary sectors to local people in order to reduce unemployment and promote interaction between neighbours. The policy was developed by the local authority in liaison with the Neighbourhood Council, the social workers of *DPJJ*,[13] the *Mission Locale* and a national voluntary youth welfare and training agency, *Association Jeunesse, Culture, Loisirs, Technique (JCLT)*. *JCLT* developed long-term youth and adult training, an extensive programme of social and cultural activities and operated a residential *foyer* for children and young people from the neighbourhood who were unable to live with their families. *JCLT* was also commissioned by the Ministry of Social Affairs to administer, locally, the *Revenue Minimum d'Insertion*, introduced in 1988 to provide income maintenance, and counselling and advice for unemployed young people. Professional workers recognized that racism and the poor reputation of the estate often made it difficult to place people in employment beyond the estate, but their emphasis on extended periods of training leading to nationally recognized qualifications meant that they had achieved some success in equipping trainees for higher-paid, skilled work in the *Département* and in Paris.

Dickens: Previous employment initiatives on the estate had reduced levels of violence while in operation. However, during the research there were no specific training or employment initiatives in operation on the estate, a problem which was exacerbated by the transfer of responsibility for youth training to employers—via the creation of local Training and Enterprise Councils—and the cessation of income support for 16- and 17-year-olds who had not secured, or had dropped out of full-time education, training schemes or employment.

Education

Flaubert: On the basis of national educational "league tables", the estate had been designated a *Zone Educationale Prioritaire* by the French Ministry of Education. This meant that additional resources had been directed towards the schools in the neighbourhood. These included additional specialist staff, additional staff hours for after-school work and the construction of a radio station which provided public service broadcasting to the surrounding region in an attempt to form closer and more positive social and economic links. In tandem with these initiatives, *Femmes Relais*, a semi-formal community organization, comprising Senegalese, North African, Kurdish, Iranian and Portuguese mothers, supported by Maghrebian community workers from the Mayor's Office, met regularly with representatives of the school, the police and the local administration to discuss the problems confronting young people, drugs, violence, racism, under-achievement, truancy, bullying etc., in the school and in the neighbourhood, and to devise collaborative, corporate solutions. *Femmes Relais*, in conjunction with *JCLT*, also offered language tuition and vocational training to parents. Meanwhile, local young people undertaking national service had been recruited by the school as "mentors" and "recreational counsellors". They also provided surveillance and protection against victimization for school students and had the effect of significantly reducing student–student violence.

Dickens: Levels of attainment in the secondary school on the Dickens Estate were roughly similar to those in the secondary school on the Flaubert Estate, *vis-à-vis* the national average. However, the implementation of the National Curriculum and Local Management of Schools had generated an enormously increased administrative load which made it increasingly difficult for the school to provide the requisite pastoral, sporting and social activities. These pressures were placing at risk the very close staff–student relationships and high standards of pastoral care for which the school was renowned. Increasingly, the school was becoming the locus and focus for violent racial conflict which spilt over from the neighbourhood. A few low-achieving white boys, those most likely to be the perpetrators of racial violence, continued to pose a serious problem to the school and, largely as a result of the pressures identified above, staff were resorting to exclusion more frequently. Feeling marginalized and scapegoated, exclusion appeared to deepen these students' frustration and anger. School students who were victimized, particularly Bengali children and young people, tended not to tell their parents, partly because they were concerned not to add to their parents' worries and partly because the only recourse available to parents was to stop their children going out. As a result, youngsters often opted to say nothing to the adults around them whom they perceived as being more or less powerless in the situation. The school, like others in adjacent areas, had attempted to respond to these difficulties by developing a Parent-Teacher Association, but mistrust amongst some Bengali parents and an apparent lack of interest amongst many others, had confounded their efforts. However, despite the formidable problems with which the school was attempting to wrestle, rather than the promise of additional support and resources, staff were "motivated" by the threat of the intervention of a Ministry of Education hit squad if standards fell further.

Inter-Agency Co-operation

Flaubert: Official initiatives to reduce victimization through inter-agency and inter-professional collaboration had been established since the early 1980s. The mayor had been central to this process and the arrangements for co-operation grew out of protracted, and continuing, negotiations between him and his fellow politicians and representatives of the adults and young people on the estate (Le Gales 1994; Jazouli 1995; Picard 1995). As we have noted, these negotiations had spawned the *Neighbourhood Council*. For its part, central government required statutory and voluntary welfare agencies, as a condition of their funding, to collaborate in projects which aimed to resolve problems of community life and neighbourhood conflict. They were required, in particular, to focus upon problems of social marginality, *Exclusion*, and to promote *Inclusion* via activities which contributed to the *Insertion* of young people into significant educational and vocational opportunities. These inter-agency and inter-professional initiatives had been institutionalized into the day-to-day practices of statutory and voluntary agencies in the neighbourhood. At the time of our research, this complex collaborative network had been evolving for eleven years.

Dickens: Public professionals from statutory agencies felt themselves to be under pressure to reconcile their commitment to inter-agency and inter-professional co-operation with their statutory responsibilities. Being required to do so within steadily reducing local authority budgets, inter-agency co-operation sometimes became another means whereby agencies would attempt to discharge or displace their statutory responsibilities. Agency priorities tended to be determined by their own "mission statements" or "quality targets", and even when problems of neighbourhood conflict were articulated, they seldom found their way on to agency "agendas". In the fields of child protection and youth justice, workers experienced an annexation of the professional task as they pursued priorities, and discharged functions specified in ever-greater detail by central government departments. This caused senior officers of the relevant departments to observe that the only response available to the council in the case of an incident of racial violence directed against a child or young person was to make the victim the subject of a child protection investigation, and to subject the perpetrator, if apprehended, to a correctional programme at the council's Youth Justice Centre. The professionals involved knew that this individualization of a profoundly social and political conflict was wholly inadequate, but felt they no longer had the means to engage with social conflict in the public domain.

Beyond this, some public professionals on the Dickens Estate were reluctant to involve the "public" in those problem-solving processes which did exist because to do so would, necessarily, bring them into a confrontation with deep-rooted inter-communal conflicts. Thus, problem-solving tended to be left to the professionals. Crime prevention programmes, *Safer Neighbourhoods*, *Safer Cities* etc., had come and gone and had, for their duration, had some effect, but because they were never seriously planned to mesh with the practices of local agencies they had little lasting impact. As a result, both professionals and local people had grown cynical about such short-term initiatives. Increasingly, agencies found themselves in competition for dwindling central government crime prevention resources which limited still further their motivation and capacity to collaborate.

Crime Prevention, Youth Justice and the Courts

Flaubert: Political, administrative and judicial systems tended to work together to render youth justice responsive to local situational, social, economic and cultural factors which might precipitate youth crime and victimization. Social prevention initiatives were institutionalized and integrated within and between local authority departments, locally-based offices of central government, central government departments, the voluntary sector and the "youth justice system". French children's judges are state employees and are expected to be active in their neighbourhoods, using knowledge gained through dealing with child care and juvenile offending cases to help focus the efforts and develop the activities of local welfare, educational, training and employment agencies. They are also enjoined to promote social *Insertion*, as a way of reducing crime and public disorder. On the Flaubert Estate they were pursuing these objectives through their membership of the management committees of local voluntary and neighbourhood organizations and regular meetings with the staff of *DPJJ*.

Dickens: On the Dickens Estate there was a clear separation between local crime prevention initiatives, which incorporated some "social", but mainly "situational", elements, and the local authority youth justice service which was wedded to an offence-focused "delinquency management" strategy. Crime prevention initiatives on the estate had been time-limited and project-based and, as such, additional rather than integral to the services provided locally by statutory and voluntary agencies. The lay magistrates approached during the research chose not to participate. Although they had sentenced young people and adults from the neighbourhood, not infrequently for racially-motivated crimes and gang-fighting, the local bench claimed to be insufficiently familiar with the neighbourhood and its problems to be of any help to the research team.

Local Politics

Flaubert: The mayor of the suburb in which the Flaubert Estate is built, like the majority of town mayors in France, served on the *Conseil National de Prévention de la Délinquance* chaired by the French Prime Minister. The mayor's office co-ordinates the expenditure of the town's share of the national Urban Policy budget with national, local and EU funds. The town has constructed a young people's resource centre, the Pagoda, on the Flaubert Estate where the mayor and his representatives met local people once a month to discuss problems of community life in general and the predicament of young people on the estate in particular. As such, the mayor's office served as a political link between the "private troubles" of the residents of the Flaubert Estate and the "public issues" which formed the basis for the development of urban policy at a national level.

Dickens: The dominant Labour group on the council was at odds with both government policy and the ideas espoused by the national party's front bench. At the time of our research, it was re-centralizing the services which had been "localized" by the previous Liberal Democrat administration. Very little information about this process had reached the electorate at this point. A sustained attempt by the secondary school on the Dickens Estate to involve local councillors in discussions about the safety of school students had proved ineffective.

49

Politics and Practice

Does politics make a difference in crime prevention and youth justice? In contrasting these two neighbourhoods we encounter one in which a politically-engaged public is devising new forms of social solidarity and another in which social atomization is accelerating. These differences have little to do with the respective scale or nature of their crime and poverty, the proclivities or potential of local residents, or the skills and abilities of the public professionals who serve them. Rather they speak to the social and political possibilities which can be opened up by a commitment from the political sphere that social cohesion and equality matter.

Since the early 1980s, local government in Britain has experienced both the introduction of "market" mechanisms into the allocation of services and a reduction and redistribution of resources in favour of central governmental control.[14] Together, both have contributed to the impotence and withdrawal of many of the youth service, education, community development and social welfare services which had previously contributed to the quality of communal life and cohesion in socially deprived neighbourhoods. The hallmark of Conservative governments in Britain between 1979 and 1997 was the development of a regulatory and administrative framework which has imposed quasi-market processes as a means of resource allocation, effectively bypassing the role played by elected, local democracy in the administration of the welfare state (Hutton 1995; Jenkins 1995). The quasi-markets of health, education and welfare aspired towards "slimline", "customer-oriented", "managerially-driven" public services, whose purpose was to be attuned to the "effective demand" of individual customers or, more usually, to the increasing variety of institutional "purchasers"—including local schools and housing associations—charged with acquiring services on their "user's" behalf. In lieu of the actual ability of users to purchase services within such markets, mechanisms have been imposed from the centre which supposedly seek to mirror the allocation which might have been attained if the market were working efficiently. Amongst the criteria which have evolved to gauge the value of public services has been an increased sensitivity to "exit"—the departure or withdrawal of users.

Yet because the means for gauging the "demand" for public services has become structurally disconnected from the alternative source of legitimacy within the local democratic process—voting—their administration has become increasingly "managerial", shaped by bureaucratically-determined "targets" in accordance with self-referential performance indicators imposed by central government (Clarke *et al.* 1994; Le Grand 1995). Although later in the process than some, these developments are now entering into the local allocation of policing and personal social services. Increasingly also, more resources—especially in the fields of crime prevention and urban regeneration—have been allocated through special programmes, operated by competitive bidding systems, in preference to mainstream programmes allocated through needs-based grants.

On the basis of our research, we would argue that the very different responses to the social dislocation of youth crime which we have observed are due in large part to the differing politics of, on the one hand, the *market project* pursued by British Conservative governments between 1979 and 1997 and, in contrast, the *solidarity project* pursued in France. The course taken by the "multi-agency approach" to crime prevention in Britain—witnessed by its failure to materialize on the Dickens Estate—is a case in point.[15] Traditionally, and certainly compared with France, there has always been a considerable degree of political autonomy and separation in the governance of local services in Britain—notably between police and local government services (Jones *et al.* 1996). Criticism during the 1970s was levelled at the inequality of the outcomes of professional discretion which such autonomy encouraged, at the conflicts which emerged about "care versus control" amongst professionals from different agencies, and at agencies' collective inability to approach crime and justice democratically.

Yet whereas initial calls for multi-agency collaboration may have reflected a "corporatist" desire to overcome the fragmentation of crime prevention practice (Crawford 1994; Hope and Shaw 1988), the effect of the combination of agency autonomy and quasi-market organization in Britain has been rather to exacerbate—or at least to fail to address—inherent inter-agency conflicts of interest over the meaning and purpose of community safety. Research on local collaborations shows a plethora of different relations and structures amongst agencies in differing areas (Liddle and Gelsthorpe 1994a, 1994b, 1994c; Home Office 1991). Since there is little variation from area to area in the way in which these agencies are formally constituted by statute, it is arguable that these differences reflect instead the varying outcomes in practice of frequent conflicts of interest and definition amongst participating agencies, some of which have been documented in detailed research case studies (Crawford and Jones 1995; Pearson *et al.* 1992; Blagg *et al.* 1988; Sampson *et al.* 1988).

Some conflict between agencies may be inevitable, springing from differential distributions of bureaucratic "power"—or capacity to mobilize resources —amongst agencies (Pearson *et al.* 1992); and different claims to professional legitimacy, "ownership", and competence in dealing with crime (Jones *et al.* 1996). Equally, mutual adjustment and accommodation may also be possible, if only to "save face" in public (Crawford and Jones 1995). Yet, as the research on the Dickens Estate suggests, the dynamic of conflict underlying inter-agency relations may stem as much from pressures being placed on individual agencies to meet their performance targets, protect their budgets and compete for marginal funds, as from anything endemic to the constitution of inter-agency relations. While the call for inter-agency collaboration may have started off as a means of overcoming inefficiency in the delivery of crime prevention and justice, this does not seem to have occurred in practice,[16] and local crime prevention "partnerships" may now be another arena in which endemic inter-agency competition takes place. It is likely that such markets can fail, or that accommodations are reached amongst agencies which do not necessarily ensure an equitable, just or effective distribution of welfare.[17]

So, are there prospects for change in Britain, and is something akin to the "French model" a likely outcome? At the time of writing, it is apparent that one of the priorities of the new Labour Government elected with a landslide majority in May 1997 will be the introduction of a Crime and Disorder Bill which, as one of its main provisions, will impose a statutory duty upon both the police and local authorities to prepare a joint "Community Safety Plan" for their areas. Such plans are to be consistent with other local plans, e.g. for policing and for Children's Services, which individual agencies are also enjoined to provide through legislation. While these proposals will give public, legal recognition to the idea of "community safety" as a product of the activities of *both* police and local government, it remains to be seen what "community safety planning" might achieve in practice. By imposing a joint responsibility, it may be that much of the grounds for institutional conflict between police and local government might be removed, inasmuch as the agencies can orientate their respective performance targets towards commonly-agreed objectives, albeit those hammered out in the negotiations leading up to the promulgation of an agreed plan. In this sense, the planning process may revive and strengthen the "corporatist" aspiration of earlier formulations of the community safety ideal, rendering a more efficient, collective response by local agencies to the common problems of order in their communities. Nevertheless, even if agencies were able to agree amongst themselves, it still remains an open issue as to whether such arrangements would lead to a greater amelioration of the exclusion which, we have argued, underpins the social dislocations of youth crime and concentrated victimization.

In addition to improving the efficiency of the local state apparatus, the task defined by Mitterrand and Bonnemaison concerned the construction, and then the institutionalization, of *a new relationship between Citizen and State* —between the political centre and the social margins. For a time, at least, the institutional infrastructure of the French Model provided a two-way conduit of power and resources along the vertical dimension linking the citizen, the community and the State. And although local agencies were central to the process of delivering community safety, they were also held accountable to the task through a two-way conduit of democratic power—through the downward transmission of power from the central State, and through the upward expression of political "voice" from the social margins.

A key issue facing the development of the local governance of community safety in Britain, then, is whether it is possible to emulate the French successes described here without the active democratic process which underpinned them. One of the distinctive features of the growth of social dislocation associated with the new poverty are *concentration effects* (Sampson and Wilson 1995; Wilson 1987)—particularly the way in which social difficulties feed off and amplify each other in a spiral of deterioration and negative feedback (Hope 1996; Skogan 1990). The experience of destabilized neighbourhoods and schools caught in these spirals is one where adverse circumstances "ratchet" together to produce compounded social dislocations. In the American case, the weak institutional infrastructure allows a freer hand to market forces, reinforced by racist practices, which constrain directly the choices of individuals (Wilson 1996). In Britain, the coupling of agency objectives to the choice decisions of individual "users" also means that agencies are ill-placed to respond in ways which could bring about stabilization and halt the ratcheting process. Indeed, the built-in incentives in the marketization approach for agencies to respond to the "effective demand" of consumers for "exit" may only serve to stimulate the process of destabilization.[18]

This brings us to the main conclusion of our paper: that the essence of the French model for tackling social dislocation lies in its local politics—especially the construction of a two-way conduit of power linking the citizen and the State. Not only does this provide a stake in society for those with no stake, but it also places local government in a pivotal position in the channel of communication and resources, and thereby also ties its agencies into a system of democratic accountability. In neither the American nor the British case does that conduit exist, though for different reasons. While the weak political infrastructure of the American ghetto exacerbates its social isolation, the marketization of the welfare infrastructure in impoverished areas in Britain has substituted "exit" for democratic "voice" as the medium of communication and the criterion for resource allocation. As such, public services are ceasing to deliver the cultural capital to the community which might enable residents to resist social dislocation and, importantly, have ceased to become the medium whereby private troubles could be translated into public issues (Mills 1957).

Notes

An earlier version of this paper was presented at the Annual Meetings of the American Society of Criminology, Chicago, IL., November, 1996. The study reported in the paper was carried out by John Pitts and Philip Smith and supported by the Economic and Social Research Council (ESRC) under its Crime and Social Order Research Programme, of which Tim Hope was Programme Director (1993–1997). All views put forward in this paper are not necessarily those of the ESRC.

1. A regular national sample survey carried out in England and Wales on behalf of the Home Office.
2. Osborn et al. 1996; Osborn and Tseloni 1995; Trickett et al. 1995b; Ellingworth et al. 1995; Osborn et al. 1992; Sampson and Groves 1989; Sampson and Wooldredge 1987.
3. Osborn et al. 1996; Osborn and Tseloni 1995; Ellingworth et al. 1995.
4. Government and housing association survey data show that the concentration of poverty in social housing has increased dramatically since the early 1980s (Page 1993: 31). At the beginning of the 1980s the average household income of council house residents was 73 per cent of the national average. At the beginning of the 1990s this had fallen to 48 per cent (Page 1993). By 1995, over 50 per cent of council households had no breadwinner (Rowntree 1996).
5. Osborn and Tseloni 1995; Ellingworth et al, 1995; Osborn et al. 1992.
6. Osborn et al. 1996; Osborn et al. 1992.
7. Osborn et al. 1996; Osborn and Tseloni 1995; Trickett et al. 1995a; Ellingworth et al. 1995; Osborn et al. 1992; Sampson and Groves 1989; Sampson and Wooldredge 1987.
8. Osborn et al. 1996; Osborn et al. 1992; Sampson and Wooldredge 1987.
9. In common with some countries. e.g. France, but unlike others, public housing in Britain has been concentrated to a considerable extent on large "estates" (Power 1993). Consequently, the economic polarization of tenure "shows up on the ground as a concentration of people with low incomes in particular neighbourhoods" (JRF 1995; volume 1: 29).

10. This is not to imply that the investment of cultural capital does not depend upon economic capital investment. As Bourdieu notes, "economic capital is at the root of all the other types of capital and that these transformed, disguised forms of economic capital, never entirely reducible to that definition, produce their most specific effects only to the extent that they conceal (not least from their possessors) the fact that economic capital is at their root" (1986: 252).

11. For which see Gilling 1997; Crawford 1997.

12. A similar process of concentration of youth poverty and a consequent explosion of crime was observed in a set of blocks on an estate in the North of England (Hope 1995b).

13. In France youth justice, child care and protection are all the responsibility of a national agency, the *DPJJ* (*Direction de la Protection Judiciaire et de la Jeunesse*). *DPJJ* trains and employs all the children's judges and court social workers in France. It works through its *Action Educative* bureaux (akin to off-site units) with children who are unwilling or unable to stay in mainstream schooling. It employs over 1000 detached/outreach youth workers and has been a lead agency in the development of the Social Prevention initiative at a local level.

14. In Britain the majority of local government expenditure on main programmes and services is financed from central taxation which is reallocated in the form of grant from central government.

15. Certainly, multi-agency working does not appear to emerge "spontaneously" in localities. On two public housing estates where local housing authorities had established locally-based offices and management structures, no formal offers of partnership were made by other agencies, especially not the police (Foster and Hope 1993).

16. For instance, see the recent report of the Audit Commission for England and Wales on the local response to offending by young people (Audit Commission 1996).

17. Bill Jordan, for example, has advanced the argument that "rational" market behaviour by social service managers responding to the new environment of cost-consciousness leads to the use of "club-like criteria for admission to or rejection from service units" (1996: 178), thereby magnifying exclusion from benefit.

18. For example, in a London secondary school, where one of the authors is presently undertaking research, rapid demographic change in the neighbourhood is reflected in rapid changes in the school roll. This is not only undermining the school's capacity to build a stable ethos but is also selectively sucking in students with behavioural difficulties—including those with histories of racist and violent behaviour—who are being transferred or excluded from other schools in the borough. Conduct problems within the school are being amplified with the concentration of such pupils. Parents with sufficient personal capital are increasingly seeking transfers of their children to other schools, staff morale is deteriorating (not least because of reductions in support services), and staff turnover increasing, replacing the more by the less experienced teachers. These interactions seem to be ratcheting together to reinforce youth violence in both the neighbourhood and the school.

References

Audit Commission (1996), *Misspent Youth . . . young people and crime*, London: Audit Commission for Local Authorities and the National Health Service in England and Wales.

Blagg, H., Pearson, G., Sampson, A., Smith, D., and Stubbs, P. (1988), Inter-agency co-operation: rhetoric and reality. In Hope, T., and Shaw, M. (eds), *Communities and Crime Reduction*, London? HMSO.

Bobbio, N. (1996), *Left and Right*. Cambridge: Polity Press.

Bonnemaison (1983), *Face à la délinquance: prévention, repression, solidarité: Rapport au prime ministre de la Commission des Maires sur la Sécurité*, Paris: La Documentation Française.

Bourdieu, P. (1986), The forms of capital. In J. G. Richardson (ed.), *Handbook of Theory and Research for the Sociology of Education*, Westport, CT: Greenwood Press.

Bursik, R. J. (1988), Social disorganization and theories of crime and delinquency: problems and prospects. *Criminology*, 26: 519–51.

Campbell, Beatrix (1993), *Goliath*, London: Methuen.

Cannan, C. (1996), The Impact of Social Development and Anti-Exclusion Policies on the French Social Work Professions *Social Work in Europe*, vol. 3, no. 2: 1–4.

Clarke, J., Cochrane, A., and McLaughlin, E. (1994), *Managing Social Policy*, London: Sage.

Coleman, J. S. (1990), *Foundations of Social Theory*, Cambridge, MA: Bleknap Press.

Cooper, A., Hetherington, R., Baistow, K., Pitts, J., and Spriggs, A. (1995), *Positive Child Protection: A View From Abroad*, Lyme Regis: Russell House.

Crawford, A., and Jones, M. (1995), Inter-agency co-operation and community-based crime prevention. *British Journal of Criminology*, vol. 35: 17–33.

De Liege, M.-P. (1988), The fight against crime and fear: a new initiative in France. In Hope, T., and Shaw, M. (eds), *Communities and Crime Reduction*, London: HMSO.

De Liege, M.-P. (1991), Social development and the prevention of crime in France: a challenge for local parties and central government. In Farrell, M., and Heidensohn, F., *Crime in Europe*, London: Routledge.

Donzelot, J., and Roman, J. (1991), Le Déplacement de la question sociale. In Donzelot, J. (ed.), *Face à l'Exclusion*, Paris: Editions Esprit.

Ellingworth, D., Osborn, D. R., Trickett, A., and Pease, K. (1995), *Prior victimisation and crime risk*, Quantitative Criminology Group, University of Manchester (also, in press, *Journal of Crime Prevention and Risk Management*).

Ely, P., and Stanley, C. (1990), *The French Alternative: Delinquency Prevention and Child Protection in France*, London: NACRO.

Esping-Andersen, G. (1990), *The Three Worlds of Welfare Capitalism*, Cambridge: Polity Press.

Feeley, M., and Simon, J. (1992), The new penology: Notes on the emerging strategy of corrections and its implementation. *Criminology*, vol. 30, no. 4: 452–74.

Felson, M. (1994), *Crime and Everyday Life*, Thousand Oaks, CA: Pine Forge Press.

Foster, Janet, and Hope, T. (1993), *Housing, Community and Crime: The Impact of the Priority Estates Project*, Home Office Research Study no. 131, London: HMSO.

Furstenberg, F. (1993), How families manage risk and opportunity in dangerous neighborhoods. In Wilson, W. J. (ed.), *Sociology and the Public Agenda*, Newbury Park, CA: Sage.

Gallo, E. (1995), The penal system in France: from correctionalism to managerialism. In Ruggerio, V., Ryan, M., and Sim, J. (eds), *Western European Penal Systems: A Critical Anatomy*, London: Sage.

Garland, D. (1985), *Punishment and Welfare*, Aldershot: Gower.

Garland, D. (1996), The limits of the sovereign state: strategies of crime control in contemporary society. *British Journal of Criminology*, vol. 36: 445–71.

Gilling, D. (1994), Multi-agency crime prevention in Britain: the problem of combining situational and social strategies. In Clarke, R. V. G. (eds), *Crime Prevention Studies*, vol. 3, Monsey, NY: Criminal Justice Press.

Gladstone, F. J. (1980), *Co-ordinating Crime Prevention Efforts*, Home Office Research Study no. 62, London: HMSO.

Graham, J. (1993), Crime prevention policies in Europe. *European Journal of Crime, Criminal Law and Criminal Justice*, vol. 1, no. 2.

Graham, J., and Bowling, B. (1995), *Young People and Crime*, London: Home Office.

Green, A. E. (1996), Aspects of the changing geography of income and wealth. In J. Hills (ed.), *New Inequalities: The Changing Distribution of Income and Wealth in the United Kingdom*, Cambridge: University of Cambridge Press.

Hagan, J. (1994), *Crime and Disrepute*, Thousand Oaks, CA: Pine Forge Press.

Hagell, A., and Newburn, T. (1994), *Persistent Young Offenders*, London: Policy Studies Institute.

Hall, S., *et al.* (1978), *Thatcherism*, London: New Left Review.

Hay, C. (1996), *Re-stating Social and Political Change*, Buckingham: Open University Press.

Hills, J. (1996), *New Inequalities: The Changing Distribution of Income and Wealth in the United Kingdom*, Cambridge: University of Cambridge Press.

Home Office (1983), *Crime Prevention: A Co-ordinated Approach*, London: Home Office.

Home Office (1991), *Safer Communities: The Local Delivery of Crime Prevention Through the Partnership Approach*, Report of a Working Group (James Morgan, Chair), Standing Conference on Crime Prevention, London: Home Office.

Home Office (1994), *The Criminal Statistics*, London: HMSO.

Home Office (1996), *Home Office Statistical Bulletin*, London: Home Office.

Hope, T. (1989), Burglary and vandalism in schools: a study of theory and practice in the prevention of crime. Unpublished PhD thesis, University of London.

Hope, T. (1995a), Community crime prevention. In M. Tonry and D. P. Farrington (eds), *Building a Safer Society: Strategic Approaches to Crime Prevention*, Crime and Justice, vol. 19, Chicago: University of Chicago Press.

Hope, T. (1995b), The flux of victimization, *British Journal of Criminology*, vol. 35: 327–42.

Hope, T. (1996), Communities, crime and inequality in England and Wales. In T. Bennett (ed,), *Preventing Crime and Disorder: Targeting Strategies and Responsibilities*, Cambridge: Institute of Criminology.

Hope, T. (1997), Inequality and the future of community crime prevention. In Lab, S. P. (ed.), *Crime Prevention at a Crossroads*, American Academy of Criminal Justice Sciences Monograph Series, Cincinnati, OH: Anderson Publishing.

Hope, T., and Foster, J. (1992), Conflicting forces: changing the dynamics of crime and community on a problem estate. *British Journal of Criminology*, vol. 32: 92.

Hope, T., and Murphy, D. (1983), Problems of implementing crime prevention. *Howard Journal*, vol. 22, 38–50.

Hutton, W. (1995), *The State We're In*, London: Jonathan Cape.

Jazouli, A. (1995), *Une Saison en banlieue*, Paris: Plon.

Jenkins, S. (1995), *Accountable to None: the Tory Nationalisation of Britain*, London: Hamish Hamilton.

Jones, T., Newburn, T., and Smith, D. J. (1996), Policing and the idea of democracy. *British Journal of Criminology*, vol. 36: 182–98.

Jordan, B. (1996), *A Theory of Poverty and Social Exclusion*, Cambridge: Polity Press.

JRF (1995), *Joseph Rowntree Foundation Inquiry into Income and Wealth*, vols. 1 and 2, York: Joseph Rowntree Foundation.

King, M. (1989), Social crime prevention à la Thatcher. *Howard Journal*, vol. 28: 291–312.

Le Gales, P. (1994), The political dynamics of European policy implementation: poverty III in Mantes-la-Jolie. *Local Government Policy Making*, vol. 20, no. 5, May: 39–44.

Le Grand, J. (1995), Quasi-markets in welfare. In Trevillion, S., and Beresford, P., *Social Work Education and the Community Care Revolution*, London: NISW.

Lemierre, R. (1994), Juvenile services of the French Ministry of Justice. *Social Work in Europe*, vol. 1, no. 2.

Liddle, A. M., and Gelsthorpe, L. R. (1994a), *Inter-Agency Crime Prevention: Organizing Local Delivery*. Paper no. 52, Police Research Group, Crime Prevention Unit Series, London: Home Office Police Department.

Liddle, A. M., and Gelsthorpe, L. R. (1994b), *Crime Prevention and Inter-Agency Co-operation*. Paper no. 53, Police Research Group, Crime Prevention Unit Series, London: Home Office Police Department.

Liddle, A. M., and Gelsthorpe, L. R. (1994c), *Inter-Agency Crime Prevention: Further Issues*. Supplementary Paper to CPU Series Paper nos. 52 and 53, Police Research Group, Crime Prevention Unit Series, London: Home Office Police Department.

Loney, M. (1983), *Community Against Government: The British Community Development Project, 1968–78—A Study of Government Incompetence*, London: Heinemann Educational Books.

McFate, K. (1996), Western states in the new world order. In K. McFate, R. Lawson, and W. J. Wilson (eds), *Poverty, Inequality, and the Future of Social Policy: Western States in the New World Order*, New York: Russell Sage Foundation.

McFate, K., Lawson, R., and Wilson, W. J. (1996), (eds), *Poverty, Inequality, and the Future of Social Policy: Western States in the New World Order*, New York: Russell Sage Foundation.

Mills, C. W. (1957), *The Sociological Imagination*, Harmondsworth, Penguin.

Noble, M., and Smith, G. (1996), Two nations? changing patterns of income and wealth in two contrasting areas. In J. Hills (ed.), *New Inequalities: The Changing Distribution of Income and Wealth in the United Kingdom*, Cambridge: University of Cambridge Press.

Osborn, D. R., Ellingworth, D., Hope, T., and Trickett, A. (1996), Are repeatedly victimized households different? *Journal of Quantitative Criminology*, vol. 12: 223–45.

Osborn, D. R., Trickett, A., and Elder, R. (1992), Area characteristics and regional variates as determinants of area property crime levels. *Journal of Quantitative Criminology*, vol. 8: 265–85.

Osborn, D. R., and Tseloni, A. (1995), *The Distribution of Household Property Crimes*. University of Manchester School of Economic Studies Discussion Paper no. 9530, Manchester: University of Manchester.

Page, D. (1993), *Building for Communities: A Study of New Housing Association Estates*, York: Joseph Rowntree Foundation.

Parti Socialiste Français (1986), *Les Murs d'argent. Manifeste contre la privatisation des prisons*, Paris; Parti Socialiste.

Pearce, J. J. (1995), French lessons: young people comparative research and community safety. *Social Work in Europe*, vol. 1, no. 3: 32–6.

Pearson, G., Sampson, A., Blagg, H., Stubbs, P., and Smith, D. (1992), Crime, community and conflict: the multi-agency approach. In D. Downes (ed.), *Unravelling Criminal Justice*, London: Macmillan.

Picard, P. (1995), *Mantes-la-jolie: Carnet de Route d'un Mairie De Banlieue*, Paris: Syros.

Pitts, J. (1995), Public issues and private troubles: a tale of two cities. *Social Work in Europe*, vol. 2, no. 1: 3–11.

Pitts, J. (1996), The politics and practice of youth justice. In Mclaughlin, E., and Muncie, J. (eds), *Controlling Crime*, London: Sage Publications/Open University Press.

Pitts, J. (forthcoming), *Discipline or Solidarity: The New Politics of Youth Justice*.

Power, A. (1993), *Hovels to High-Rise: State Housing in Europe since 1850*, London: Routledge.

Rowntree Foundation (1996), *The Future of Work: Contributions to the Debate*, York: Joseph Rowntree Foundation.

Sampson, A., Stubbs, P., Smith, D., Pearson, G., and Blagg, H. (1988), Crime, localities, and the multi-agency approach. *British Journal of Criminology*, vol. 28: 473–93.

Sampson, R. J., and Groves, W. B. (1989), Community structure and crime: testing social disorganization theory. *American Journal of Sociology*, vol. 94: 774–802.

Sampson, R. J., and Wilson, W. J. (1995), Toward a theory of race, crime and urban inequality. In Hagan, J., and Peterson, R. D. (eds), *Crime and Inequality*, Stanford, CA: Stanford University Press.

Sampson, R. J., and Wooldredge, J. D. (1987), Linking the micro- and macro-level dimensions of lifestyle-routine activity and opportunity models of predatory victimization. *Journal of Quantitative Criminology*, vol. 3: 371–93.

Skogan, W. G. (1990), *Disorder and Decline: Crime and the Spiral of Decay in American Neighborhoods*, New York: Free Press.

Thorpe, D., Smith, D., Green, C., and Paley, J. (1980), *Out of Care*, London: Allen and Unwin.

Trickett, A., Ellingworth, D., Hope, T., and Pease, K. (1995), Crime victimization in the eighties. *British Journal of Criminology*, vol. 35: 343–59.

Wacquant, L. (1996), The comparative structure and experience of urban exclusion: "race", class and space in Chicago and Paris. In K. McFate, R. .Lawson, and W. J. Wilson (eds), *Poverty, Inequality, and the Future of Social Policy: Western States in the New World Order*, New York: Russell Sage Foundation.

Wieviorka, M. (1994), Racism in Europe: unity and diversity. In Ratsani, A., and Westwood, S., *Racism, Modernity, Identity on the Western Front*, Cambridge: Polity Press.

Wilson, W. J. (1987), *The Truly Disadvantaged: The Inner City, the Underclass and Public Policy*, Chicago: University of Chicago Press.

Wilson, W. J. (1996), *When Work Disappears: The World of the New Urban Poor*, New York: Knopf.

Young, J. (in press), From inclusive to exclusive society: nightmares in the European Dream. In V. Ruggiero, N. South, and I. Taylor (eds), *Crime and Social Order in Europe*, London: Routledge.

Dangerous Futures: Social Exclusion and Youth Work in Late Modernity

Alan France and Paul Wiles

Abstract

The paper contrasts the role and structure of youth work in modern and late modern societies. Modern societies linked citizenship to inclusion in production and youth work helped the transition of young people from childhood to inclusion into the labour market and citizenship. When postwar full employment eased these transition processes then youth work concentrated on leisure provision and dealing with the small numbers of excluded young people. Late modern societies redefine citizenship in terms of market choices but also create increasing risks, which a declining state can no longer manage, and a growing use of social exclusion as a form of social control. These changes demand a new role and structure for youth work.

Keywords

Youth work; Social exclusion; Citizenship; Social control

Social Change and Late Modernity

There is an ongoing debate within the social sciences about present processes of social change and whether we are living in "new times" (Turner 1990; Bauman 1992). Postmodernists argue that we are in a new age: one distinctly different from the world of modernity (Lyotard 1984). Critics challenge this view by claiming that continuity and stability still abound and that the idea of "post" anything is unhelpful for understanding the present (Habermas 1987). However, without taking sides in this debate (which can sometimes be simply semantic), it is clear that society at the end of the twentieth century is undergoing significant change. Giddens (1991), while rejecting the postmodern mantle argues that an explanatory, more productive term is that of "late

Address for Correspondence: *Paul Wiles, Department of Criminology, University of Sheffield, Crookesmoor Building, Conduit Road, Sheffield, S10 1FL.*

modernity". We prefer such a concept because it captures both continuity and change, recognizing that modernity was never a project which remained static (Habermas 1987). Changes in our present social arrangements can, at least heuristically, be examined in terms of the transition from modernity to late modernity (Giddens 1991). This paper aims to explore the implications of this issue for the future role of youth work. In the discussion that follows we will identify how social, economic and political change is creating tensions for locally-funded Youth Services and youth workers. We then conclude by highlighting a number of changes Youth Services may have to make if they are not only to survive but flourish.

Modernity and Citizenship

Giddens characterizes modernity as a post-traditional society that involves the establishment of post-feudal institutions and modes of behaviour. Modernity, in this sense, refers to the introduction of three main developments: industrialism, capitalism and the growth of the nation state. Industrialism is conceptualized as the creation of material power and machinery in the production process which affects social relations. Capitalism, on the other hand, is the development of commodity production involving both competitive product markets and the commodification of labour power. Neither of these undertake surveillance responsibilities, although both can have a function of instilling discipline in the modern citizen either through the exchange of money or through controlling labour power.

The third and most important development of modernity has been the growth of the nation state. This has had a number of key functions. First, the nation state undertakes what Giddens calls the "territoriality of surveillance", while also having the monopoly of control over legitimate violence. Second, it creates organizations that regulate social relations across time and space, and third, it is a key actor in protecting its citizens. The nation state can therefore be seen as having the potential to provide and protect freedom and liberty, while also having the power to impose discipline and order on its citizens (for a fuller discussion of these themes, see Foucault 1977; and Habermas 1987).

Modernity is often believed to have achieved its full potential, at any rate in Britain, in the postwar period. With aid from the nation state, capitalism and industrialism provided stability of social relations and the full commodification of labour power. Discipline and control were maintained through greater labour opportunities, increased wages and a claimed fairer distribution of society's resources through the social wage.[1] Work or paid employment, therefore, became the defining factor in the identification of the citizen. To be a worker or wage-earner was seen as essential to being a part of the modern project. The nation state aided this process in a number of ways. First, it supported the notion of "full employment" for all by creating jobs and resources for economic growth. Second, the nation state increased the possibilities for inclusion by expanding citizenship rights, not only in terms of employment rights but also social, political and civil rights (Marshall 1950). Third and finally, the state took greater responsibility for the management of individual risk and security by offering universal social services and education.

60

This risk management and social inclusion was aided by the creation of financial benefits for the unemployed and the poor through the development of social assistance and unemployment benefit.

Youth, Citizenship and Modernity

As far as young people were concerned the postwar period, up until the 1960s, was a time when their "social integration"[2] was a central aim of the state. National policy documents proposed that the state had an obligation to its young citizens to create opportunities for their integration into mainstream society (Board of Education 1940). During the early postwar years inclusion of the young was to be achieved by greater employment opportunities and the improvement of the transition from school to labour market (Ministry of Education 1947; see also Davis 1990). Access to adult citizenship was therefore co-ordinated by the state through the labour market.

But while the rhetoric emphasized the social justice of inclusion and citizenship, there were also economic motives for wanting to pursue such policies. As the postwar economy grew, so did the demands for unskilled and semi-skilled labour. For example, Davies (1986) shows that much of the postwar social democratic project was, in reality, a response to the needs of employers and industry. Policy documents such as the Crowther (1959) and Newsom (Central Advisory Council for Education (England) 1963) reports recommended that changes in education were made to improve the skill levels and abilities of the young. Education policy increasingly focused attention on skill shortages as Britain's economy seemed to be losing its international competitiveness.

The policy of social inclusion, therefore, was greatly influenced by the needs of industry and the labour market. This is not to say that this was a problem for young people or the state. Clearly, the shortage of labour was to the advantage of both. Young people benefited from having clear pathways to adult citizenship[3] while discipline and control of the young was undertaken by employers and the labour market.

Youth Work in Modernity

The establishment of youth work can historically be located in the middle class movements of the Victorian era. Smith (1988) argues that the roots of youth work lie in the early "improving movements" of the middle and educated classes in the late nineteenth century. Many of these developments were linked to either the evangelical movement or the efforts of the Jewish community to improve the working class. This saw a massive growth of youth clubs and activities run by organizations such as the Boys Clubs, the Scouting movement, and the Boys Brigade.[4] These youth movements were part of a much wider attempt to improve the physical and moral health of the industrial, urban proletariat. Anyone who has read, for example, Baden Powell's *Scouting for Boys* will know how it mixes play-based activity with stern moral lectures and instructions on healthy living. This mix would have seemed less odd to its original readers than it does to us today since a powerful popular ideological cocktail of muscular Christianity, popular neo-Darwinian evolutionary ideas and eugenics provided an integrated reading of moral and physical well-being.

Youth work was clearly seen as having a major role in the character-building of the young working class. Butters and Newell, writing in the late 1970s, argued that this tradition continued to dominate the history of youth work and so aided the status quo by ensuring that middle-class values were passed down to working-class youth. As they state: "If enough character is produced by education and youth work, the mature citizens that emerge will find a way to make the institutions of the country run smoothly and humanely" (Butters and Newell 1978: 41).

The formal establishment of youth work into the state welfare system was undertaken much later, towards the end of the Second World War. Concerns about the impact of the war on young people and the support by the incoming Labour administration for the bipartisan policies on welfare and education which had emerged during the war, meant that youth work was seen as having a key role in implementing social policies of inclusion. Much of the discussion, at that time, focused on how youth work could play a central role in the "training of the young for citizenship" (Ministry of Education 1945). The new national education system was to take responsibility for educating those under 15, but youth work was given the role of ensuring that young workers, aged between 16 and 21, were trained for citizenship. What this meant in reality was that youth work was seen as a site of intervention where opportunities existed for the state to reinforce national norms and values and develop the responsibilities of citizenship (Smith 1988: 39). Inclusion for the young was conditional upon fulfilling obligations, such as undertaking paid work, and accepting the norms and values of the nation state. Youth work was seen as the ideal mode for such intervention because of its access to young people through leisure. Youth workers' ideal of voluntarism also gave them a unique relationship with young people and the opportunity to encourage citizenship, especially amongst the most disadvantaged.

The legal establishment of youth work within the state was undertaken in the 1944 Education Act.[5] The Act required local authorities to meet the needs of young people, but the legislation laid down no minimum standards or statutory obligations and instructed them to have regard to existing voluntary provision. The nature and extent of youth work, therefore, was left to be defined at local level.[6] The extent of youth work, as a service aimed at aiding social inclusion of the young, therefore, was limited from the start. Astley (1987) suggests that part of the failure of youth work arose not from the lack of enthusiasm by senior civil servants, but from the lack of political will by the politicians of the day to put in the required resources (1987: 26). Davies (1986: 98), on the other hand, suggests that limited funds were given to youth work because the general growth of the postwar economy led to the success of the inclusion project which meant that young people seemed less dangerous than had been feared.

The High Point of Modernity

It was out of this initial failure that contemporary youth work emerged. By the end of the 1950s it was recognized that it had lost its direction, had failed to fulfil its initial promise and that social change now required a new form of practice (Albemarle Report 1960). It was not suggested that youth work abandon the project of inclusion, but that it needed to deliver this in different ways.

At the end of the 1950s the very success of modernity created a number of new problems for the nation state and the Youth Service. As Eric Hobsbawm (1994) points out, the late 1950s and early 1960s were the period when the "teenager" was discovered and youth was created as an autonomous category;[7] as a result, he argues, of the success of modernity. Large numbers of young people benefited from increases in educational opportunities and full employment and this gave them greater autonomy, both as thinkers and consumers. The most visible public signs of this were the new cultural practices and political radicalism of the 1960s. Abrams (1961) points out that teenagers had been the main beneficiaries of the postwar economic boom. Full employment and increasing youth wages had created the affluent teenager who had greater spending power than previous generations. This in turn made possible the development of a new consumer youth market. However, it initially existed as a single, undifferentiated youth market. Not only was the teenager born, but also a market in youth fashion and music which transcended the existing social distinctions of class. The new teenager, therefore, not only created more generational conflict but also undercut existing structures of power and authority.[8] Expanding numbers of university students also shaped a greater intellectual and ideological autonomy from parents and tradition. The success of modernity, therefore, was important in creating "youth" as an autonomous category and in helping ultimately to create some of the conditions for late modernity.

It was in this context that youth work developed a set of working practices which are still influential today. At the centre of the changes was the Albemarle Report (1960). This was the vehicle by which modern youth work was established. The Albemarle Committee were asked to review the success of youth work and to recommend its future direction. As many commentators have rightly pointed out, the Albemarle Report set a radical agenda for the future of youth work (Davies 1986; Smith 1988; Davis 1990; Astley 1987). It rejected the character-building approach, arguing that such a method was out of touch with young people and did not reflect their needs in the modern world:

> these particular words [service, dedication, leadership and character-building] now connect little with the realities of life as most young people see them: they do not seem to "speak to their condition". They recall the hierarchies, the less interesting moments of school speech days and other occasions of moral exhortation. (Albemarle Report 1960: para 145).

The Committee suggested that if the Youth Service[9] was to attract greater numbers of participants, then it had to make radical changes. Of central concern to Albemarle was the impact of the new consumerism on young people. The use of youth clubs had declined and the fact that the Youth Service was only attracting 1 in 3 young people was a major concern. To increase their membership Albemarle proposed that youth clubs would have to compete with the new commercial leisure facilities. This led to a massive investment in youth work facilities and staffing to enable youth workers to compete with the expanding leisure market. Not only were facilities to be modernized, but the type of activity young people were to be offered was also to change. As Davies summarizes:

> A key aim was to reach those "many young [people] who leave school lonely and estranged, (para 184) and to "help many more individuals find their way better, personally and socially" (para 138). This too was to be done through contemporary activities—skiffle and washboard groups were specially mentioned. (Davies 1986: 100).

As the above quotation highlights, Albemarle was concerned not only with the cultural adjustment of the many (Butters and Newell 1978), but also with those young people who felt excluded from an increasingly affluent society. While unemployment was not a significant issue, there was a growing concern about the "unattached": that is those young people who had little contact with the Youth Service. In answer to this problem Albemarle recommended that the Youth Service needed to develop alternative ways of working with those on the margins of society who were at risk of moving into delinquency. The result of this was the adoption of working practices, such as detached work, which had been pioneered in the inner-city missions of the USA.[10]

Not only did Albemarle recommend that youth work shift its emphasis to helping young people come to terms with the modern world, it also proposed that it should focus on young people's social needs rather than their needs for skills training and informal instruction (Davies 1986). The result was the establishment of what has become known as "social education".[11] While the term has always been controversial (see: Butters and Newall, 1978, Davies, 1986 and Smith, 1988), it is now seen as central to professional youth work practice (Smith 1988). Social education is an extension of the child-centred schooling tradition, which encourages self-determination, into youth work. Smith suggests that "social education is a particular type of learning process [usually taking place in informal contexts] and/or an attempt to achieve an internal change of consciousness such as the achievement of maturity" (Smith 1988: 91). The approach differed from character-building in being a shift from "personal adjustment to person-centredness". Social education, therefore, had clear links to the growing individualism of modernity and its social democratic ideal which encouraged an expansion of the social and political inclusion of citizens. Social education was aimed at developing young people as individuals and so ensuring their participation in this new, more inclusive political process.

Late Modernity and Citizenship

We now turn to the different world of late modernity. We have already pointed out that the nature of late modernity is much debated, although it is broadly accepted as involving fundamental changes in the way contemporary developed societies are organized. Roche (1992), for example, highlights an expansion of neoliberal economics, the growth of globalization and technology, and the declining role of the nation state, whilst Wagner (1994) argues that the first clear indication that modernity was moving into a new phase was the global economic crisis of the 1970s. However, for present purposes three aspects of late modernity are of particular importance.

One indicator of late modernity is what Giddens and others call the growth of the "risk society" (Giddens 1991; Beck 1992). Late modernity is characterized by a risk culture in which both lay actors and technical specialists use the concept of risk and its management to organize their world. In order to try and control risks the future is continually drawn into the present by means of the reflexive organization of knowledge. However, whilst people in late modernity attempt to manage and reduce risk, the nature of the society in which they live continually throws up new risks. As Giddens argues, ". . . high modernity . . . is apocalyptic not because it is inevitably heading towards calamity, but because it introduces risks which previous generations have not had to face" (Giddens 1991: 4). He focuses especially on new environmental risks, but another key area where risk has increased is the labour market. Since the mid-1980s globalization and technological change have led to decreased labour market security. Three main trends are evident. First, whereas modernity at its height believed full employment could be achieved and maintained, late modern societies are now characterized by unpredictable levels of employment and unemployment. There is a recognition that full employment may be unsustainable and some unemployment structural (Pixley 1993). Not only does this create insecurity for the unemployed, but it also creates fear amongst those workers employed in industries that are at the forefront of economic restructuring. Second, the notion that employment careers are for life and that mobility is within a company career structure has diminished. Instead, greater emphasis is placed on the development of individual biographies in which citizens negotiate their way through life by changing direction at different points in time (Beck 1992).[12] Third, in so far as new jobs are created, then they are predominantly within the service sector rather than in manufacturing. Service jobs, however, have traditionally offered limited job security, are often part-time, sometimes subcontracted, often unskilled, and provide limited opportunities for career advancement and development. Also, they are frequently culturally perceived as women's jobs.[13] From work being a stable focus for managing risks and the focus of citizenship participation in modernity, in late modernity work itself is risk-bearing and is decreasingly able to bear a central position fo managing other risks and citizenship.

A second trend in late modernity is the declining role of the state. At a macro level this has led many commentators to talk of the "hollowing out" of state power by its being eroded both at the supra state and local levels. More parochially, in Britain, important shifts in the relationship between the citizen and the state have been taking place. At one level this has happened because of the influence of neo-liberal economics and philosophy in which individual freedom is conceptualized as the absence of state control (Hayek 1994; Friedman 1962; Mead 1986; Murray 1989). Whilst ironically the neo-liberal project in Britain has not led to a reduction in state control,[14] it has been used to justify government reducing its responsibilities for providing the social rights of citizenship (Lister 1990; France 1996) and, in particular, abandoning the goal of full employment. In Britain, after the 1979 election of a Conservative government, the principles of state management of the economy and the protection of employment were replaced by free market economics in which employment levels were to be determined by the market. Whether these changes were in fact driven by ideology has been questioned. A more pragmatic interpretation of this restructuring recognizes that fundamental difficulties were embedded in the economic crisis of the mid-1970s, the employment crisis of the 1990s and the demographic shifts which began to undermine the funding basis of the postwar welfare system. Regardless of which interpretation is preferred, the clear outcome is that the state has taken less responsibility for providing the benefits of citizenship or for ensuring the full inclusion of its citizens.

A third aspect of late modernity surrounds the meaning of "inclusion". With the restructuring of paid work and the changing citizen/state relationship other notions of inclusion have been prioritized. Consumption and lifestyle have become important indicators of personal and collective indentity. Giddens, for example, argues that in late modernity "lifestyle" takes on a particular significance in which individuals have to negotiate a diversity of options. The opportunity to do this arises as social life is made more "open" and lifestyle choice becomes increasingly important in the construction of self-identity and daily activity. What we wear, what we own, what music we listen to, what we read and what leisure pursuits we engage in, become central aspects of our individual identities. Citizenship is shaped increasingly not by our relationship with the state but by our lifestyle choices—that is, what we consume. While Giddens recognizes that these choices are constrained by the standardizing features of capitalist production, he also highlights the declining extent to which traditional group membership any longer constrains individuals making lifestyle choices. Institutional groups, such as the family, school or workplace were used in modernity as central vehicles for developing and maintaining collective goals and for curtailing the actions of their members by enforcing group loyalty. Such groups were important social defences against deviance, but late modernity erodes their power.

In spite of giving priority to individuals, nevertheless exclusion has become a common feature of late modernity. Previously, inclusion was a necessary requirement of capitalist production and served the function of discipline and control. However, in late modernity advanced economies often have surplus labour because they have reduced their dependence on unskilled work. Inclusion, therefore, is no longer economically so important. At the same time the state has abdicated its responsibility for inclusion, arguing that it is for the individual to gain inclusion through making choices in the market. But market forms of distribution are not built around notions of inclusion, since their main interest is profit maximization. Furthermore, the reduction of state welfare has reduced the capacity of the poor and other marginalized groups to participate in such market choices (Lister 1990).

Youth and Citizenship in Late Modernity

Young people have been particularly susceptible, in a number of ways, to this

66

growth of exclusion. First, as the state reduces its responsibilities for inclusion young people are finding that the pathways to adult status and autonomy are being replaced wih extended forms of dependency (Jones and Wallace 1992; France 1996). Since the early 1980s many legal rights of the young have been removed. Whilst historically it has always been unclear how young people's rights help them gain adult citizenship (Franklin 1986), nevertheless the end period of modernity in Britain increasingly recognized the importance of such rights (Marshall 1950).[15] However, in late modernity political rights have been separated from social rights. Political rights have become a formal status separated from any notion of substantive rights to social justice. Citizenship is now attached to formal legal rights (such as voting or legal due process) but separated from any notion of social rights (such as a right to work or welfare)—in other words, the welfare state is being replaced by a liberal state with strictly limited involvement in civil society. Indeed, the neo-liberals have argued that social rights undermine formal legal rights since they create dependency on the state (Hayek 1944; Friedman 1962; Mead 1986; Murray 1989).[16] The result of this shift has been a reduction of young people's social rights in areas such as housing, employment and social insurance. This has led, not to adult independence, but greater dependence on the family and higher expectations by both the state and adults that the young should undertake certain obligational duties before they become full citizens (France 1996). This exclusion from citizenship affects groups of young people differently. Those most affected are young people already on the margins. For example, being poor, working-class and with limited education or employment increases the experience of exclusion (France 1996; Coles 1995; Jones and Wallace 1992; Lister 1990). This is not to suggest that exclusion from citizenship is only experienced by the poor. Other groups, such as students, may also find the routes to adult autonomy blocked, since changes in housing benefit and income support, and the freezing of the student grant have led to increased dependency on parents.

Youth and the Labour Market in Late Modernity

Young people are also experiencing other forms of exclusion. Since the early 1980s there has been a growing body of evidence to show that young people are being excluded from the labour market. While unemployment has recently been on the decline,[17] evidence shows that young people are more likely not to have a paid job and to be unemployed for longer periods (Unemployment Brief 1994). For example, unemployment in the late 1980s amongst 25–34-year-olds averaged 11 per cent, while unemployment in the 16- to 19-year-old age group averaged 20 per cent (General Household Survey 1995). Unemployment amongst 16- and 17-year-olds is even more entrenched: nationally, 1 in 6 are unemployed, but in Yorkshire and Humberside the figure is 1 in 4 (Unemployment Brief 1994).

In late modernity the demand for youth labour is reduced, first, because technical advances have reduced the dependency on the traditional utility of youth labour: that is active muscle power. Second, international competition and globalization of production ensures that cheap labour can be gained from sources other than British young people. Finally, what is now wanted is not single-skilled permanent employees but flexible, multi-skilled workers who can be brought into the production process as and when demand requires (Wyn and White 1997).[18] The return, therefore, to fulltime secure employment for the young seems unlikely (Beasley 1991). This form of exclusion further exacerbates problems of transition to adulthood and so exclusion from citizenship.

Youth and Education in Late Modernity

Exclusions from education are also increasing. Evidence suggests that over the last seven years there has been an increase in formal school exclusions. The Department for Education and Employment's own research has shown that 12,458 young people were excluded from schools in the 1994/5 academic year, as opposed to 2,910 in 1990/1 (Department for Education and Employment 1995). Over 80 per cent of exclusions were in secondary schools, of which 45 per cent were from years 10 and 11. Parsons (1996) suggests that figures from the DfEE study show that over 5,000 exclusions are of 15- and 16-year-olds who, once excluded, do not return to school. If informal exclusions were also included then the figures would be much worse. Indeed, Booth (1996) suggests that relying upon formal definitions alone diverts attention from the extent of informal exclusionary practices used in schools which are not recorded. It is not entirely clear why exclusions have been increasing. However, late modernity demands high skill levels as the price for social inclusion simply because there is little demand for the labour of the unskilled. The emphasis in education, therefore, has shifted towards higher skill training through devices such as the national curriculum, educational testing and league tables. In such a system the unskilled or the unwilling are simply disruptive of educational goals and have been increasingly removed through either formal or informal exclusion.[19]

Employment opportunities for the young school-leaver have changed dramatically. The consequences of this are twofold. First, with little prospect of paid employment many young people see school as "boring" and "irrelevant" (France and Wiles 1996; John 1996). The result is disruptive behaviour, high levels of truancy and underachievement (Stirling 1996; Booth 1996). Second, whilst employment opportunities for the young have decreased, the state has argued that a growing economy depends on developing the skills of the most able and so has encouraged the development of policies of selection, both between schools and within schools. In such an environment exclusion of the disruptive or less able is in danger of being seen as an acceptable price so that the needs of the most able can be concentrated upon. Exclusion is tacitly encouraged by policies that aim to ensure the most able get the best education possible (Blyth and Milner 1996).

Youth, Space and Social Control in Late Modernity

One aspect of the growth of risk in late modernity is that feelings of insecurity are increasingly responded to by creating locations of trust—small bubbles of security in an insecure world (Bottoms and Wiles 1995). Sometimes these are created by displays of technical control and the management of risk (especially by the new technologies of crime control). More important, for this essay, is the use of geographical segregation and control by business to reassure potential customers about their security. Cities were always made up of areas which generated different degrees of risk, but developers and businesses have become increasingly sophisticated in creating "security bubbles" for their customers, whether these be women-only hotels, guarded car parks or privately-policed shopping malls. Such security bubbles use exclusion of those who are believed to be potentially threatening to reduce fear and risk.

The use of exclusion depends on private property rights since you can only lawfully exclude people from private property. This is the very antithesis of the public law rights of civic society in modernity. Modernity achieved order and control through the inclusion of all citizens in a public realm of social interaction and discourse which was celebrated through a wealth of public facilities and access. Ideals of citizenship rights under modernity were enshrined in a public law which aimed to guarantee this public aspect of civil society. Security in modernity, therefore, was based on universal citizenship rights in a shared public domain, the existence of which was the sign of a civilized society.

Security in late modernity, however, is achieved by offering customers services and facilities in a private space from which undesirables can be excluded. The result is that many of the facilities of late modernity, such as shopping malls or leisure facilities, are no longer public (even though many of the public may use them) but private (what is often called "mass private property"). Security is now one aspect of the contractual bargain made between customer and supplier in the market and each individual is free to enter into whatever such contracts are on offer.

This shift has had two important implications for young people. First, those most often excluded from mass private property are young people. A large private shopping mall will have thousands of exclusions per year and most of those will be of young people. Young people will be targeted in this way partly because statistically they are responsible for a lot of crime, but also because youths, especially groups of young males, are usually seen as threatening by adults.[20] There is a clear danger that as mass private property increases young people, or rather particular groups of young people, will be excluded from many of the locations where the key market lifestyle choices of the new citizenship are being made. Even more worrying is that most of the public law rights which were developed as part of the modernity project, and which protected young people from exclusion, are now being evaded by the use of private law devices. This is especially dangerous in a country like Britain which, because it has never had a formal, written constitution, has never really had positive rights (as most other legal systems of modernity provided) but only the much weaker notion of negative rights—that is, you may do whatever is not lawfully forbidden.

As more facilities are provided in private space, the public realm shrinks, both metaphorically in the sense that proportionately less facilities are available in the public rather than the private realm, but also literally in that previously public facilities, such as parks or swimming pools, are sold off to private institutions. At the same time other private realms are resorting to closure to reinforce their distinction from a shrinking public realm. For example, universities, although always legally private institutions, used to operate as if they were public, often positively encouraging access; but now they are increasingly closed off and their separateness guarded by private police. Even the architecture of late modernity symbolizes closure and exclusion. Modernity placed buildings in the middle of sites with publicly accessible lawns surrounding them, but late modernity puts building around the edges of a site with enclosed courtyards or atriums. The celebration of the public realm has been replaced by that of private, controlled space. Those young people and others who are excluded from these private places will have to compete for the shrinking and increasingly second-rate public space and facilities. There is a danger that some young people will be forced to spend their time in a public realm where lifestyle choices are few and where problematic populations are concentrated who can only be controlled by increasingly assertive public policing.

Youth and Crime in Late Modernity

The connection between young people and crime is not a new feature of late modernity. Modernity recognized the importance of the links between youth and crime and all societies have worried about the lawlessness of youth. However, a part of modernity's inclusion project was to recognize that such lawlessness could be contained by the disciplines provided by employment and adult responsibilities and citizenship. Criminality was something young people did grow out of and therefore was best responded to by maximizing those factors which linked to inclusion and maturity. At the end period of modernity it was even recognized that involvement with the criminal justice system could make these processes of inclusion more difficult by stigmatizing young people, and so juvenile justice policy developed the notion of "minimum intervention" in response to youth crime.

Late modernity is increasingly excluding some young people from precisely those institutions which, in modernity, bolstered maturity and reduced offending. Not surprisingly, therefore, recent evidence suggests that those desistance factors which we believe reduced offending by young people in modernity, no longer seem to work for young males (Graham and Bowling 1995). The rate of youth crime is increasing and no longer seems to be declining so obviously with age. The result has been that criminal justice policies of minimum intervention have been all but abandoned and a new, more oppressive response to youth crime is on the agenda (Newburn 1996). More generally, there is an increasing public focus on reducing youth criminality but without much recognition that the main outcome of youth criminality is youth victimization and fear. Young people suffer personal crime victimization rates which adults would regard as intolerable (Anderson *et al.* 1994; Brown 1995; Mayhew *et al.* 1993), and as a result have a well-grounded fear of crime (see Hough 1995).

70

Youth Work in Late Modernity

Youth work adapted itself to changes during modernity. It shifted from a voluntary service aimed at character-building and helping the poor to an increasingly public service aimed at social inclusion and citizenship, to a public outreach service to the casualties of affluence and the provider of education aimed at self-development. However, it does not seem to us that youth work, and especially the public Youth Service, has yet adapted successfully to the changes of late modernity. Much of the rhetoric and working practices of youth work remain those from the end period of modernity. As we have argued, these were developed in response to a world that has now fundamentally changed. For example, youth work moved away, in the affluent 1960s, from being centrally focused on youth clubs to increasingly using detached work. Yet today unemployed young people, excluded from much private leisure space and provision, may welcome something similar to the facilities which the old youth clubs used to provide.

The task now is to attempt to analyse the structural locations within which youth workers could operate in late modernity. There are a number of obvious headings for this analysis which have come out of the above discussion. For example, should youth work even exist in late modernity? Should the Youth Service attempt to deliver a universal service for all young people? Is social education still a useful goal for youth work? Is detached work still a useful working method? Is youth work best delivered as a public (statutory) service?

Is youth work still needed?

If one accepts a neo-liberal ideology of late modernity then there is little purpose for youth work and certainly not for a public, state-funded Youth Service. This is so, either because what youth work provides is better provided by commercial leisure facilities (as evidenced by young people's clear preference for such facilities over those provided by the Youth Service), or because state-funded youth work actually prevents the very thing that is needed—namely, young people taking responsibility for their own lives. The inadequacy of this neo-liberal position is that it assumes that the market will provide for all young people and therefore ignores the problems of exclusion and structural unemployment in late modernity. Unless one is prepared to abandon a portion of young people to foraging on the margins of a society built upon consumer choice then the neo-liberal answer will not do.

However, a more radical response might be that unless we are prepared to do something about structural unemployment (by, say, positively encouraging inefficient use of labour in non-globalized parts of the economy, such as in petrol stations or personal services), or exclusion (by, say, legally reinforcing the pre-eminence of public law and rights over certain previously private space) then youth work cannot solve the problems which have been identified for some young people. The inadequacy, at least in part, of this position is that it ignores the weakening of the state under late modernity and assumes that in a global world such changes can be delivered as a matter of national political will.[21]

If youth work has a role, it is neither by ignoring the structures of late modernity nor by thinking that they can be easily changed. Although it is dangerous to hypothesize the collective views of contemporary youth workers, they do seem often to operate with a naive radicalism (France and Wiles 1995). If youth work is going to survive it needs to develop a more sophisticated understanding of its place in the political economy of late modernity. The very uncertainties of late modernity make this difficult, but then these are the same uncertainties which young people are having to negotiate in their daily lives.

Should youth work be a universal service?

Youth work shifted from being a nineteenth-century service aimed at the working-class poor to being a universal service and the route to citizenship in a postwar world. Contemporary youth work has tended to keep the rhetoric of being a universal and voluntaristic service, but the reality is now different. As far as public youth work is concerned, cuts in local authority youth service budgets have meant that it can no longer attempt to deliver a universal service and a much reduced service has had to target its delivery in terms of need (France and Wiles 1996; Maychell *et al.* 1996). Furthermore, an increasing proportion of the public Youth Service budget comes via central government programme funding for projects with quite specific types of work, such as the Youth Action Scheme (see France and Wiles 1996). The voluntary sector has similarly had to target limited resources, and its fund-raising often depends on appealing for support for clearly targeted work. Youth work, in other words, no longer offers a universal service and even its voluntarism has been brought into question by targeted programme work.

In reality this *de facto* shift fits with the nature of late modernity which, as we have seen, provides a wide variety of goods and services as the basis for a citizenship based on choice. The idea of a state-provided universal youth service is about as relevant today as the state-run nationalized industries of the immediate postwar period. Nobody today would try and sell a product to *all* young people but instead would concentrate on different products for different groups of young people. This is the world of choice in which youth services must operate and although those it mainly works with may have more limited market choices than their contemporaries, they still inhabit a social world of choice. Youth work needs to develop a much more clearly targeted notion of service delivery. It will be unsuccessful with universal offerings but instead needs to provide services which are carefully tailored to market segments, as are all the other offerings to young people. The Youth Service has to decide who it is providing a service for, before it can decide what that service ought to be.

Is social education any longer useful?

The difficulty with social education as provided by the Youth Service is that it was always a slippery concept. Like some other phrases—such as "holistic"—it was rather loosely used by youth workers, often without either agreed or precise meaning, and sometimes seemed to stand for little more than "what youth workers do". However, three general points can be made. First, social education was a process which was meant to encourage self-development so that the individual could play a full part in the world. Second, at the time it was developed other forms of education, such as schools, colleges and universities, only encompassed a small minority of the youth population throughout the transition to adulthood and so youth work could fill this gap with social education. Finally, it was useful in the professional development of youth work because its use of "education" and "curriculum" gave its members entry into the world of professional education and hence higher status.

Late modernity is a very different context for social education. The gap in young people's education which social education sought to fill is now very much smaller as an increasing proportion of each youth cohort stay in formal education of one kind or another. The ideal of personal development has now extended into a general societal individualism of market choice. The employment advantages which successful social education may have once endowed young people with will no longer make up for a lack of formal skills in a world of structural unemployment. Even the professional gains seem less worthwhile now, given the changed status of school teachers.

There is a remaining role for something like social education, but its recipients are much more likely to be those who have failed to stay in other forms of education. To be part of the excluded, or/and the unskilled (or of limited skills) in late modernity is to be in the most disadvantaged market position and hence disadvantaged in other areas also. Such young people are likely to face a world of long bouts of unemployment and little security. Unless they can learn to construct meaningful life biographies for themselves in these circumstances then they are in danger of suffering the kind of physical and mental traumas that we already know afflict the long-term unemployed. To help with this situation is a real challenge for youth workers. Offering skills training, links to TECS etc. is important but if not very carefully done can raise expectations of employment which if not met can be personally destructive. Ironically, when other forms of education seem to have given up the classical notion of "education for life" in favour of raw skills-provision, this is exactly what social education provided by youth work needs to be. Late modernity is shifting social status from class notions tied to employment, to lifestyles tied to market choices. For excluded and disadvantaged young people their problem is not unemployment *per se* but that this denies them the resources to make market lifestyle choices. Here is a wonderful opportunity for social education to help develop a new range of lifestyle choices for young people with routes of access other than market payment. This will not be easy because globalized marketing messages will create a desire for market provision, but young people are surely no less able than adults to filter such messages through to realistic personal choices. Late modernity may be a new set of structural constraints on our lives but we can still exercise human choice, and that is what social education can encourage.

Is detached work still useful?

Detached work was originally developed as a working method in order first, to make contact with those young people who would not come to youth clubs (more properly outreach work), or to work with those who had been excluded from such clubs and latterly, to work with young people in the natural setting of the streets. Detached work was a method *par excellence* for finding and working with small minorities of deviant youth who were never joiners but creatures of street-based peer group culture. As youth workers increasingly focused on such youth, detached work became a major working method —indeed, it almost became a fetish of professional virility. However, in many places now youth clubs hardly exist, disadvantaged young people are easy to identify but for many of them their problem is often that they spend too much of their time on the streets and would like to get indoors (Brown 1995). Detached work will remain a useful working practice for workers who are targeting deviant or troublesome minorities, but the majority of young people in late modernity who would benefit from youth work are not in this category—indeed, one of the aims of working with them is to stop them becoming so excluded from mainstream society.

Youth work needs to broaden its repertoire of skills and even recapture those skills of centre-based work which the profession once prized. Detached work is a useful method for certain types of youth work but should not be fetishized as *the* method.

Should youth work be a state service?

Given the problems for some young people in late modernity which we have catalogued, a civilized response might appear to be that youth services must be provided by the state as a matter of social justice. However, this response ignores not merely the changing nature of the state itself but also the history of state provision.

The public Youth Service, when criticized, has frequently pointed out that it has never been placed on a proper statutory basis because no level or standard of service has ever been laid down, nor has it been properly funded. A more detailed statutory framework may well come, but mainly because it is the route by which government could take a more direct control over the nature and quality of youth work. However, it does not follow that any more money would be provided, and the crisis in state welfare spending caused by demographic shifts, combined with the financial strategy of the new Labour government makes this unlikely. The Youth Service, therefore, needs to find sources of funding outwith the state. In order to find this funding the present gulf between the public and voluntary youth work sectors is going to have to be closed.

The history of the public Youth Service, compared to the voluntary sector in general, has not always been one of clear advantages. Like any public provision it has sometimes been over-bureaucratic, slow in responding to the rapidly-changing needs of young people and often inefficiently managed. A mixture of the state setting standards for training and service delivery, backed up by an inspectorate system, together with mixed public and private funding, and services mainly provided on a fixed-term programme basis seems a likely outcome to current policy rethinking. This would have the advantage of the state underwriting quality whilst allowing the flexibility and speed of change which youth services in late modernity will need if they are to be successful.

Conclusion

Late modernity is creating major problems for youth services, but rethinking the nature of the Youth Service is possible. What this requires is acceptance by youth workers (and especially those in the statutory sector) that change is a necessity. Some local Youth Services have taken up this challenge but many remain locked into inflexible historical structures and the political rhetoric of universalism. Such positions are not going to save youth work. If the Youth Service is to survive then it must engage with the new problems of late modernity.

Notes

1. This argument does not mean that a "fairer" society was, in reality, created. There is ample evidence to suggest that large sections of the population failed to benefit from these developments. The important point here is that a claim to justice was made as a legitimating device.

2. Social integration was the term used, after the Second World War to describe "social inclusion". The idea being proposed was that young people should take their place in society. In such a perspective the social order would remain unchanged. Hierarchies of class and gender were to remain in place and young people would find their "natural place" through becoming adults with responsibilities and obligations (especially to the family). For a good discussion of the distinction between the two terms see Levitas (1996).

3. Of course, what this does not take into account is the gendered notion of inclusion. Davis (1990) highlights this contradiction by showing how the attitude to girls changes over time. In the period of expansion politicians and policy-makers argued for the training and integration of young women into the labour market but when the economy contracted arguments concerning the importance of family life and motherhood dominated.

4. Smith also argues that while much of the literature in this area concentrates on movements that aimed to improve the young working-class male, other less-known organizations, that catered for young women, did exit. For example, one of the earliest movements the Leman Street Girls Club formed in 1883 and the Girls Friendly Society founded in 1874.

5. The "Butler Act": so called because it was passed by Rab Butler, Conservative Education Minister during the wartime coalition government. This is still the formal base of contemporary youth work.

6. It is widely argued, by youth workers, that the failure to give youth work a statutory base has undermined its ability to provide a quality national service for young people.

7. This is not to suggest that the concept of "youth" or "adolescence" was new. Others have shown how historically such categories evolved (see for example Springhall 1986; and Musgrove 1964). The point Hobsbawm is making is that generational differences became clearly evident and distinctions between youth and adulthood were born out of both conflictual perspectives as to how society should be ordered and the development of the consuming teenager.

8. See for example the analysis of the Birmingham Contemporary Cultural Studies

Centre in the mid-1970s.
9. Youth Service in this context, is not a national term. There has never been a national Youth Service, only local authority-run services, but it is common to talk about "the Youth Service" rather than youth services.
10. Detached work has a long and illustrious history (one that has not yet been fully illuminated). Albemarle was a major watershed for the professional establishment of detached work within British youth work, especially within mainstream public services.
11. Social education has a longer history, but it was not until after the Albemarle Report that it became mainstream (or accepted as professional practice). For example, see Smith (1988) for an excellent discussion on the development of this form of practice.
12. How widely such developments are taking place is not always clear. A central weakness of writers such as Beck and Giddens is their limited attention to empirical detail. However, there are more empirically-grounded accounts of late modernity, such as that by Lash and Urry (1994).
13. This is partly because service provision is sometimes associated with traditional domestic service jobs but also because unskilled service jobs do not rely on the traditional unskilled male job attributes of physical strength and toughness.
14. Under the Conservative governments from 1979 the central state strengthened its power against local power centres and extended its control, either directly, or via a growing number of quangos staffed by placemen.
15. How far such debates actually influence youth policy is arguable. Davies (1986) has argued that it was mere rhetoric.
16. The argument as to whether the implementation of policies of substantive justice creates dependency is not new. For an excellent discussion on the same debate in the nineteenth century, see Stedman Jones (1971).
17. While it is generally accepted that unemployment is decreasing, controversy exists over by how much. The calculation of such figures has been greatly restructured since the early 1980s, making historical comparisons difficult.
18. The growth of such a workforce is most evident within the service sector (Allen and Massey 1988), although it can also be identified in manufacturing.
19. Much of the evidence of the late 1950s and early 1960s suggests that the tripartite system, because it was designed to provide training for different segments of a full-demand labour market, operated with less exclusion.
20. Interestingly, groups of youths are also seen as threatening by young people themselves (not surprising when one remembers that most interpersonal crime by young people is against other young people) and therefore they may also welcome such exclusionary practices.
21. Of course the effects of globalism can be attacked by supra-state political will or supra-state law. For example, the attempt by the EU to impose working conditions through the Social Chapter—attacked, of course, by the Conservative government on precisely the grounds that you cannot buck the global market without paying a high price in relative inefficiency.

References

Abrams, P. (1961), *The Teenage Consumer*, London: London Press Exchange.
Albemarle Report (1960), *The Youth Service in England and Wales*, Cmnd 6458, London: HMSO.
Allen, J., and Massey, D. (1988), *The Economy in Question*, London: Sage.
Anderson, S., Kinsey, R., Loader, I., and Smith, C. (1994), *Cautionary Tales: Young People, crime and policing in Edinburgh*, Aldershot: Avebury.

Astley, J. (1987), *Youth Service policy making in the 1950s, in Youth and Policy*, no. 19.

Bauman, Z. (1992), *Intimations of Postmodernity*, London: Routledge.

Beasley, B. (1991), Transitions to nowhere: the effects of government policies on young working class people's access to employment/training, in White, R., and Wilson, B. (eds), *For Your Own Good, Young People and State Intervention*, Bundoora: Latrobe University Press.

Beck, U. (1992), *Risk Society: Towards a New Modernity*, London: Sage.

Blyth, E., and Milner, J. (1996), Exclusions: Trends and Issues, in Blyth, E., and Milner, J. (eds) (1996), *Exclusion From School*, London: Routledge.

Board of Education (1940), *The Challenge of Youth* (Circular 1516), London: HMSO.

Booth, T. (1996), Stories of exclusion: natural and unnatural selection, in Blyth, E., and Milner, J. (eds) (1996), *Exclusion From School*, London: Routledge.

Bottoms, A., and Wiles, P. (1995), Crime and insecurity in the city, in C. Fijnaut *et al.* (eds), *Changes in Society, Crime and Criminal Justice in Europe, Vol. 1*, Antwerp: Kluwer.

Bottoms, A., and Wiles, P. (1996), Understanding crime prevention in late modern societies, in T. Bennett (ed.), *Preventing Crime and Disorder: Targeting, Strategies and Responsibilities*, Cambridge: Institute of Criminology.

Brown, S. (1995), Crime and safety in whose "community", in *Youth and Policy*, Spring, no. 48.

Butters, S., and Newell, S. (1978), *The Realities of Training*, Leicester: National Youth Bureau.

Central Advisory Council for Education (England) (1963), *Half our Future: A Report* (The Newsom Report), London: HMSO.

Coles, B. (1995), *Youth and Social Policy: Youth, Citizenship and Young Careers*, London, UCL.

Crowther Report (1959), *15 to 18 Year Olds*, London: HMSO.

Davies, B. (1986), *Threatening Youth*, Milton Keynes: Open University Press.

Davis, J. (1990), *Youth and the Social Condition of Britain*, London: Athlone Press.

Department of Education and Employment (1995), *More Willing to School: An Independent Evaluation of the Truancy and Disaffected Pupils GEST Programme*, London: Department for Education and Employment.

Foucault, M. (1977), *Discipline and Punish*, New York: Pantheon.

France, A. (1996), Youth and citizenship in the 1990s, in *Youth and Policy*, no. 53.

France, A., and Wiles, P. (1995), Whose side are they on? Youth workers and the practice of crime control. Paper given to *Loughborough British Criminological Conference*.

France, A., and Wiles, P. (1996), *The National Evaluation of Youth Action*, London: Department for Education and Employment.

Franklin, B. (1986), *The Rights of Children*, Oxford: Basil Blackwell.

Friedman, M. (1962), *Capitalism and Freedom*, Chicago: Chicago University Press.

Giddens, A. (1991), *Modernity and Self-Identity*, Cambridge: Polity Press.

Graham, J., and Bowling, B. (1995), *Young People and Crime*, London: HMSO.

Habermas, J. (1987), *The Philosophical Discourse of Modernity: Twelve Lectures*, tr. F. Lawrence, Cambridge: Polity Press.

Hayek, F. V. (1944), *The Road to Serfdom*, London: Routledge and Sons.

Hobsbawm, E. (1994), *Age of Extremes: The Short 20th Century*, London: Michael Joseph.

Hough, M. (1995), *Anxiety about Crime: Findings from the 1994 British Crime Survey*, London: Home Office, Research and Planning Unit Report 147.

John, P. (1996), Damaged goods? An interpretation of excluded pupils' perception of schooling, in Blyth, E., and Milner, J. (eds), *Exclusion From School*, London: Routledge.

Jones, G., and Wallace, C. (1992), *Youth, Family and Citizenship*, Milton Keynes: Open University Press.

Lash, S., and Urry, J. (1994), *Economies of Signs and Space*, London: Sage.

Levitas, R. (1996), The concept of social exclusion: the new Durkeimian hegemony, *Critical Social Policy*, vol. 16(1).

Lister, R. (1990), *The Exclusive Society: Citizenship and the Poor*, London: Child Poverty Action Group.

Lyotard, J.-F. (1984), *The Post-modern Condition*, tr. G. Bennington and B. Massumi, Manchester: Manchester University Press.

Marshall, T. H. (1950), *Citizenship and Social Class*, Cambridge: Cambridge University Press.

Maychell, K., Pathak, S., and Cato, V. (1996), *Providing For Young People*, Slough: NFER Press.

Mayhew, P., Aye Maung, N., and Mirrlees-Black, C. (1993), *The 1992 British Crime Survey*, London: Home Office.

Mead, L. (1986), *Beyond Entitlement: The Social Obligations of Citizenship*, New York: Free Press.

Ministry of Education (1945), *The Purpose and Content of the Youth Service*, London: HMSO.

Ministry of Education (1947), *School and Life: A First Enquiry into the Transition from School to Independent Life*, London: HMSO.

Murray, C. (1989), *The Emerging British Underclass*, London: Institute of Economic Affairs.

Musgrove, F. (1964), *Youth and the Social Order*, London: Routledge and Kegan Paul.

Newburn, T. (1996), Back to the future? Youth crime, youth justice and the rediscovery of "Authoritarian populism", in Pilcher, J., and Wagg, S., *Thatcher's Children*, London: Falmer Press.

Parsons, C. (1996), Permanent exclusions from schools in England in the 1990s: trends, causes and responses, in *Children and Society*, vol. 10: 177–86.

Pearson, G. (1983), *Hooligan: A History of Respectable Fears*, London: Macmillan.

Pixley, J. (1992), *Citizenship and Employment*, Cambridge: Cambridge University Press.

Roche, M. (1992), *Rethinking Citizenship*, Cambridge: Polity Press.

Smith, M. (1988), *Developing Youth Work*, London: Macmillan.

Springhall, J. (1986), *Coming of Age: Adolescence in Britain*, London: Gill and Macmillan.

Stedman Jones, G. (1971), *Outcast London*, London: Penguin.

Stirling, M. (1996), Government policy and disadvantaged chlidren, in Blyth, E., and Milner, J. (eds), *Exclusion From School*, London: Routledge.

Turner, B. (1990), *Theories of Modernity and Post Modernity*, London: Sage.

Wagner, P. (1994), *A Sociology of Modernity: Liberty and Discipline*, Routledge: London.

Wyn, J., and White, R. (1997), *Rethinking Youth*, London: Sage.

Anti-racism and the Limits of Equal Opportunities Policy in the Criminal Justice System

David Denney

Abstract

In this paper some of the evidence relating to the incidence of racial discrimination in the criminal justice system will be critically examined. It will be argued that equal opportunities policies have been adopted in the British case with the stated aim of tackling the exclusionary effects of racial discrimination. The notion of equal opportunities has been contested not least by those who have advocated anti-racist approaches towards discrimination. Anti-racism has been represented by some of its advocates as reflecting a critique of the authentic source of racism which is loosely defined in terms of social structure and capitalist social relations. The case for reconstituting anti-racism in such a way as to make it relevant to the lives of black offenders will be made. Finally, a framework for developing policies based upon the implementation of specific and clearly stated rights will be made.

Keywords:

Anti-racism; Opportunities; Discrimination; Exclusion; Rights

Neither I nor my friends ever set out to be criminals or villains, nor wished to go to jail. But such is society's hatred for those who are not of their pigmentation or of their beliefs that we had no choice but to rebel against the system. (Trevor Hercules, 1989)

Introduction

The above quotation illustrates the lack of power that black people feel they have over their own lives, and the way in which the criminal justice system appears to perpetuate social exclusion through the reproduction of racial divisions. Equal opportunities policies and, more latterly, anti-racism have been presented by their advocates as tools for tackling the worst effects of

Address for Correspondence: *David Denney, Department of Social Policy and Social Science, Royal Holloway, University of London, Egham, Surrey, TW20 0EX.*

racism. Both concepts have also been the subject of fierce debate and criticism. The impact of both anti-racism and equal opportunities in the struggle against social exclusion within the British criminal justice system is the focus of this discussion.

Some of the evidence relating to racial discrimination in the criminal justice system will be examined in relation to sentencing, prisons and the practices of various key professionals. Three basic propositions will then be developed in an examination of the emergent debates in this area. First, it will be argued that both equal opportunities policies and anti-racism are complex concepts which have strengths and limitations. Second, generic explanations of inequality which conflate race with disability, gender and class are problematic, particularly when applied to the criminal justice system. Finally, the case for developing a rights-based approach to counter discrimination in the criminal justice system will be used to demonstrate how equal opportunities policies and anti-racism might be reconstituted.

Discrimination in the Criminal Justice System

The incidence of racial discrimination and other forms of discrimination is now well documented in the criminal justice system. Although space does not permit a full examination of the complexities of research in this area, it is important to remember that discrimination is not confined to the area of race, but exists also in the areas of physical disability, learning impairment, gender and sexual orientation.[1]

The literature relating to black people[2] and the criminal justice system is probably the best researched, and consequently presents the most complex picture (Reiner 1989; 1993; NACRO 1991; Hood 1992; Fitzgerald 1993; Smith 1994). Some studies carried out during the 1980s appeared to indicate that there was little if any real racial element in the sentencing of people (McConville and Baldwin 1982; Crowe and Cove 1984). While it is the case that black people are more likely to receive custodial sentences with fewer previous convictions when compared with white people, when variables like offence type, age, and the nature of the criminal history are taken into consideration, the differences to some extent are diminished. Other factors which could contribute to the overrepresentation of black defendants in the criminal justice system include unemployment and high levels of policing in black communities.

On the other hand, although seriousness is a possible factor in explaining differences in the length of custodial sentences, it does not explain the difference in the use of other non-custodial disposals. Some research has suggested that racial discrimination is the crucial factor in the sentencing process. Hudson found considerable disparity in sentencing for most common offences of theft and burglary. Young unemployed black people in particular seemed vulnerable to high tariff sentences even in relation to "run of the mill" offences (Hudson 1989). Magistrates are more likely to commit black than white people to Crown Court in relation to offences which are triable either way (i.e. magistrates or crown court), which results in heavier sentencing if convicted (Fitzgerald 1993; Moxon 1988). These and other findings suggest that discrimination is a factor which affects black people detrimentally in the sentencing process.

Roger Hood's influential study of race and sentencing suggested that 80 per cent of the overrepresentation of black men in the criminal justice system could be accounted for by the disproportionate numbers appearing before the crown courts. This reflected decisions made at lower courts and the seriousness of the offences. The remaining 20 per cent could be accounted for by differential treatment by the courts, and other factors influencing the severity of the sentence, including the higher proportion of black defendants pleading not guilty. A complex picture emerged in that all black offenders had a 5 to 8 per cent higher chance of being sent to prison than white whilst black people of Asian origin had a 4 per cent lower probability. A higher proportion of black women, some 6 per cent, were sentenced to custody, but this was explained by the characteristics of the cases (Hood 1992).

Within the prison system black people are more likely to encounter discrimination, often finding themselves at the bottom of a complex prison pecking-order (Genders and Player 1989). Some 53 per cent of black and 14 per cent of white prisoners reported that they had been badly treated in prison (NACRO 1991). One-third of black inmates are reported to have been victims of racial attacks. Approximately 25 per cent of black prisoners reported that they had been victimized on an average of four occasions. Half of black and Asian inmates claimed that they had been unfairly treated during disciplinary proceedings in prison on racial grounds (Burnett and Farrell 1994).

In 1995 black males constituted 11.6 per cent of the total prison population, whilst 20.45 per cent of women in prison are black (Home Office 1996a). If foreign nationals are excluded from these figures the percentage reduces to 9.9 of the total prison population for black men and 11.6 for women. These figures should be compared with the 5.6 per cent of the general population who are designated black (NACRO 1991). As in the research relating to sentencing, the evidence that such disparities are the direct result of discrimination is not clear-cut. If the outcomes of parole applications are examined, according to the Home Office the results are likely to be similar for black and white inmates (Home Office 1994b). It should be remembered that much of the parole process occurs within the prison system.

Considerable research interest has also been focused upon professional practices and black representation within occupations which are associated with the criminal justice system. On 1 December 1995 there were 5 "ethnic minority" circuit judges, 12 recorders, 9 assistant recorders, and 4 stipendiary magistrates. Some 5 per cent of lay magistrates in 1995 were of "ethnic minority origin". In 1995 6 per cent of barristers in practice were of "ethnic minority origin" (Home Office 1996c). Although the generic term "ethnic minority" does not adequately reflect the number of black recruits to the legal profession and magistracy, it would seem fair to infer from these figures that black people constitute a small minority of lawyers in the British case. The relatively low numbers of black recruits to the legal profession generally could be explained by a reluctance on the part of black people to enter a profession which is widely regarded as exclusive and hierarchical. It might also reflect the lack of wider educational equality for black people.

The policing of black people has been a highly contentious area which has generated a literature spanning two decades (Hall *et al.* 1978). Since 1986, all police forces have collected information on racial incidents. Since 1993 there has been a 5 per cent increase in such incidents according to Home Office figures, which may be partly attributable to improvements in recording practices. The total number of racial incidents recorded in England and Wales for 1994/5 was 11,876 (Home Office 1996b).

Within the police it would appear that relatively few black people rise swiftly through the ranks. At present what were referred to by the Home Office as "ethnic minorities" make up 1.7 per cent of the police force in England and Wales. There are no "ethnic minorities" above the rank of chief superintendent (Home Office 1996b). Given the incidence and severity of racially motivated attacks, and the overrepresentation of black people in the Criminal Justice system generally, the need to have more black officers in positions of strategic managerial importance in the police force would appear to be self-evident.

Home Office evidence suggests that there has been some increase in the representation of black people in the probation service. In 1988 there were 127 black probation officers constituting 1.9 per cent (Denney 1992). Figures for 1995 suggest that this figure has now increased to 5.8 per cent (Home Office 1996c). It is still unclear from the available evidence what proportion of black probation officers hold senior positions within the service. In reviewing the evidence dating from 1976 on probation practice and black people, three major strands can be discerned.

1. Probation officers perceive black offenders in a manner incorporating various degrees of prejudice and racism, which constitutes discriminatory professional behaviour.
2. Probation officers who are aware of anti-racist practices in the probation service and the wider criminal justice system are constrained by the sanctions imposed by the courts and the wider criminal justice system. Quasi-professional conventions lead them to include some irrelevant and exclude some relevant material in reports on black offenders. Such practices could increase the possibility of some black offenders receiving custodial sentences.
3. Differences in the content and tone of pre-sentence reports[3] are indicative of an attempt to present the reality of black offending behaviour as perceived by the black offender (Denney 1992).

Reiner (1989; 1993) in a comprehensive analysis of race and criminal justice has argued that racism may be one factor among many which lead to discrimination in the criminal justice system. The current evidence available leaves open the question of the possible effects of other variables such as age, gender and class. The most plausible suggestion made by Reiner is that both racial discrimination and black offending patterns have played a part in the overrepresentation of black people in the criminal justice system.

Equal Opportunity: Origins and Development

What impact, if any, have equal opportunities policies had upon the criminal justice system? In order to begin to answer this question, the origins and development of the concept need to be understood. "Equal opportunity" is often ascribed to Tawney, who believed essentially that human beings were of equal worth, a premise which probably stemmed from his religious beliefs. For Tawney there should be equal access to all basic necessities of life. He was aware that it was possible to have "equal opportunities of becoming unequal" (quoted in Deakin and Wright 1995). Tawney acknowledged that whilst individuals differed profoundly, a "civilized society" would aim at eliminating inequalities, the source of which lay not in individual differences but in the way in which society is organized. Individual differences are more likely to find productive expression in a society where social inequalities have been diminished. Equal opportunities policies are linked to the elimination of discrimination. Taylor and Baldwin (1989) have conceptualized discrimination in terms of the systematic use of power by some groups which devalue other, less powerful groups on the basis of perceived difference. Such differences can be conceptualized in terms of "race", ethnic or national origin, religion, age, gender, class, sexuality or disability.

Legal backcloth

Equal opportunities policies seek to respect rights, have understanding of diversity, and counter unfairness. Although one can look to Tawney for a basic all-encompassing notion of equal opportunity, the idea has come to have differing meanings as it has developed over time. All equal opportunities policies, according to Mason and Jewson, have a number of common characteristics. The policy must involve a formal programme with procedures which can be demonstrated to be fair. The policy must also be implemented on a day-to-day basis and must be seen to be effective (Mason and Jewson 1992).

In reality, government policies related to discrimination have tended to be reformist and simultaneously accompanied by legislation which seeks to control the entry of black people into the country. The 1948 Nationality Act, during a postwar labour shortage, ensured the right of those holding colonial passports as well as of those holding passports issued by independent Commonwealth countries to enter the UK freely, to settle and find work whilst enjoying full political and social rights. The goal of assimilation continued until 1962, when the Commonwealth Immigrants Act, and later the 1968 Commonwealth Immigrants Act withdrew the right of settlement for those who did not have a close connection. The 1981 British Nationality Act, although ostensibly designed to clarify the concept of British citizenship, in practice further tightened entry restrictions. Legislation based upon an equal opportunities approach passed through Parliament in 1965 and 1968. The current legislation contained in the 1976 Race Relations Act makes it an offence to publish or distribute written material or use language in any public place which is threatening or offensive to black people or likely to incite racial hatred (Denney 1981).

Section 95 of the Criminal Justice Act 1991 requires the Secretary of State in each year to publish such information as "he" considers "expedient" for the purposes of "facilitating the performance by persons engaged in the criminal justice system in a way which avoids discrimination against any persons on the grounds of race or sex or any other improper grounds" (Home Office 1992).

A new offence of intentional harassment was introduced under Section 154 of the 1994 Criminal Justice and Public Order Act which amended the 1986 Public Order Act. The new offence was meant to address more serious cases of harassment. In the case of R v Ribbans, Dugley, Ridley, the Court of Appeal ruled that it was appropriate for a court to deal with any offence containing a proven racial element in such as way as to reflect the gravity of racial harassment as an aggravating feature.

Variations on a theme

Edwards has argued that there are two distinct ways of seeing equality of opportunity. Firstly, everyone irrespective of their morally arbitrary characteristics should have the same opportunities to develop their lives as they wish, or to pursue their chosen life plans.

The second formulation Edwards argues is quite distinct, encapsulating the idea that every individual should have an equal opportunity, unfettered by arbitrary boundaries like race or ethnicity, to compete for a given goal or a scarce resource. The glittering prizes constitute what Edwards refers to as the rewards system and are allocated on the basis of merit (Edwards 1990).

The essential distinction between these two concepts can be extended to incorporate a discussion of the appropriate role of the state in creating equal opportunities. The first emphasizes equality of opportunity and state intervention to create fullness of life for all. The latter reflects the possibility of placing a greater responsibility on the individual to create opportunities for her- or himself. Here the state has a more modest responsibility, to ensure that a level playing field is created for competition to take place. The stated aim of the first proposition can be regarded as equality of outcome, whilst the second approach aims to ensure equality of initial opportunity.

One can add to these two ideas a third free market minimal approach to equal opportunities. Market principles during the 1980s and 1990s wesystem. Examples of market principles in the criminal justice system are now manifest, with, for instance, the possibility of wages being paid to prisoners which would enable them to make a contribution to their own accommodation, privatization of the prison escort service, and also the contracting out of prison services to the private sector (Cavadino and Dignan 1994).

Neither equal opportunities nor anti-racism figured in the decision to move the criminal justice system towards the private sector. The reduction of public expenditure through competitive tendering was the prime and unequivocal aim. The existence of inequality from this perspective is recognized, but is to some degree accepted on the basis that it constitutes an inevitable, albeit undesirable, result of market forces. Inequality is not created by the deliberate misallocation of resources since such a position would be blatantly unjust. However, to demand justice from a society dominated by market competition would be unrealistic and absurd from this perspective. In a society in which the idea of markets has over the last decade taken on an almost sacred mantle, neither anti-racism nor equal opportunities has been given the highest priority. The advocates of free markets in public services acknowledge that policies designed to curb the exclusionary effects of inequality should exist, but not at the cost of detrimentally affecting the free interplay of market forces.

This approach can be seen in government rhetoric. In a Treasury policy document entitled *Competing for Quality* it is simply asserted that "Competition is the best guarantee of quality and value for money" (Treasury 1992: 1). In official discourse such an equation now appears to be so self-evident that no further official elaboration is thought justified. Consequently, equal opportunities policies within the criminal justice system are minimalist.

The equality of initial opportunity approach is to some extent evident in the two dominant currents within legal thinking which have been described by Smith (1994). Firstly, there is the idea that existing rules should be applied regardless of outcome. Second, and conflicting with this idea, is the proposition that legal procedures which effectively punish a higher proportion in one social group over another are essentially unjust, and the system should be regulated so as to achieve equal outcomes.

Both positions are fraught with problems. The first position poses difficulties, since in some cases it might be possible to make some changes to the system so as to equalize outcomes. Smith uses the example of the disproportionate number of black people who are refused bail on the basis of family circumstances. The justification for using family circumstances in relation to bail is not made explicit in the courts, and such criteria could probably be changed in an attempt to reduce inequality of outcome. On the other hand, the proposition that courts could administer a system based upon an aimed reduction in penalization for any group would in itself create further inequalities in the legal process.

Table 1 summarizes the fundamental principles upon which the variants of equal opportunities in the criminal justice system are based.

Criticisms of equal opportunities policies

Equal opportunities can appear attractive to those who manage the criminal justice system, in that they can be associated with quality and "good management". Equal opportunities can also be used as a tool by management to give the impression that an organization is tackling discrimination. The aims of equal opportunities policies are frequently minimalist and defined so widely as to be devoid of meaning.

Difficulties have arisen with the way in which equal opportunities policies have been implemented in practice. There has been a significant failure to identify the goals of equal opportunities in organizations. Also there has been a tendency to focus on changing the historically disadvantaged groups themselves rather than the organization (Blakemore and Drake 1996).

It still remains the case in the criminal justice system that the professionals, whether they be representing the police, probation or prison departments are

Table 1

	Minimal market equal opportunity approach	Equality of initial opportunities	Equality of outcome
Causes of inequality	Inevitable in market economy, unintentional	Unbridled markets	Greed, social inaction and mal-organization
Remedies	Statements of intent on equal opportunities, market interplay, individual effort Business-like management techniques to ameliorate inequality	Access to lifelong training	Increased taxation in state-funded programmes designed to combat disadvantage and unfairness
Implications for the criminal justice system	Limited support for some offenders and ex-offenders in a market- or quasi-market-led economy	Impartial application of rules to all groups	Regulation to counter unfairness

often the sole arbiters of complaints made against them (Broad and Denney 1996).

Equal opportunity policies, according to some writers, fail to address social exclusion and oppression; neither do such policies seek to equalize power, merely to individualize problems (Dominelli 1996).[4] Oppression, it is argued, focuses directly on the power relations which give some individuals the power to discriminate against certain social groups, whilst equality of opportunities is essentially reformist.

Equal opportunities policies seek to respect, have understanding of diversity and counter unfairness, consulting user groups with regard to types of provision and individual needs. In other words, the equal opportunities approach seeks to bring about changes within existing structural arrangements. Equal opportunity, it is sometimes argued, represents the postmodern condition characterized by specialist, individualized, fragmented and contractual service provision (Dominelli 1996). Anti-racist policies, by contrast, emphasize the importance of transforming the systems which create oppression and the dominant ideological discourse which legitimates negative beliefs about particular user groups.

The Development of Anti-racism

It is a matter of some debate why, during the 1980s, it appeared that equal opportunities policies, and to a lesser extent anti-racist policies were being developed in local authority-run education and social services departments.

Anti-racism has not figured dominantly in criminal justice policy given the adoption of minimal equal opportunities policies. One of the few examples of anti-racism having been adopted within the criminal justice system was in relation to the training of probation officers. In 1991 probation training was still regulated by the Central Council for Education and Training in Social Work, and the Rule and Requirements for the Diploma in Social Work (CCETSW 1991). With specific respect to probation officers CCETSW unequivocally stated that at the point of qualification a probation student must be able to:

> Demonstrate and operate antiracist, antisexist and other forms of discriminatory policy and practice in order to enable them to work effectively within a multiracial and multicultural society. (CCETSW 1991: 40).

Subsequently (1995), CCETSW adopted a policy more akin to equal opportunities, but in any case probation training was removed from generic social work education and the regulation of CCETSW in 1996.

Criticisms and limitations of anti-racism

A concerted media campaign directed at attempts being made by CCETSW to implement anti-racist and anti-discriminatory policies followed articles published in "quality" newspapers.[5] The idea of "political correctness" was presented as exclusively emanating from the left of British politics. Dominant regulatory discourse fundamentally affecting the criminal justice system with origins on the right of British politics (e.g. market testing of services, curfews) was not presented by the media as being politically correct. The essence of the populist critique of anti-racism rests upon the supposed emergence of a form of intellectual neo-Stalinism. Such ideas are supposedly backed by a corpus of undifferentiated certainties, sanctioned and then promulgated by an institutionalized thought police situated within local authority education and social service departments, some institutions of higher education and quangos like the Central Council for Education and Training of Social Workers (Amiel 1992, Phillips 1993a; 1993b).

The significance of the popularization of political correctness is questionable, but could have provided fuel for the government to justify the restructuring not only of aspects of the criminal justice system, but of all forms of personal social services. The differences in approach are summarized in table 2.

Anti-racism has been attacked from a number of other more theoretical perspectives. Gilroy in a withering attack argues that anti-racism fails to locate racism as being at the core of British politics. Anti-racism as developed in

Table 2

	Equal Opportunities	*Anti-racism*
Causes of racism	Prejudice values misunderstanding ignorance	Structural oppression race gender class
Solutions	Respect for individuals, quality assurance, monitoring. Formal procedures which create fairness. Implementation of policy on a day to day basis.	Demonstrate anti-racism in practice; promotion of non-discriminatory and anti-oppressive practices.

Britain has done little more than to provide a "coat of paint" since it has been located outside social and political life. Racism constitutes an unfortunate

"excrescence on a democratic policy which is essentially sound, and it follows from this that with the right ideological tools and political elbow grease, racism can be dealt with once and for all leaving the basic structures and relations of British economy and society essentially unchanged" (Gilroy 1990: 74).

Anti-racists are according to Gilroy doubly mistaken in that they fail to recognize, as equal opportunities policies do, the importance of social justice and democracy in the battle against racism. Some forms of anti-racism also reduce and trivialize the rich experience of black life to "nothing more than a response to racism". This then leads towards a reductionist conception of black people as victims.

Like Gilroy, Ballard argues that anti-racism conflates racial divisions with class divisions. Any such limiting explanation suggests, according to Ballard, that the "victims" of exclusionism lack the capacity to change their own destiny.

Some anti-racist writers have argued that overemphasizing the importance of cultural barriers in the creation of discrimination can divert attention from institutional practices which serve to perpetuate racism. This critique of cultural pluralism developed in the early 1980s, although some writers have continued to make such a criticism of the culturalist position throughout the decade (Bourne and Sivanandan 1980).

In answer to this, Ballard argues that the ethnocentric preoccupation with urban proletarianization is not sufficiently cognizant of the part that differing cultures have played in the "extraordinary effectiveness" of the resistance to hegemony demonstrated by the "migrant minorities". Creative human energy can be effectively utilized to circumvent or resist oppression. Hegemonic ideologies which oppress can be challenged through the establishing of alternative conceptualizations of reality based on what Ballard refers to as mental, spiritual and cultural resistance (Ballard 1992).

Webb argues that anti-racism has constructed a new "moral universe" for both service users and service providers; an authoritarian form of puritanism, a "moral crusade" which aims to "reconstruct practices, and thoughts". Puritanism aims to expose and eradicate the evils of discrimination. Like the pre-Restoration puritanism which derived its certainty from divine scripture, the new puritanism gains inspiration from a secular equivalent. However, while this may have been the case in some earlier anti-racist writing, the reductionism which characterizes some forms of anti-racist writing is being increasingly challenged (Macey and Moxon 1996).

There is very little evidence relating to the effectiveness of anti-racist training in the criminal justice system in this country, since the emphasis in the main has been on the development of equal opportunity policies. Indeed, very few countries have developed distinctly anti-racist programmes in the area of criminal justice. An exception to this is Canada, where elements of anti-racism have been incorporated into both training and practice, but with disappointing results. Research into the Ottawa police anti-racism programme indicated that it was unlikely to change the behaviour of police officers. Other Canadian research into effectiveness of anti-racist training in the Canadian criminal justice system supports this view (QPO 1995).

Reformulating anti-racism

One possible conclusion that can be drawn from these criticisms is that anti-racism is not redundant, but needs to be reconstituted in order to take cognizance of the differing meanings which have been ascribed to the term racism.

Table 3 indicates some of the differences between unreconstituted and reconstituted forms of anti-racism. The table reflects some of the difficulties involved in defining racism which are unacknowledged in much of the anti-racist literature. The manifestations, and implications for the criminal justice system, are also shown in relation to a reconstituted form of anti-racism. It can be seen that the overrepresentation of black people in the system is not simply the result of individual racism which is determined by an all-encompassing notion of ideology, but related to a dominant view of black culture as constituting a threat to an imagined wholly-British society. Anti-racism has thus been presented as an overdetermined model, which racializes all or most aspects of professional conduct in the criminal justice system. This reduces complex questions to the level of slogans which can then be utilized by governments seeking to restructure public services in the direction of the market. Unreconstituted anti-racism possesses a sense of absolute certainty bordering on the evangelical. This has led to more recent calls for a non-reductionist form of anti-racism to be adopted (Macey and Moxon 1996: 303). Even more worrying is the distinct possibility that anti-racism also fails to take into account the voice of service users who have experienced discrimination.

Table 3

Varieties of anti-racism

	Reconstituted	*Unreconstituted*
Racism defined	Nation as a unified and cultural community	Prejudice and power. Conceptions of biological inferiority and superiority
Manifestations of racism	Cultural	Anti-collectivist
Defining characteristics	Separation of class and race	Conflation of class and race; equal opportunities cultural relativism.
	Tentative—race at the centre of political life;	Certainty—race a discrete conceptual category
	Multidimensional	Monocausal, monolithic
Crime and criminal justice	Crime related to dominant view of system of deviant black culture, constituting a threat to essence of imagined civilized wholeness of British cultural greatness	Black people over-represented in the criminal justice system created by individual and institutional racism

In the mid-1980s it appeared as if a new quasi-antidiscriminatory academic industry was developing which worked to the benefit of consultants and trainers, rather than the recipients of services.

Looking to the Future: Equality, Rights and the Development of the Criminal Justice System

Efforts to implement Section 95 of the 1991 Criminal Justice Act can be seen in the work of the Criminal Justice Consultative Council (CJCC) which comprises senior officials from all the criminal justice agencies, relevant government departments, and the legal profession. This has led to the publication of fifty recommendations for action with respect to discrimination across the criminal justice system. Attention has been directed towards the influence of race in bail decisions, sentencing decisions, more detailed "ethnic monitoring", training of staff including the judiciary and magistracy, monitoring of particular police procedures, most notably stop and search, and greater employment equality in all areas of the criminal justice system. Much of the substance to these proposals is based upon monitoring which has itself come under criticism. If monitoring does not take place criminal justice agencies leave themselves open to the charge of ignoring discriminatory behaviour. Ethnic monitoring on the other hand can be seen as unduly intrusive. When introduced into the probation service it was regarded by

NAPO as unacceptable in that it used questionable ethnic categories to create a supposed relationship between skin colour and discrimination. What was more urgently required according to NAPO was a monitoring of the impact of anti-racist policies on probation practice.

Towards rights in the criminal justice system

Equal opportunities policies in the criminal justice system barely reach a minimal level. We have seen that although procedural justice and fairness may be the stated aim of policies, the manner in which the policy is implemented, and the lack of reference to specific rights, still disadvantages particular groups. Wilding (1994) warns of the dangers associated with the implementation of complex and expensive organizational backup for rights enforcement, and questions the ultimate usefulness of charters of rights to protect the service provider. Wilding also warns against the overemphasis on the adversarial struggle for rights which could detrimentally affect the user–provider relationship. An example of this would be the level of trust that can exist between probation officer and client. It has been argued that the need for more rights is clear in today's criminal justice system in which punishment is so frequently emphasized. Clear enforceable rights could perform a mediating function between good intention and practice in the criminal justice system. The goals of Section 95 of the 1991 Criminal Justice Act are more achievable when rights are related to both the financing and administration of the public services. This is to some extent accepted by the Home Office. In a Home Office report on the workings of Police and Criminal Evidence Act codes of practice it is acknowledged that with regard to the questioning of suspects, "More information is to be given to the suspect about the right to legal advice and there is more detailed guidance about putting rights into practice" (Home Office 1992: vi).

Prisoners in the Netherlands and Germany have the right to take disputes regarding procedures and disciplinary matters to an independent ombudsperson. This has, according to Cavadino and Dignan, changed the mood within prisons in those countries from one of riotous discontent to the reduction of prisoners' sense of injustice. The right to fair and independent procedures for pursuing grievances is fundamental if Britain is to move from increasing levels of punishment towards consistency (Cavadino and Dignan 1994).

There needs to be an independent complaints body which includes the brief to investigate allegations of racial discrimination, against the police, prisons and probation. This would require the appointment of an independent ombudsperson, independent of services, to receive and investigate specific complaints relating to discriminatory practices. Reference has been made above to the disadvantage suffered by black prisoners, particularly with regard to the disciplinary procedures. Changes introduced in 1990 which were meant to address the gross inadequacies in enforceable standards are marginally less cumbersome than the old. Woolf rejected the idea of a prison ombudsperson to whom prisoners could make their complaints at any stage, on the basis that it was unnecessary if there were satisfactory grievance and disciplinary procedures. However as Cavadino and Dignan argue, this is a "big if" (Cavadino and Dignan 1994).

Equal opportunities policies cannot be rejected simply on the basis of being liberal and woolly, since they embody the crucial concept of rights. They do need to have more specified objectives, and measurable outcomes which are then made public. Although this happens nationally in the publications emanating from the Home Office which relate to Section 95, continuing evidence of racial discrimination in the criminal justice system strongly suggests that headway still needs to be made in relation to the manner in which day-to-day practices reflect good intentions.

All service users should have the right to receive service only from staff who have completed anti-discriminatory training courses which have been independently assessed. The roots of institutional discrimination are laid down in training by professional conventions which can differentially affect black people. Training should enable all staff, including judges and magistrates, to examine critically the ramifications of institutionalized discrimination in relation to penal policy, rights and procedures under the anti-discriminatory legislation such as it is, as well as aspects of relevant criminology. Service users should also have the right to express a written and/or verbal opinion on the outcome and quality of service they have received through, for example, an exit survey or evaluation form given to users (Broad and Denney 1996).

However, the recommendation made by the CJCC that equality service management groups should be formed in order to devise good practice fails to recognize that satisfactory procedures do not yet exist to consider complaints against the police. Sanders has argued: "Police rule breaking is normal and not deviant" (Sanders 1994: 811).

Conclusion

It has been argued that both anti-racism and equal opportunities policies have failed to tackle seriously racial discrimination within the workings of the criminal justice system. In many respects both concepts suffer from a lack of conceptual clarity, and are thus open to attack from all sides of the political spectrum. They appear to make elaborate global critiques of existing practices, whilst offering few practical possibilities for the future. Without considering the impact of good intentions on service users, both anti-racism and equal opportunities policies could become empty polemical statements of intent.

A rights approach with all its possible pitfalls, does hold out some hope for the future. Given the election of a new government with a commitment to the establishment of more clearly stated and enforceable rights for service users in the public sector, it may well be that the future offers black people a greater possibility of gaining equal treatment within the criminal justice system, and ultimately more control over their own lives.

Notes

I have been greatly assisted in developing ideas relating to equal opportunity by discussion with Judith Glover of the Roehampton Institute, London.

1. In the *Handbook* of criminology, containing some 1246 pages covering a wide variety of criminological issues, no reference is made to disabled people (Macguire *et al.* 1994). On 19 October 1993, 0.45 per cent of prison service employees were recorded

as being disabled, which falls short of the Cabinet Office target of 3 per cent (Home Office 1994a). The Home Office do not categorize prisons into those which do or do not have provision for disabled prisoners. No data are kept relating to the total number of prisoners who have disabilities in total or in each standard age group. In April 1991 a NAPO subgroup on disabled people wrote to all probation areas seeking information about policies on disability. Only one met the conditions laid down under the 1944 Employment of Disabled Persons Act which requires 3 per cent of disabled staff to be employed (Bodlovic 1992). People with learning impairments, who are also neglected in criminology, are particularly easy targets when demands exist to secure a conviction at any cost. In the case of Stefan Kiszko, vital forensic evidence which could have cleared him at his original trial was withheld. As a result he was convicted in 1976 of murder, but freed by the Court of Appeal in 1992. He died in 1993, whilst in May 1994 a senior police officer and a forensic scientist, both now retired, who had been instrumental in the case were both charged with attempting to pervert the course of justice. Women commit fewer, and less serious, crimes than men, and are represented in smaller numbers within the criminal justice system (Heidensohn 1994). Women in the criminal justice system are subjected to multiple "discursive oppression" which is dependent upon the inability and/or refusal of a number of authorized definers (who empirically, may be either men or women) "to hear or listen to communications which are incongruent with professionally legitimated modes of expression about female conditions of existence" (Worral 1990: 162). With regard to sexual orientation, no specific legislation exists to make discriminatory behaviour against gay and lesbian people an offence. Clause 28 of the local government legislation prohibited local authority employees from promoting homosexuality in their services.

2. The term black has come under close scrutiny, particularly by those who have criticized anti-racist positions which developed through the 1980s. The words "black people" are often used to denote persons of Afro-Asian or Caribbean descent irrespective of birth, who consider themselves to be of such descent. Fevre (1984) points out that some may argue that Asians are not black; Asians do not look like people from Saigon or Tokyo. Terms like "black" and "white" emphasize that to be recognized as non-white is to be treated differently from those with white skin. It is in relation to the manner in which black people are distinctly identifiable and treated differently by those employed in the criminal justice system that the term black is used here.

3. Pre-sentence reports are written by probation officers and provide the courts with a social history of the offender concentrating on such aspects as education, employment, and the circumstances and attitude towards the offence. They also usually contain a recommendation on how the case should be dealt with by the courts.

4. Dominelli has recently defined anti-oppressive social work practice for instance in terms of

> a form of social work practice which addresses social divisions and structural inequalities in the work that is done with people whether they be users (clients) or workers. AOP aims to provide more appropriate and sensitive services by responding to people's needs regardless of their social status. AOP embodies a person concerned philosophy; an egalitarian value system concerned with reducing the deleterious effects of structural inequality upon people's lives; a methodology focusing on both process and outcome; a way of structuring relationships between individuals that aims to empower users by reducing the negative effects of social hierarchies on their interaction and the work they do together. (Dominelli 1996: 170)

5. Following the decision of Norfolk County Council adoption panel to refuse Jim and

Roma Lawrence permission to adopt a "mixed race" child in July 1993 it was argued that the drive to eradicate all "politically incorrect" attitudes was an abuse of power and a corruption of traditional liberal values of open-minded education and honest inquiry (Phillips 1993a; Amiel 1992).

References

Amiel, B. (1992), Lady Bountiful Lethal Little Society List, *Sunday Times*, 11 October.

Ballard, R. (1992), New Clothes for the Emperor: The conceptual nakedness of the race relations industry in Britain, *New Community*, vol. 18, no. 3: 481–92.

Blakemore, K. and Drake, R. (1996), *Understanding Equal Opportunity Policies*, London: Harvester Wheatsheaf.

Bodlovic, M. (1992), Disability-responses of probation areas to a survey by sub-group on disability, *NAPO News*, vol. 36: 4–5.

Bourne, J. and Sivanandan, A. (1980), Cheerleaders and ombudsmen: the sociology of race relations in Britain, *Race and Class*, vol. 21: 331–52.

Broad, B. and Denney, D. (1996), User's rights and the Probation Service: some opportunities and obstacles, *Howard Journal of Criminal Justice*, vol. 35, no. 1: 61–76.

Burnett, R. and Farrell, G. (1994), *Reported and Unreported Incidents in Prisons*, Occasional Paper 14, Centre for Criminological Research, University of Oxford.

Cavadino, M. and Dignan, J. (1994), *The Penal System*, London: Sage.

CCETSW (1991), *Rules and Requirements for the Diploma in Social Work* (Paper 30), second edition, London: Central Council for Education and Training.

Chappel, A. (1995), Disability Discrimination and the Criminal Justice System, *Critical Social Policy*, issue 42: 19–34.

Crowe, I. and Cove, J. (1984), Ethnic minorities and the courts, *Criminal Law Review*: 413–17.

Deakin, N. and Wright, A. (1995), Tawney in George, V. and Page, R. *Modern Thinkers on Welfare*, Hemel Hempstead: Harvester Wheatsheaf.

Denney, D. (1981), Race and Crisis Management, in Manning, N. (ed.), *Social Problems and Welfare Ideology*, Aldershot: Gower.

Denney, D. (1992), *Racism and Antiracism in Probation*, London: Routledge.

Dominelli, L. (1996), De-professionalising social work: anti-oppressive practice, competencies and postmodernism, *British Journal of Social Work*, vol. 26: 153–75.

Edwards, J. (1990), What purpose does equal opportunity serve?, *New Community*, vol. 17, no. 1: 19–35.

Fevre, R. (1984), *Cheap Labour and Racial Discrimination*, Aldershot: Gower.

Fitzgerald, M. (1993), *Ethnic Minorities and the Criminal Justice System*, Royal Commission on Criminal Justice System, Research Study 20, London: HMSO.

Genders, E. and Player, E. (1989), *Race Relations in Prisons*, Oxford: Oxford University Press.

Gilroy, P. (1990), The end of anti-racism, *New Community*, vol. 17, no. 1: 71–83.

Hall, S., Critcher, C., Jefferson, T., Clarke, J. and Roberts, B. (1978), *Policing the Crisis: Mugging, the State, Law and Order*, London: Macmillan.

Heidensohn, F. (1994), *Gender and Crime*, in Maguire, M., Morgan, R. and Reiner, R. (eds), *The Oxford Handbook of Criminology*, Oxford: Clarendon Press.

Home Office (1992), *Three Year Plan for the Probation Service, 1993–1996*, London: HMSO.

Home Office (1994a), *Equal Opportunities: Annual Progress Report 1992/1993*, London: Home Office.

Home Office (1994b), *Parole Recommendations and Ethnic Origins*, Home Office Statistical Bulletin 2/94, London: Home Office.

Home Office (1996a), *The Prison Population in 1995*, Home Office Statistical Bulletin 14/96, London: Home Office.

Home Office (1996b), *Policing and the Public in England and Wales*, Home Office Research Findings 28, London: Home Office.

Home Office (1996c), *Race and the Criminal Justice System 1995*, London: Home Office.

Hood, R. (1992), *Race and Sentencing: A Study in the Crown Court*, London: Commission for Racial Equality.

Hudson, B. (1989), Discrimination and disparity: the influence of race on sentencing, *New Community*, vol. 16, no. 1: 21–32.

Macey, M. and Moxon, E. (1996), Antiracist and antioppressive theory, *British Journal of Social Work*, vol. 26, no. 3: 297–314.

Maguire, M., Morgan, M. and Reiner, R. (eds) (1994), *The Oxford Handbook of Criminology*, Oxford: Clarendon Press.

Mason, D. and Jewson, N. (1992), Race, Equal Opportunities and Employment Practice—Reflections in the 1980s prospects for the 1990s, *New Community*, vol. 19, no. 1: 75–99.

McConville, F. H. and Baldwin, J. (1982), The influence of race on sentencing in England, *Criminal Law Review*: 652–58.

Moxon, D. (1988), *Sentencing Practice in the Crown Court*, Home Office Research Study 103, London: Home Office.

NACRO (1991), *Race and Criminal Justice*, Briefing, London: National Association for the Care and Resettlement of Offenders.

Phillips, M. (1993a), Oppressive urge to stop oppression, *Independent*, 1 August.

Phillips, M. (1993b), Antiracist zealots drive away recruits, *Observer*, 1 August.

QPO (1995), *Report of the Commission on Systematic Racism in the Ontario Criminal Justice System*, Toronto: Queen's Printer for Ontario.

Reiner, R. (1989), Race and Criminal Justice, *New Community*, vol. 16, no. 1: 5–21.

Reiner, R. (1993), Race, crime and justice: models of interpretation, in Gelsthorpe, L. and McWilliams, W. (eds), *Minority Ethnic Groups in the Criminal Justice System*, Cambridge: Cambridge University Institute of Criminology.

Sanders, A. (1994), From suspect to trial, in Maguire, M., Morgan, R. and Reiner, R. (eds), *The Oxford Handbook of Criminology*, Oxford: Clarendon Press.

Smith, D. J. (1994), Race, crime, and criminal justice, in Maguire, M., Morgan, R. and Reiner, R. (eds), *The Oxford Handbook of Criminology*, Oxford: Clarendon Press.

Taylor, P. and Baldwin, M. (1989), Travelling hopefully: anti-racist practice and practice learning opportunities, *Social Work Education*, vol. 10, no. 3: 5–32.

Treasury (1992), *Competing for Quality*, June, London: HMSO.

Wilding, P. (1994), Maintaining quality in human services, *Social Policy & Administration*, vol. 28, no. 1: 57–72.

Worral, A. (1990), *Offending Women*, London: Routledge.

Probation and Social Exclusion

David Smith and John Stewart

Abstract

The paper begins with a brief discussion of the value of the term "social exclusion", before drawing on quantitative (survey) and qualitative (interview) evidence to suggest that young people on the caseload of the probation service are, in general, excluded from the full range of social goods. The basis of this exclusion is not only in poverty and unemployment, but in social and personal insecurity, lack of access to the benefits of education and training, and housing and health problems. It is argued that despite their exclusion these young people have predominantly conventional hopes and aspirations, and that there is therefore no reason to believe that a programme for their social inclusion and reintegration would be doomed to fail. The paper then reviews some aspects of present practice in probation which may tend to increase rather than reduce the exclusionary pressure on those with whom the service works, by stigmatizing and marginalizing them through a narrow focus on their offending. It concludes by suggesting strategies for more inclusionary and integrative practice in the areas of anti-custodialism, restorative justice and reintegrative shaming, community safety, and help with access to education, training and health services. The paper considers what local inter-agency structures are needed to support intensive work on offending, and sketches some characteristics of a probation service committed to social inclusion.

Keywords:

Probation; Offenders; Unemployment; Exclusion; Reintegration

In this paper we will be concerned with the uses which can be made of the concept of social exclusion in understanding the situation and experience of offenders in contact with the probation service, and in developing ideas about what kinds of strategy the service might most helpfully adopt in response. We will draw on quantitative and qualitative evidence to show that on most interpretations of the concept most of the people with whom the service works can be thought of as excluded from the full range of goods associated with

Address for Correspondence: *David Smith, Department of Applied Social Science, Lancaster University, Cartmel College, Lancaster, LA1 4YL.*

citizenship, not only by virtue of their status as offenders but through other experiences of marginalization and deprivation. We will also suggest, however, that there is little evidence from this sample of offenders to support the idea that they are part of a threatening "underclass" defined by values and attitudes at odds with prevailing social norms and by various symptoms of moral decline. We will then discuss some recent work on probation and social work practice to suggest some ways in which the service could (and perhaps does) contribute to the further exclusion of offenders, before suggesting a number of approaches which, in our view, would help to reduce the impact of the "exclusionary processes" (Carlen 1996: 106) to which they are subject.

Perhaps we should say at the start roughly where we stand in relation to some recent debates about the value of the term "social exclusion" and other concepts often associated with it. We are aware of the complaints of some critics that the term glosses over various continuing social divisions which are inherent in capitalist societies, and sympathetic to the argument that "social exclusion" should mean something more than exclusion from the labour market (Levitas 1996); it also seems clear that in some usages "social exclusion" and the kindred terms of social cohesion, social solidarity, integration, interdependence and so on have become part of a possibly seductive but actually vacuous Eurospeak. Despite this, we are broadly sympathetic to the communitarian, solidaristic commitments which lie behind the comparatively recent acceptance of this kind of language in debates on social policy in Britain, and are cautiously optimistic that the thinking behind it will have a positive practical influence on the social and penal policy of a Labour government. We also think that the concepts of social inclusion, (re)integration and interdependence have had fruitful results in recent developments in criminological theory and criminal justice practice (Braith-waite 1989; Burnside and Baker 1994; Nellis 1995) and that, at the very least, a sense of the exclusionary forces working on many (officially known) offenders is important if the social and personal context of offending is to be understood (as we think it should be). There are, we shall suggest, good reasons for thinking that the narrow focus on "offending behaviour" and on enforcement which the probation service has been encouraged to adopt in recent years is both theoretically and practically inadequate (and that it is likely on its own to fail to achieve the reduced offending rates to which it aspires), and we are therefore sympathetic to those who have argued for going "beyond offending behaviour" (Drakeford and Vanstone 1996). We hope to have retained a due academic and political scepticism in our interpretation of social exclusion in this context, and are certainly hostile to versions of communitarianism (Etzioni 1993) which stress defensive stigmatization and marginalization rather than inclusion and integration; but whether, despite this, we have fallen victim to the "punk Durkheimianism" of which Levitas (1996) complains is for the reader to judge.

How are Offenders Socially Excluded?

Recent surveys of the social and personal circumstances of offenders known to the probation service all tell a similar story of deprivation, poverty, stress and personal difficulties (Pritchard *et al.* 1992; National Association of Probation Officers 1993; Stewart and Stewart 1993). While social exclusion has important dimensions other than those associated with unemployment and the poverty which results from it, there is little dispute that Townsend (1979) was right to point to the various ways in which poor people are excluded from full participation in socially valued activities. Tables 1, 2 and 3 present findings from the survey by Stewart and Stewart (1993), which was based on questionnaires completed by probation officers from almost every English region in January 1991 on young adult offenders aged 17, 20 and 23. The survey collected data on 1,389 individuals who were in contact with the service in January 1991.

Table 1

Source of income currently received, or expected
on release from custody (January 1991)

% of age groups	17	20	23	all ages	
				N	%
Wages, full or part-time	18	21	22	276	21
Training scheme allowance	20	5	3	105	8
Income Support, Hardship	20	66	67	748	56
Another benefit	3	7	10	98	7
One-off payments	14	6	4	96	7
Subsidies from individuals	27	8	4	151	11
No income at all	27	3	2	114	9
(multiple responses*) N	315	614	414	1343	

* Multiple response means that individual cases may be included under more than one category as applicable to their situation.

Table 1 shows that just over a fifth of the sample were in paid work at the time of the survey. The majority were on Income Support or another benefit, while a substantial minority had no income at all, or were living on money from a variety of sources of doubtful reliability. Of those who did have a reasonably regular source of legitimate income, 20 per cent had some of this income directly deducted at source to pay off Social Fund loans, fuel and rent arrears. More than half of those with a known regular income actually received under £30 a week for their own needs and those of any dependants. Those with the lowest income were unemployed single people, and particularly 17-year-olds disqualified from benefit, who were living either on their own or within extended families which were supporting them. Many families, too, were badly off: tables 2 and 3 show that nearly half of parents with responsibility for children had a family income of less than £60 a week. Overall, 54 per cent of these young people had debts in addition to any covered by direct deductions, usually in the form of outstanding fines (37%), poll tax arrears, and catalogue debts. The general impression was one of poverty and financial pressure; in

98

Table 2

Weekly income currently received (January 1991)

% of households	single	nuclear couple	extended family	all types N	%
Nothing	8	4	18	110	13
£1 to £19	5	1	6	41	5
£20 to £29	48	19	38	306	37
£30 to £39	17	6	12	99	12
£40 to £59	7	17	4	58	7
£60 to £79	3	19	6	70	8
£80 to £99	6	10	6	56	7
over £100	7	18	9	86	10
N	198	143	485	826	

Table 3

Weekly income currently received (January 1991)

% of age group	17	20	23	all ages N	%
Nothing	38	5	4	114	13
£1 to £19	12	2	2	41	5
£20 to £29	14	49	39	318	38
£30 to £39	16	11	9	101	12
£40 to £59	4	8	7	59	7
£60 to £79	8	7	11	70	8
£80 to £99	4	7	10	59	8
over £100	4	10	17	86	10
N	222	395	231	848	

Note: Weekly income does not include housing benefit.

many cases the situation was so uncertain that no specific weekly income could be recorded.

Only 10 per cent of young offenders in the survey had a weekly income of over £100; two-thirds had less than £40. Arnold and Jordan (1996) are in no doubt that this demonstrable poverty represents a worsening of conditions over the past thirty years, and that its consequences include social exclusion. According to them, today's probation clients are much less likely to have a job, and much less likely to have access to adequate resources and services for a secure, healthy lifestyle in the mainstream of society. They are far more likely to suffer deprivation and exclusion—in other words, they are not different people, but people in much more desperate circumstances, who have therefore resorted to more desperate measures (Arnold and Jordan 1996: 30–1). There is evidence to support their claim that the financial circumstances of offenders have become relatively more impoverished since the 1960s. Davies (1969), reporting the results of a survey of probationers in 1965, allows a comparison of known income then and in 1991. The basis for the comparison is the appropriate weekly social security payment for a single person, the most common household type in both surveys. This rose in the 26-year period by a factor of 9.1, from £3.175 to £28.80, and table 4 shows the result of multiplying Davies's income bands by this figure.

Table 4

Weekly income of probationers
in 1964–5, at 1990–1 rates

Nothing	3%
Under £36.40	12%
Up to £72.80	33%
Up to £109.20	32%
Up to £145.60	14%
Up to £182	3%
Over £182	2%
N	461

Source: Derived from Davies
(1969), table 5.31.

The proportion of probation clients with no income at all was more than four times as high in 1991 as in 1965; and Davies (1969: 61, 81) found that 59 per cent of the probationers in his sample were in employment, compared with 21 per cent in 1991. Davies was able to conclude that, in general, the problems of probationers in 1965 were not material ones, and to argue specifically that they were not, in today's language, "excluded". On the contrary, "There was every indication, indeed, that the probationers and their families were for the most part well in the mainstream of Britain's economic affluence" (Davies 1969: 31). This conclusion may have been over-optimistic even at the time Davies reached it; certainly no one could possibly argue this of the probation caseload of the 1990s. The surveys by Stewart and Stewart (1993) and the National Association of Probation Officers (1993) both found that 64 per cent of their samples were unemployed, and even those who were working in the former were estimated, on the basis of interviews with a smaller sample, to be earning an average of £106 a week. If *one* source of social exclusion is lack of regular, legitimate employment, then probation clients are disproportionately likely to experience it, and we consider below what the service might do to increase their chances of participation in the labour market.

We should note, too, that the risk of social exclusion as a result of unemployment is not evenly distributed, in the probation caseload or in the general population. According to the 1991 census, male unemployment was higher among all ethnic minority groups except the Chinese than among whites, and the discrepancy was even more marked for young males, who make up the bulk of the probation caseload. For example, among males aged 16–24, 37.5 per cent of black Caribbeans and 41.5 per cent of black Africans were unemployed in 1991, according to the census, compared with 17.4 per cent of whites in the same age group (Home Office 1994). Since the highest population concentrations of ethnic minorities are in parts of the country with relatively low overall rates of unemployment, the gap in employment opportunities between whites and minority ethnic groups is even greater than the national figures suggest. To ignore the exclusionary effects of unemployment would therefore be to run the risk of ignoring an important element of the experience of racism, which neither the probation service nor the criminal justice system as a whole can afford to do (Hood 1992; Home Office 1994).

Apart from unemployment and poverty, Stewart and Stewart (1993) found that the young offenders in their sample had experienced or were experiencing various other forms of exclusion, as well as those associated with the status of "offender". Most obviously, and most closely related to subsequent employability, many had either been excluded or had excluded themselves from most of the opportunities provided by education and training: 80 per cent had left school with no qualifications at all (compared with 8 per cent of the general population), and 16 per cent had effectively left school before the minimum legal age. Graham and Bowling (1995) found that offending among young people was strongly associated with persistent truancy and with exclusion from school, especially in the rare cases of permanent exclusion. Cause and effect are hard to disentangle here, and both persistent truancy and the kind of behaviour which leads to exclusion from school may be best thought of as part of a range of disruptive and antisocial behaviour which also includes delinquency: Graham and Bowling conclude that exclusion was probably both a cause and a result of offending. "Exclusion" from school is one of the formal legal mechanisms by which troublesome people can be deliberately barred from participation in citizenship (the most obvious case being imprisonment), and it is hard to believe that it does not increase the risk of further offending. In this connection, Graham and Bowling remark (1995: 90) that recent policies may "inadvertently" have contributed to the sharp increase in the use of exclusion between 1991 and 1994, and note that in 1995 only 5 per cent of local authorities had any policies to prevent exclusion. We suggest below what such policies might look like, and argue that the probation service should participate in their development.

As some of the quotations below from young offenders suggest, problems at school were often associated with problems at home. Among the social goods from which many offenders are excluded is that of a stable, loving and caring family life. Like the National Prison Survey (Dodd and Hunter 1992), Stewart and Stewart (1993) found that a far higher proportion of known offenders than of the general population had had some experience of local authority care (26 per cent compared with 2 per cent), suggesting (at the very least) some unhappiness and stress within their families. Care need not, perhaps, always entail exclusion, but there is no doubt that many young people find the process of leaving care and returning to "normal" community life difficult, and that many are expected to achieve this transition in poor health, with few educational qualifications, and largely on their own (Department of Health 1991; Stein and Carey 1986). Leaving care, like leaving custody (Paylor 1995), is a housing "pressure point" (Stewart 1996), and there is no doubt that the disrupted and difficult family relationships of many young offenders lead to problems in finding safe, secure and healthy accommodation, which compound the difficulties common to young people in finding affordable independent housing. Another indicator of family stress in Stewart and Stewart's survey was that while 46 per cent of the sample were currently living with one or both of their parents, or intended to do so on release from prison, only 17 per cent had done so all their lives; family conflict and the young person's own behaviour, rather than any positive developments such as a move into tertiary education, were the most common reasons given for leaving home.

Finally, and distressingly, Stewart and Stewart (1993) found that 22 per cent of their sample were assessed by their probation officers as chronically incapacitated through some form of disability, illness or addiction. This seems an astonishingly high figure for a population none of whom was older than 23, but the health risks and needs of young people known to the probation service have been highlighted by other studies (Pritchard *et al.* 1990; 1992), and their implications for probation practice and policy are suggested later in this paper. The exclusionary effects of illness and disability hardly need to be spelt out, and these are likely to be exaggerated when the health problem is thought to be the sufferers' own fault, the result of their wickedness or at least carelessness. Just as problems at school are linked with problems at home, so health problems can be both the cause and the effect of unemployment: the links between long-term unemployment and heroin use have been established (e.g. Pearson 1987), and unemployment is also associated with an increased risk of the ultimate self-exclusion of suicide (Pritchard 1995).

Some Experiences of Exclusion

Here we turn to the accounts of their experiences given by a structured sample of 58 young offenders interviewed in probation centres, offices and hostels in 1991 and 1992 to provide a qualitative complement to the survey cited above. Many told stories of past abuse or neglect and of past and present poverty and stress. Life had always been difficult, a matter of survival and day-to-day coping in which any long-term plans (as opposed to vague aspirations) were hopelessly unrealistic. May (all names are fictional) summed up the fatalistic assumptions which can come from growing up poor in a world dedicated to consumption:

> "I had no money, my family had no money, but that weren't really the point. I just had no money, I was brought up around no money and I thought that's the way it's going to be for the rest of my life. I'm just going to be a nobody in society."

She took her exclusion for granted, as a mere fact of life. Others fought back against deprivation and abuse, like Andy, who left home *"when I was fifteen. They were going to put us in a home, so I left at fifteen after giving them a kicking. I took fifteen year of getting beaten up off them, so I says 'Right, my turn'. I says, 'If you hit me again I'm going to hit you back', so I did and I left. Coppers arranged for us to stop at my nan's.* [Well before that he] *kept running away all the time. Went out to stop getting a good hiding. Locked in your bedroom and that.* [After talking about his brother he returns to his mother:] *And then she got married again. And they had a kid. So when she had him, we were pushed out even further."*

Although in many cases their experiences of deprivation were extreme, there are recognizable elements in the accounts of these young people which suggest that they too participate in the "mixed economy of welfare", move between formal and informal networks of care and support, and have relatives who feel some sense of the obligations associated with kinship (Finch and Mason 1992; Paylor and Smith 1994). Often, though, neither source of care had worked very well, as in Dean's account:

"I lived in Somerset. My mum got divorced from my real dad, and then we moved down to Wales when I was about three months old. My mum got married to another bloke in Wales. She had another kid. And then my step-dad kept abusing me. It was then my mum couldn't control me in Wales and she moved me into Social Services in Wales, put me into a couple of foster homes and I kept running away. My grandma, granddad from Nottingham offered to foster me, so the rest of my life I've been brought up by them . . . I've never seen my real dad since I was born . . . With my step-dad beating me up and abusing me, it got to me quite a lot at school, I was picking on everyone at school. [He left his grandparents' home at 16:] *I wasn't getting on with my granddad too well, because he was alcoholic. If I wanted to stay out at my girlfriend's, he'd come home, find out I'm not in, I'd go back and we'd just start arguing. Then one day we just ended up fighting, so I just left home."*

He went on to a chldren's home, from which he was excluded for criminal damage, and then to a hostel; from there he moved to a bedsit, where he accumulated rent arrears: *"it was a private landlord, and he was getting pissed off with it, and I had to move out of there and live with my friends, two of my good friends who live in Nottingham."* The friends had moved on, leaving Dean in Nottingham, and now the responsibility of the probation service rather than Social Services.

In an account like this there is a strong sense of one calamity being piled on another; one can imagine a young person somehow dealing with any one of these traumatic events, but not all of them, against the diurnal round of routine poverty. This, in common with many of the interviewees' accounts, is a story of survival, like the stories of the young homeless people interviewed by Carlen (1996: 106), who stresses the "primarily conventional aspirations and social needs" of the young homeless, and their insistence that being homeless "does not mean that one is anti-social". Surviving, for the young offenders interviewed, often required considerable ingenuity in the pursuit of conventional social goods, as in Linda's account of how she and the friend with whom she shared accommodation managed:

"Tina don't sort of take say £20 off me every single week, you know. If there's no milk or there's no electric I'll go and buy it or we'll go halves on it. She'd rather do it like that. Say one week she ain't got the money to go and get milk, bread or whatever, or electric and I have, I'll do it. I've got no clothes and I'm starting to build up my clothes, trying to—hair spray, personal things, footwear. Most of it does go on going to look for jobs. That's where it mostly goes and all my fines I pay. The thing is there's a fiver for fines. Say I get £60, that's £55 plus a fiver to my mum for my catalogue, that's fifty, by the time I've got some bits and bobs for the food I like to eat, it's gone then."

Although the aspirations of most of these young people are conventional (and see Heath (1992) and Gallie *et al.* (1994) for further evidence that the alleged "underclass" and the long-term unemployed generally express conventional views and values), they are not always well equipped to achieve them on their own. One can only guess at what difference the right kind of support at the right time might have made in the following cases, where the young people lost jobs they liked and valued as a result of inability to persevere through periods of boredom or difficulty. Linda regretted losing a job in a private nursing home:

"They wanted me to go there so they gave me a uniform and I started two days later. Because my work was so good, they put me on to their paybooks, so instead of YTS money I got nearly £100 a week . . . But after eight months I started messing around and drinking so I couldn't be bothered to get up for work. But I still get really upset about that because that was the most brilliantest job I've ever had."

Guy also had his regrets:

"I've had two good jobs since I left school. First when I left school, accounts, YTS accounts on the [name of newspaper]. *Paper, good job. Cocked it up."*
Q: How long did that go on for?
"A good couple of months, three quarters of a year."
Q: And when you say you "cocked it up", what did you do?
"You don't realize how good a job is until you leave it."
Q: How did you mess it up?
"I don't say I messed it up, I just couldn't be bothered."
Q: So what does that mean? You didn't go?
"No, I just couldn't be bothered to carry on with it in the end. Couldn't be bothered to do this for the rest of my life. And then I went to a TV licensing place down town . . . That was a good job, that. One or two blokes in the office and that, like, you know. Just couldn't be bothered. I don't know. Got the sack for it . . . It were just a case of boredom."
Q: Yeah. Do you regret leaving?
"Yeah, I regret leaving a few of my jobs, or two of them, those two. I ain't going to get them again."

To show that young offenders have (predominantly) much the same ideas as the law-abiding of what the goods of citizenship are, is to show, among other things, that, given the opportunity and the support, which they will often need, they are capable of being socially included.

How the Probation Service can Reduce (and Promote) Social Exclusion

We will begin this section with an indication of the ways in which the probation service might actually contribute, and perhaps is contributing, to the (further) social exclusion of those with whom it works. Essentially our position is that, especially in the penal policy climate which prevailed during Michael Howard's time at the Home Office, probation practice which is exclusively focused on individual offenders, which demands that they and not their social circumstances should change, and which neglects the social and personal context in which their offending becomes intelligible, is likely to have this effect. Drakeford and Vanstone (1996: 3) make the point when they criticize the convenient

> idea that individual moral responsibility exists within a vacuum some-how detached from the circumstances in which people find themselves . . . Within this way of thinking "offenders" clearly occupy so residual a category of citizenship as to endorse the spirit of moral superiority which suffuses the idea of one human being "confronting" or "tackling" the behaviour of another.

Our position is perhaps slightly different, in that we think that offenders' behaviour (when antisocial, harmful or abusive) should at times be tackled and confronted (just as one may wish to do with friends, relations and colleagues at times), but that if this were *all* that probation officers do (which it is not, but which it might become if some present trends continue) then the effect would be further to stigmatize, marginalize and exclude people who (we have shown above) are likely to have had quite enough experience of such processes from sources other than the criminal justice system. What we (like Drakeford and Vanstone) object to is the language of hostility and aggres-sion—or warfare—which has been increasingly used not just to describe what probation officers are supposed to do but how the public at large are meant to feel about offenders (Currie 1996; Stern 1996). The language may be dismissed as political rhetoric, but the point is that rhetoric has real effects: "The deeply offensive image of young criminals as hyenas is a self-fulfilling prophecy: given no other role, that is what they will become" (Arnold and Jordan 1996: 41). The probation service will contribute to this process if it does not successfully resist the current pressure to deny that offenders too are citizens, members of some community (Currie 1988), and have claims upon us by virtue of their membership.

Should anyone doubt that the rhetoric of authoritative voices can have effects in the real world, it is useful to consider the fate of the 1991 Criminal Justice Act and how its aims were subverted well before corrective legislation was introduced with unusual speed in 1993. The 1991 Act, with its commitment to just deserts sentencing and its conception of probation as punishment in the community, is among the influences which have encouraged a focus on offending behaviour in isolation from its social context, but there is no doubt that its aims were compatible with much of what the probation service had traditionally argued for, particularly a reduction in the use of custody. The Home Office's own monitoring showed clearly that in the first months after its implementation the Act did have the intended effect (a lower use of custody, and a higher use of fines and community sentences); equally, the monitoring showed that when the Act was exposed to public criticism from (among others) a new Home Secretary, and once sentencers began to get a message from government that prison need not be a sentence of last resort, these trends were very quickly reversed (Home Office 1993), marking the start of the increasing reliance on imprisonment which is the most notable penal development of the mid-1990s.

Prison, as we noted above, is the most definitive form of social exclusion which the law allows, and a probation service committed to reducing the impact of exclusionary forces needs to be committed in principle to what Nellis (1995) calls "anti-custodialism", and able to bring the principle to life as a practical influence on sentencers' decisions. Raynor (1991) found, as had others (e.g. Moxon 1988), that in the Crown Court the effect of social inquiry reports was to change the distribution of non-custodial sentences, rather than to reduce the use of custody; indeed, for a substantial group of defendants the availability of a report increased rather than reduced the risk of a prison sentence. Without the benefit of reports, sentencers' favoured non-custodial measures were fines and suspended sentences, which were hardly ever suggested by probation officers. Their recommendations were for probation and community service and, if the court was unpersuaded by this advice, the result tended to be a prison sentence. Commenting later on this research, Raynor (1996) notes that compared with juvenile justice practitioners, who could point to substantial and influential achievements in reducing the use of custody, probation officers tended to be reluctant to believe that they could influence the workings of the criminal justice system, and therefore were rarely interested in monitoring the system's local operations or the effects of their own interventions. He concludes that we "cannot influence systems if we do not even know the immmediate consequences of our own inputs" (1996: 18), and knowing what these are, as part of a systematic effort of monitoring and quality control, is surely a basic responsibility of a service which believes in the virtues of community sentences and the vices of custody. There is evidence (Gelsthorpe and Raynor 1995) that better reports are more likely to produce less exclusionary sentences (i.e. less use of custody and more use of community-based measures), so that, if the service is serious about social inclusion, quality control of pre-sentence reports is essential. Reports which are careless and incompetent (or, worse, stigmatizing and rejecting) can make the service part of the exclusionary experience which, of course, need not end with the prisoner's release (Raynor *et al.* 1994: 38–42).

Without claiming to have exhausted the ways in which the probation service can fail to help, or can actively make things worse, we turn now to ideas, many of them derived from recent developments in practice, as to how the service might mitigate the exclusionary pressures which are such a prominent part of offenders' lives, before as well as after they become (officially) offenders. As with the discussion above, we make no claim that what follows represents an exhaustive treatment of the possible strategies open to the service; however, we will briefly outline, in turn, some promising approaches (using the categories employed by Nellis, 1995) under the headings of restorative justice, community safety, education and employment, and health (we have already discussed anti-custodialism). We will conclude with some broader reflections on what a probation service committed to combating social exclusion might look like. A recurring theme is that practice aimed solely at getting offenders to reform their ways is necessarily limited and is likely to be stigmatizing; instead the service needs to broaden its range and begin to contribute what it distinctively has to offer to inter-agency strategies in each of the areas we discuss.

Restorative justice

Suddenly, it seems, everyone is committed once again to restorative justice. The idea, usually expressed in practice as victim–offender mediation, was taken up in Britain by a number of enthusiasts, probation officers amongst them, in the 1980s, and was briefly supported by the Home Office (Marshall and Merry 1990). The principle was not new, and indeed the practice of mediating disputes was familiar enough to many practitioners not only in the probation service but in, for example, the police and the youth service; what was new was its higher public profile and the optimism of some of the pioneering figures that informal means of settling disputes could substantially replace (rather than be an adjunct to) the formal processes of criminal justice (Smith *et al.* 1988). The projects of the 1980s had in common a sense of the formal system as literally excluding not only offenders but victims from meaningful participation in resolving what, following Christie (1977), could be thought of as their own conflicts, and a commitment to reconciliation between the parties in dispute and the restoration of harmonious relations within a shared community. The aim was to provide a forum in which both victims and offenders could be helped to shed these stigmatizing and outcast statuses through the giving and receiving of apology and forgiveness, and (more ambiguously) to encourage offenders to make some kind of material compensation to their victims. Despite some good evidence that both parties often found mediation helpful and productive, the projects' location (in the main) within the criminal justice system, and the fact that they were run by agencies whose traditional identification was with offenders' rather than victims' interests, led to conflicts and uncertainties of aim which ultimately proved too difficult to resolve. The practice of mediation survived in various settings, however, for example as an element of the diversionary strategy for young offenders in Northamptonshire, where it was singled out for praise by the Audit Commission (1996) as a more constructive (and economical) response to minor offending than prosecution.

Nellis (1995: 185) argues that the probation service has no real choice about whether it should support a restorative approach to justice, because an interest in the welfare of offenders will lack political credibility and support if it is not complemented by a demonstrable concern with the needs and interests of victims. There are, however, other reasons for believing that restorative principles should increasingly inform probation practice. Whatever precise shape they assume in practice, restorative approaches necessarily involve setting offending within an intelligible human and relational context, and are therefore not open to the criticism that they abstract offending from the circumstances which give it meaning. On an optimistic reading of the recent revival of interest not only in victim–offender mediation but in the less private, more communitarian approach of family group conferencing, one can also argue that the practice of the 1990s is better-founded theoretically than that of the 1980s, particularly when it draws upon John Braithwaite's (Durkheim-ian!) theory of reintegrative shaming (Braithwaite 1989; 1994; Braithwaite and Mugford 1994). There are potential connections to be developed with the concrete and relational emphasis of feminist ethics applied to criminal justice (see Heidensohn (1986) for an original if tentative indication of where this might lead). Ethically, too, it is difficult to see how the probation service can decline to apply to victims the same respect and care which it has traditionally sought to bring to its work with offenders (Raynor and Vanstone 1994)—particularly if it can be shown that something "works" in the sense of reducing the risk of reoffending, and we can more or less specify what this is (McGuire 1995).

While convinced of the value of restorative principles and their place within an overall commitment to inclusionary rather than exclusionary practices, then, we should however add a cautionary note. There must be a risk that family group conferencing, which originally developed in a quite specific social and cultural context (McElrea 1994), will be taken up uncritically by probation officers and others who are understandably attracted to the idea, and either transplanted to settings in which it cannot thrive or used for purposes other than the empowerment and reintegration which it was meant to achieve. Shaming is a dangerous weapon in the wrong hands, or wrongly handled, and there is no reason why the practice of restorative justice any more than any other aspect of the service's work should be protected from rigorous monitoring of its effects. Recent optimism about the effectiveness of some forms of practice is almost exclusively based on evaluations of centre-based intensive groupwork with offenders on enhanced probation orders, and there remain huge tracts of probation work which research has hardly begun to explore. At the very least, it is important that the new wave of enthusiasts for restorative justice should learn from the confusions and mistakes of their 1980s' predecessors.

Community safety

The probation service has not always been clear about what the "wider work in the community" which it has been officially encouraged to undertake since the early 1980s (Home Office 1984) might amount to in practice, but increasingly (and coherently with concern for victims which has developed over the same period) activity in this area has crystallized around involvement in initiatives in crime prevention, or, as it has come to be known, community safety (Geraghty 1991; Home Office 1991; Sampson and Smith 1992). Although some (e.g. Gilling 1996) have remained sceptical about whether this is the best use of the service's resources, and indeed whether the social (as opposed to situational) approaches to crime prevention which are the service's strength are really necessary, we believe that there are good reasons why probation should seek to play a part in community safety programmes — especially if it is serious about reducing the exclusionary forces to which offenders (and potentially, whole neighbourhoods and segments of the population) are subject. The divisive, repressive and exclusionary possibilities of situational approaches to crime prevention have long been recognized (Cohen 1985), and the message is as important now as then—or more important, given the all-party commitment to "zero tolerance" policing, the enthusiastic pursuit of deliberately exclusionary policies such as the eviction of offenders from council housing, and the proposed extension of courts' powers to impose curfews and electronic tagging on offenders and their parents. The *Guardian* of 10 April 1997 carried a timely reminder from Charles Pollard, Chief Constable of Thames Valley Police, that "zero tolerance" wrenched from its original context of domestic violence and applied to petty offenders and their public incivilities could mean exactly the kind of repressive policing which Scarman (1981) argued had sparked the Brixton riots. Inevitably, this kind of policing targets particular and visible social groups, mainly those who are already most marginalized and vulnerable both to exclusion and to victimization (and including those newly criminalized as much for who they are as for what they do under the Criminal Justice and Public Order Act of 1994).

We do not mean to suggest that petty incivilities should always be disregarded, or that it is impossible to police them sensitively and effectively; and we are aware of the criticism of some writers, notably Ken Pease (e.g. Pease 1994), that the more "social" crime prevention becomes, and the more stress that is put on the need for co-ordinated inter-agency action, the vaguer become the objectives of the enterprise, and the more it shifts its targets from crime prevention to broader social policy goals. But we believe that this kind of drift is avoidable, and indeed that the involvement of the probation service can make it less likely, because the service's expertise (of which it should be collectively more confident than perhaps it is) lies in its understanding of offending patterns, offenders' lifestyles, and the criminogenic potential of the stresses to which poor and marginalized people are exposed. Pease himself some time ago endorsed the idea that the probation service's access to particular kinds of knowledge about offenders and offending meant that it could make a distinctive contribution to co-operative crime prevention efforts (Laycock and Pease 1985), and it seems likely that community safety projects which are run without probation participation will be needlessly impoverished. Further, the probation service has long experience of inter-agency working (because it cannot work at all without the co-operation of others) and of fruitful partnerships with other organizations (Smith *et al.* 1993) which it can put at the service of others, not least to help them be clear about what they should avoid.

Access to the benefits of education and training is not only a good in itself but is likely to be strongly associated with increased employability. We saw above that the use of school exclusions has increased in recent years, and while the causal links between educational failure and offending, and still more between unemployment and offending, are complex, there seems little doubt that unemployment is associated at the individual level with a greater propensity to offend (Farrington *et al.* 1986) and that high local rates of long-term unemployment, especially among young men, contribute to high rates of crime, disorder and unhappiness (Campbell 1993; Downes 1993). Recent work by one of the present authors on two Scottish projects for persistent juvenile offenders suggests some elements of an effective inter-agency commitment to reducing exclusion from school and increasing employment chances. The Freagarrach Project, supported by the Scottish Office and run by Barnardo's in Central Region, was conceived as part of a broader inter-agency strategy for young people in trouble. An important element of this was the commitment by the Education Department to find ways of reducing school exclusions and encouraging reintegration into mainstream education. Teachers with experience of children with special needs were used to train their colleagues in mainstream schools in handling difficult behaviour. Teachers were seconded to the office of the Reporter to the Children's Hearings to identify referrals associated with school problems and respond to them quickly; the Freagarrach Project itself was guaranteed access to places in a special educational unit designed to help children back into normal education. The second project, also supported by the Scottish Office and run in Fife by Apex Scotland, aims to help young people acquire a more positive view of education and training and to give them some experience of employment. Working with persistent offenders who have almost all failed in or been excluded from the education system, the project has achieved some notable successes, while also encountering problems in sustaining the interest and motivation of young people through a quite demanding curriculum. It may be that the best place for projects working directly on young people's employability is as an adjunct to those working more conventionally on offending behaviour. At any rate, both projects exemplify an inclusionary, integrative approach in which young offenders are helped back from the margins of citizenship and sociability, and illustrate something of the need for specialized and intensive projects to be sustained by a supportive and coherent inter- agency network (for an indication of why this matters see Raynor and Vanstone (1996)). In the case of the Apex project, as with any project which aims to provide a route into employment, the supportive network needs to include a range of employers willing to participate in the reintegration of offenders and the restoration of their community membership; probation services have been active, and perhaps should be more active now, in developing such networks (Drakeford and Vanstone 1996: 62–7)). *Mutatis mutandis*, we think that the probation service could learn from these initiatives north of the border.

We noted above the findings of recent surveys of the probation caseload which showed a high prevalence of disability, illness, addiction and risky behaviour. Hitherto, much discussion of the links between the criminal justice system and health services has concentrated on mentally disordered offenders and on finding ways of giving practical effect to the official policy that they should be diverted from courts and penal institutions and into appropriate health services (Department of Health and Home Office 1991). The health needs of offenders known to the probation service are not confined to this group, however, as Farrar (1996) has recently noted. The probation service is in regular contact with people who are at high risk of various kinds of health impairment, notably those associated with substance misuse and poverty, many of whom are unlikely to seek help from the health services on their own initiative and are at greater than average risk of finding that they are unwelcome when they do, because their ailments are liable to be seen as self- inflicted, their behaviour may not promote tranquillity in a surgery waiting room, and any improvement may depend upon changes in behaviour which they may be reluctant to make. Recent talk of partnerships has focused mainly on probation's links with the "independent sector", and the importance of partnerships with the health services has tended to be comparatively neglected (Orme and Pritchard 1996); but, without expecting probation officers to take on responsibility for everything, one can argue that work on these partnerships promises both to contribute to community safety broadly conceived and to improve access to health services (and thus to better health) for people whose behaviour involves risk to themselves as well as to others. Farrar (1996) discusses some ways in which the service could become a more attractive partner for the health services, notably by being confident and explicit about its achievements in "reducing public harm"; and the relevant knowledge and skills to make partnerships work are, as we noted above, already part of the service's repertoire.

Conclusion: The Look of a Probation Service Committed to Reducing Social Exclusion

Our stress throughout this paper has been on the need for probation practice to be understood as involving much more than face-to-face work with identified offenders if it is to be capable of reducing the exclusionary pressures experienced by most of the people with whom it works. The recent revival of optimism in the possibility of effective practice (McGuire 1995) is certainly preferable to, and more rational than, the pessimism which preceded it, but the focus on only one kind of practice, itself a potential contributor to social exclusion, has tended to leave other aspects of probation work relatively unexamined. How, then, might the service begin to reverse the recent trend of withdrawal from the poor and sometimes desperate communities in which its clients live (North *et al.* 1992), and start to make social solidarity, integration and inclusion more than distant aspirations?

We suggest that progress along these lines, relevent to the themes we have discussed above, should include:

- decentralization—probation offices should as far as possible function as community resources, located in the areas they are meant to serve;
- accessibility—instead of fortresses defended by arrays of situational crime prevention devices, probation offices should be open and accessible, and offer a wide range of services and resources (advice, information, child care, facilities for fun and adventure);
- diversification—probation services should employ a wider range of people with a wider range of skills, including youth workers, community workers, trainers and "social pedagogues" (in appropriately European terminology);
- networking—the service should build on its existing skills and experience to develop a range of supportive links with the resources on which any intensive work on offending behaviour depends for its success;
- knowledge and its dissemination—the messages about what works in intensive groupwork are now widely, though certainly not universally, understood within the service, but little is known by anyone, and nothing is known by many, about what works best in (for example) community service, individual supervision (do some probation officers get better results than others, and what makes the difference?), pre-sentence reports and interventions in court more generally, partnerships, community safety, and restorative justice.

Whether the service can make this kind of progress depends, of course, not only on its own capacity for change but on the political support it can attract. Both, but especially the latter, remain uncertain. Nevertheless, the election of a Labour government whose ministers do not disdain the language of social inclusion and exclusion, and whose Home Secretary has at least tentatively supported the principle of restorative justice, suggests that the prospect of political backing for developments such as those we have outlined may be better than it has been for some time.

References

Arnold, J. and Jordan, B. (1996), Poverty. In M. Drakeford and M. Vanstone (eds), *Beyond Offending Behaviour*, Aldershot: Arena.

Audit Commission (1996), *Misspent Youth: Young People and Crime*, London: Audit Commission.

Braithwaite, J. (1989), *Crime, Shame and Reintegration*, Cambridge: Cambridge University Press.

Braithwaite, J. (1994) Resolving crimes in the community: restorative justice reforms in New Zealand and Australia. In C. Martin (ed.), *Resolving Crime in the Community: Mediation in Criminal Justice*, London: ISTD.

Braithwaite, J. and Mugford, S. (1994), Conditions for successful reintegration ceremonies: the case of juvenile offenders, *British Journal of Criminology*, 32(1): 139–72.

Burnside, J. and Baker, N. (eds) (1994), *Relational Justice: Repairing the Breach*, Winchester: Waterside Press.

Campbell, B. (1993), *Goliath: Britain's Dangerous Places*, London: Methuen.

Carlen, P. (1996), *Jigsaw: A Political Criminology of Youth Homelessness*, Buckingham: Open University Press.

Christie, N. (1977), Conflicts as property, *British Journal of Criminology*, 17(1): 1–15.

Cohen, S. (1985), *Visions of Social Control*, Cambridge: Polity Press.

Currie, E. (1988), Two visions of community crime prevention. In T. Hope and M. Shaw (eds), *Communities and Crime Reduction*, London: HMSO.

Currie, E. (1996), *Is America Really Winning the War against Crime and Should Britain Follow its Example?*, London: NACRO.

Davies, M. (1969), *Probationers in their Social Environment*, Home Office Research Study 2, London: HMSO.

Department of Health (1991), *Patterns and Outcomes in Child Placement*, London: HMSO.

Department of Health and Home Office (1991), *Review of Health and Social Services for Mentally Disordered Offenders and Others Requiring Similar Services* (The Reed Report), London: Department of Health/Home Office.

Dodd, T. and Hunter, P. (1992), *The National Prison Survey 1991*, London: HMSO.

Downes, D. (1993), *Employment Opportunities for Offenders*, London: Home Office.

Drakeford, M. and Vanstone, M. (eds) (1996), *Beyond Offending Behaviour*, Aldershot: Arena.

Etzioni, A. (1993), *The Spirit of Community: Rights, Responsibilities and the Communitarian Agenda*, New York: Crown.

Farrar, M. (1996), Probation in the community. Paper to the First Annual Colloquium of the Probation Studies Unit, University of Oxford, 17 December.

Farrington, D. P., Gallagher, B., Morley, L., St Ledger, R. J. and West, D. J. (1986), Unemployment, school leaving and crime, *British Journal of Criminology*, 26(4): 335–56.

Finch, J. and Mason, J. (1992), *Negotiating Family Responsibilities*, London: Routledge.

Gallie, D., Marsh, C. and Vogler, C. (eds) (1994), *Social Change and the Experience of Unemployment*, Oxford: Oxford University Press.

Gelsthorpe, L. and Raynor, P. (1995), Quality and effectiveness in probation officers' reports to sentencers, *British Journal of Criminology*, 35(2): 188–200.

Geraghty, J. (1991), *Probation Practice in Crime Prevention*, Crime Prevention Unit Paper 24, London: Home Office.

Gilling, D. (1996) Crime prevention. In T. May and A. A. Vass (eds), *Working with Offenders: Issues, Contexts and Outcomes*, London: Sage.

Graham, J. and Bowling, B. (1995), *Young People and Crime*, Home Office Research Study 145, London: Home Office.

Heath, A. (1992), The attitudes of the underclass. In D. J. Smith (ed.), *Understanding the Underclass*, London: Policy Studies Institute.

Heidensohn, F. (1986), Models of justice: Portia or Persephone? Some thoughts on equality, fairness and gender in the field of criminal justice, *International Journal of the Sociology of Law*, 14: 187–98.

Home Office (1991), *Safer Communities: The Local Delivery of Crime Prevention through the Partnership Approach* (The Morgan Report), London: Home Office.

Home Office (1993), *Monitoring of the Criminal Justice Act 1991: Data from a Special Data Collection Exercise*, Statistical Bulletin 25/93, London: Home Office.

Home Office (1994), *Race and the Criminal Justice System 1994*, London: Home Office.

Hood, R. (1992), *Race and Sentencing: A Study in the Crown Court*, Oxford: Clarendon Press.

Laycock, G. and Pease, K. (1985), Crime prevention within the probation service, *Probation Journal*, 32(1): 43–7.

Levitas, R. (1996), The concept of social exclusion and the new Durkheimian hegemony, *Critical Social Policy*, 46: 5–20.

Marshall, T. F. and Merry, S. (1990), *Crime and Accountability*, London: HMSO.

McElrea, F. (1994), Justice in the community: the New Zealand experience. In J. Burnside and N. Baker (eds), *Relational Justice: Repairing the Breach*, Winchester: Waterside Press.

McGuire, J. (ed.) (1995), *What Works: Reducing Reoffending. Guidelines from Research and Practice,* Chichester: Wiley.

Moxon, D. (1988), *Sentencing Practice in the Crown Court,* Home Office Research Study 103, London: HMSO.

National Association of Probation Officers (1993), *Probation Caseload: Income and Employment. A Study of the Financial Circumstances of 1331 Offenders on Probation Supervision,* London: NAPO.

Nellis, M. (1995), Towards a new view of probation values. In R. Hugman and D. Smith (eds), *Ethical Issues in Social Work,* London: Routledge.

North, J., Adair, H., Langley, B., Mills, J. and Morten, C. (1992), *The Dog that Finally Barked: The Tyneside Disturbances of 1991—A Probation Perspective,* Newcastle: Northumbria Probation Service.

Orme, J. and Pritchard, C. (1996), Health. In M. Drakeford and M. Vanstone (eds), *Beyond Offending Behaviour,* Aldershot: Arena.

Paylor, I. (1995), *Housing Needs of Ex-offenders,* Aldershot: Avebury.

Paylor, I. and Smith, D. (1994), Who are prisoners' families?, *Journal of Social Welfare and Family Law* 16(2): 131–44.

Pearson, G. (1987), Social deprivation, unemployment and patterns of heroin use. In N. Dorn and N. South (eds), *A Land Fit for Heroin? Drug Policies, Prevention and Practice,* London: Macmillan.

Pease, K. (1994), Crime prevention. In M. Maguire, R. Morgan and R. Reiner (eds), *The Oxford Handbook of Criminology,* Oxford: Oxford University Press.

Pritchard, C. (1995), Unemployment, age, gender and regional suicide in England and Wales 1974–90: a harbinger of increased suicide for the 1990s?, *British Journal of Social Work,* 25(6): 767–90.

Pritchard, C., Cox, M. and Cotton, A. (1990), Analysis of young adult clients in probation and social services caseloads: a focus on illegal drugs and HIV infection, *Research Policy Planning,* 8(2): 1–8.

Pritchard, C., Cox, M., Godson, D. and Weeks, S. (1992), Mental illness, drug and alcohol misuse and HIV risk behaviour in 214 young adult probation clients: implications for policy, practice and training, *Social Work and Social Sciences Review,* 3(2): 150–62.

Probation Service in England and Wales (1984), *Statement of National Objectives and Priorities,* London: Home Office.

Raynor, P. (1991), Sentencing with and without reports, *Howard Journal of Criminal Justice,* 30(4): 293–300.

Raynor, P. (1996), The criminal justice system. In M. Drakeford and M. Vanstone (eds), *Beyond Offending Behaviour,* Aldershot: Arena.

Raynor, P., Smith, D. and Vanstone, M. (1994), *Effective Probation Practice,* Basingstoke: Macmillan.

Raynor, P. and Vanstone, M. (1994), Probation practice, effectiveness and the non-treatment paradigm, *British Journal of Social Work,* 24(4): 387–404.

Raynor, P. and Vanstone, M. (1996), Reasoning and rehabilitation in Britain: the results of the Straight Thinking on Probation (STOP) programme, *International Journal of Offender Therapy and Comparative Criminology,* 40(4): 272–84.

Sampson, A. and Smith, D. (1992), Probation and community crime prevention, *Howard Journal of Criminal Justice,* 33(2): 105–19.

Scarman, Lord (1981), *The Brixton Disorders,* London: HMSO.

Smith, D., Blagg, H. and Derricourt, N. (1988), Mediation in South Yorkshire, *British Journal of Criminology,* 28(3): 378–95.

Smith, D., Paylor, I. and Mitchell, P. (1993), Partnerships between the independent sector and the probation service, *Howard Journal of Criminal Justice,* 32(1): 25–39.

Stein, M. and Carey, K. (1986), *Leaving Care,* Oxford: Blackwell.

Stern, V. (1996), Let the ex-cons back in, *Guardian*, 2 May: 15.

Stewart, G. (1996), Housing. In M. Drakeford and M. Vanstone (eds), *Beyond Offending Behaviour*, Aldershot: Arena.

Stewart, G. and Stewart, J. (1993), *Social Circumstances of Younger Offenders under Probation Supervision*, Wakefield, ACOP.

Townsend, P. (1979), *Poverty in the United Kingdom*, Harmondsworth, Penguin.

Criminal Policy and the Eliminative Ideal

Andrew Rutherford

Abstract

Any study of the uses of elimination is necessarily an excursion into the darker regions of criminal policy. The eliminative ideal strives to solve present and emerging problems by getting rid of troublesome and disagreeable people with methods which are lawful and widely supported. Much of this article provides a historical overview of some of the most significant episodes of the potent and perennial pull of elimination, notably Britain's use of Australia and the island of South Andaman, France's involvement in New Caledonia and Guiana, and Russia's reliance upon Siberia. Rather more detailed attention is given to Germany between 1933 and 1938. This first phase of German concentration camps brought together many elements of the eliminative ideal, including an ever-widening range of perceived internal enemies, but also the lip-service paid by the authorities to legality and public legitimacy. Finally, reference is made to contemporary developments in California and, at least by implication, to Britain. The eliminative ideal sits all too comfortably with contemporary pressures for social exclusion, and, invariably, its most explicit and brutal expression is to be found within the realm of criminal policy.

Keywords:

Elimination; Criminal policy; Transportation; Social exclusion; Internal enemies

Introduction

In his book *Scum of the Earth*, Arthur Koestler describes how he was arrested by the Parisian police in October 1939 and taken to the Roland Garros Stadium which had been converted into a provisional camp for the detention of "undesirable aliens". Those detained included many people from the arts and some of the leading intellectuals of the day from across Europe. He recalled that shortly afterwards the French newspapers carried a Ministry of Information press briefing to the effect that as a result of the internment of "the foreign rabble which for years had infested the capital" the amount of robbery and other crime had suddenly dropped. Koestler wryly observed that the

Address for Correspondence: *Andrew Rutherford, Faculty of Law, University of Southampton, Highfield, Southampton, SO17 1BJ*

French government, in merely following an ancient recipe, had discovered a welcome diversion for the general discontent (Koestler 1991: 89–90).

This ancient recipe and its modern variations go to the core of what is referred to in this article as the "eliminative ideal". Put bluntly, the eliminative ideal strives to solve present and emerging problems by getting rid of troublesome and disagreeable people with methods which are lawful and widely supported. The pursuit of this ideal is not confined to criminal policy, but it is within this particular realm that it takes its most explicit and direct form. Over recent years, as developments in Britain have increasingly borrowed from American criminal policy, notions of elimination have moved very much to the fore. In particular, the Crime (Sentences) Act 1997 has provided for mandatory minimum prison terms, including life sentences, in blatant imitation of the wave of legislative activity across the United States. This statute, which was broadly supported by both main political parties, must be regarded as the final nail in the coffin of calm and constructive approaches to criminal policy which has characterized the latter 1980s.[1]

A distinction needs to be made between elimination and extermination. The eliminative disposal of troublesome people, at least in the first instance, falls short of death. However, in practice the dividing line between elimination and extermination is often blurred and with high mortality rates as regular features of elimination, it is a social rather than physical death which is imposed through the enforced removal to a place from which there is little, if any, prospect of return. As Daniel Jonah Goldhagen has recently argued, the universe of the socially dead has long been occupied by people other than slaves. He concludes that members of a society conceive of the socially dead as being bereft of some essential human attributes and undeserving of essential social, civil and legal protections. Furthermore, they are treated in a manner that denies them the *possibility* of receiving social honour, which is a requisite for becoming a recognized and full member of a social community (Goldhagen 1996: 168–9). The form taken by the eliminative ideal is subject to constant change, but, in one guise or another, it invariably lurks not far below the surface of criminal policy.

This staying power, an impressive feature of the eliminative ideal, is particularly evident in surveying the historical course of criminological theory. Such a survey might begin with that child of the Enlightenment, Cesare Beccaria and his extraordinarily influential essay *On Crimes and Punishments* of 1764 in which he insisted on a proportionate response by the law to crime. But Beccaria also justifed the retention and, indeed, urged the extension of eliminative measures. In calling for the abolition of the death penalty, Beccaria had in mind the need for something therefore "*worse* than death". He argued that slavery for life would be every bit as effective a deterrent as breaking on the wheel. Indeed, lifelong slavery would produce "the salutary terror which the law wants to inspire". He added: "That intensity of the punishment of lifelong slavery as substitute for the death penalty possesses that which suffices to deter a determined soul. Neither fanaticism nor vanity dwells among fetters and chains, under the yoke or in an iron cage, when the evildoer begins his sufferings instead of terminating them" (Radzinowicz 1948: 277–300). Nor did the eliminative ideal have any less appeal to the positivist school which, reflecting the social Darwinism of its day, so dominated criminological theory around the turn of the last century. Scholars such as Raffaele Garofalo had no compunction in advocating the death penalty for offenders shown to be "forever incapable of social life". While acknowledging that extermination "has always excited public indignation when inflicted for offences not seriously violating the moral sense", Garofalo advocated that for the more serious offenders among this group, elimination must take the form of life imprisonment or transportation. But contrary to Beccaria, he explicitly rejected proportionality as setting limits upon the court's sentencing powers (Allen 1960: 266).

For good measure, in the years leading up to the First World War attention must be given to the contribution of Franz von Liszt, professor of criminal science at the University of Berlin. In von Liszt's opinion, every offender convicted for a third time should, without exception, be designated an "incorrigible habitual offender". He wrote that "as we do not wish to hang and we cannot transport, what is left is detention for life or for an indeterminate period. Furthermore, such prisoners should be held under exceptionally severe conditions and as cheaply as possible, even if prisoners 'went down under it'" (Radzinowicz 1991a: 40–1). Eighty years later, in January 1994, we find that latter-day academic Prince of Darkness, John J. DiIulio, Jnr, professor of politics and public affairs at Princeton University and tireless advocate of "prison works" through incapacitation, writing for the *Wall Street Journal* an article entitled "Let 'em rot", in which he contents that the United States is soft on crime. According to DiIulio, "By every measure, the anti-incarceration elite has been winning its tug of war with the public on crime . . . America has crime without punishment . . . get-tough politics is good crime policy" (DiIulio 1994).[2]

By any rational consideration of contemporary American criminal policy DiIulio's conclusions are nothing less than extraordinary. There are at least three reasons why this is so. First, there has been a quantum leap in the national prison and jail population, which has quadrupled since 1970, and by mid-1997 stood in excess of 1.6 million. This translates into a rate per 100,000 inhabitants of over 550, which is close to that of Russia and more than five times that of most European countries. Furthermore, there is a racial aspect to all of this: the imprisonment rate for white Americans is 306 per 100,000 inhabitants compared with, for African-Americans, 1,947 per 100,000—a rate which is six times higher than for whites. The pace of growth in the number of people sent to prison and the length of time they stay there is unprecedented in American history and shows no sign of slowing down or being more even-handed in its selection processes. Projections have been made of a prison population within the next two decades of 3 to 7 million, which would take it comfortably past today's Chinese total of somewhere between 4 and 5$^1/_2$ million. A second feature of the American scene is the new generation of mandatory life-sentencing statutes—generally referred to in the baseball lingo as "three strikes and you're out", and which have now been adopted by some twenty-five states and by the federal government. The provisions vary from one jurisdiction to another, but the overall aim is to insist that very long sentences, usually 25 years to life, are imposed where there are two earlier convictions for violent offences. In some states the third strike does not have to involve any violence. Finally, there are increasingly intrusive and austere conditions within many prisons, often taken to their most degrading degree within the so-called "supermax" institutions.

Many leading criminologists unequivocally reject both DiIulio's analysis and prescription, and over recent years have voiced alarm about the direction of criminal policy in the United States. For example, Sir Leon Radzinowicz, who lives in America, wrote in 1991 that he had no hesitation in affirming that the American system of criminal justice belonged to the lowest category among the democratic countries of the world. He warned of a gravitation towards short-cut solutions usually identified with authoritarian systems of criminal justice (Radzinowicz 1991b: 439). Two years later, Nils Christie of the University of Oslo warned that the major danger of crime in the United States and other modern societies is not so much of crime itself, but rather that the fight against it will pave the way to totalitarian developments. For Nils Christie, "the risks are great that those seen as core members of the dangerous population may be confined, warehoused, stored away, and forced to live their most active years as consumers of control" (Christie 1993: 171).[3] He makes the crucial point that this can be done democratically and under conditions of strict legal control. But "Gulags Western-Style", to use Christie's phrase, speaks to the potent and perennial pull of elimination as a central theme of criminal policy. Viewed in this way, what is happening in America and perhaps elsewhere today represents not so much a new departure but rather the re-emergence of the eliminative ideal in a virulent guise.

Historical Background

A brief historical exploration of selected episodes of elimination as an instrument of criminal policy serves to better our understanding of its resilience and seductive appeal. The origins of criminal law, a number of scholars contend, are to be found in the slave punishments of ancient Greece. Not only was slavery itself a form of punishment, but punishments once only applicable to slaves were, in due course, extended to other groups. By the Middle Ages galley slavery was extensively used as a punishment in Spain, France and some other maritime countries. For example, the fleet of Louis XIV required no less than 10,000 oarsmen, prompting a decree that there be a search for "all malefactors, gypsies, vagrants, sturdy beggars, discharged soldiers, salt bootleggers and other disreputable fellows for commitment to the galleys" (Sellin: 1976). Later groups to be sentenced to galley slavery for life included three and a half thousand Protestants found attending religious services. With the obsolescence of the galley fleets other forms of penal banishment were sought. In large part, colonial ambitions pointed the way to transportation, and from the early fifteenth century, Portugal began transporting people to North Africa and later to its colonies in the West Indies, Brazil and elsewhere. Spain and Holland followed, and Denmark attempted to put Greenland to similar use during the eighteenth century, but this very brief experiment was quickly aborted after many of the twenty-four transportees died as a result of malnutrition and inadequate shelter.[4] But from the close of the eighteenth century it was Britain, France and Russia which vigorously took the lead in transportation, whether it was simply exile or exile combined with imprisonment and other punishments.

Britain's involvement in transportation stretched across 340 years. It began shipping people to America under the Vagrancy Act of 1597 (which enabled courts to banish or send to the galleys, rogues, vagabonds and sturdy beggars) and ended in India just before the outbreak of the Second World War. With regard to America precise numbers of people so transported are unknown, but between 1717, when the courts were given powers to sentence felons to transportation to America, and 1775 some 30 to 40 thousand people found themselves on the other side of the Atlantic, mostly in Maryland and Virginia. But with the burgeoning slave trade from Africa the enthusiasm of the colonists for transportees from Britain began to wane. Perhaps, as those perceptive German sociologists George Rusche and Otto Kirchheimer suggested: "Once transportation ceased to pay, the colonists realized that it was a shameful business unworthy of them" (Rusche and Kirchheimer 1939: 61). The *coup de grâce* came abruptly with the American War of Independence and for some years thereafter many prisoners were placed on to boats not going anywhere—severely crowded and disease-ridden hulks moored on the Thames, and in the docks at Plymouth, Portsmouth, Gosport and elsewhere. Several leading figures of the day, including Jeremy Bentham and John Howard, were convinced that reason and humanity dictated the construction of penitentiaries. Howard believed that "the settled object in all such houses should be to make men better; at least, more *useful* subjects" (Howard 1929: 162). But the penitentiary campaign was to little avail, and in 1782 the government let it be known that "new measures were about to be taken" which made unnecessary prison construction. Much to the chagrin of Bentham, transportation was firmly back on the agenda. Putting the problem of crime out of sight made no sense to him: if there was to be punishment it had to be seen to be done. He parodied the government's position thus: "I rid myself of the sight of you, the ship that bears you away saves me from witnessing your sufferings—I shall give myself no more trouble about you" (Bowring 1843: i.497). With characteristic flair, some years later Bentham urged that a fleet be sent out to bring the convicts home.

Australia, 1787–1868

The British statute of 1784 allowed for "removal overseas", leaving it to the Privy Council to fill in technical details such as the actual destination. Although the Gambia, Nova Scotia and the Cape of Good Hope were among the candidate sites considered, the final choice of that "hulk the size of a continent", as Robert Hughes was to describe his native Australia, was probably never in doubt. Claimed for Britain in 1770 it was to the same shores of eastern Australia where Captain Cook had landed that the First Fleet set sail from Portsmouth on 13 May 1787. Commanded by Captain Arthur Phillip of Lyndhurst, the fleet of eleven ships and its 741 convicts (191 of whom were women), arrived at Botany Bay eight months later after a 15,000-mile journey. Over the next eighty years 750 ships followed, leaving their human cargo in

New South Wales, Van Diemen's Land (now Tasmania), and at the penal settlement on Norfolk Island, 900 miles off the eastern coast of Australia. Official lists are incomplete, but the most careful count puts the number shipped to Australia at 163,021 persons, of whom some 2,800 died of disease or in shipwrecks en route. During this period, smaller numbers of people were also deposited in naval hulks moored off Barbados, Jamaica and the Leeward Islands.

A few of the very early transportees to Australia had already been sentenced to imprisonment, and these people were returned to court to be re-sentenced to transportation, much to their understandable distress. Sarah Mills shouted at an Old Bailey judge who had just announced why she was to be taken to Portsmouth: "I would rather die than go out of my own country to be devoured by savages." But under the threat of execution she and several other women prisoners changed their minds. A Bow Street magistrate, writing to the Home Secretary, admitted it was unlawful to tamper with the sentences in this way but added that "the public will be happy to get rid of them" (Ignatieff 1989: 91). Most of the people transported to Australia resembled the British prison population today—they were young men in their late teens or twenties with convictions for property offences. But there were also 25,000 women transported which, proportionately, was five times higher than the number of women currently in prison. As Deirdre Beddoe has argued, a perverse positive discrimination operated to adjust the gender gap, resulting in women being dispatched to Australia much more readily than men guilty of the same crime (Beddoe 1979: 176).

There were also some very young children. Extrapolating from Leslie Robson's sample of 6,000 transportees there were, in all, some 1,720 children aged 14 or under of whom a handful were aged 10 and a few perhaps even younger. Among the children sent to Australia was John Halfpenny, a 12-year-old from Staffordshire who was described as a bootmaker's boy of four feet two inches tall and convicted for stealing money. And at the other end of the age spectrum there was 70-year-old William Sandplant, a woolcomber from Leicester, sentenced for stealing sugar and wool. The women, almost all convicted of property offences, including Elizabeth Mayo, sentenced in Hereford for stealing ribbon from a shop (Robson 1965). By 1839, 134 offences carried the penalty of "removal overseas", and as Leon Radzinowicz and Roger Hood have observed, transportation to Australia was "clearly not simply a measure against serious crime but more generally a measure of elimination of those likely to continue to commit small crimes" (Radzinowicz and Hood 1986: 484–5).

The available data also strongly suggest that persons of Irish extraction were massively overrepresented among those transported. Of Robson's sample, 55 per cent were tried in England, 33 per cent in Ireland and most of the remainder in Scotland. And when place of birth is used, the picture is even more startling: 47 per cent were Irish, 43 per cent were English and 9 per cent Scottish. For example, Mary Butler, along with a friend, was convicted for stealing a basket and some beans in Covent Garden. The victim, as was at the time the practice, prosecuted the case, and told the court that the defendants had "plotted in Irish", and because he understood the language he was able to catch them trying to get vegetables for nothing. People from Ireland also formed the majority of those transportees best described as political offenders (Robson 1965: 78–9). George Rudé has identified 3,600 people as being transported for political offences, one in forty-five of the total who arrived in Australia. Of these political offenders about 60 per cent were from Ireland, 33 per cent from Britain and 4 per cent from Canada (these 130 Canadians, amongst whom there were a number of American citizens, had taken part in the rebellions of 1838–9). Among the political offenders from England and Scotland there were Luddites, Chartists, "swing rioters" as well as people arrested in the Bristol riots of 1831 and the Welsh Rebecca riots of a decade later. Irish political prisoners were among the first arrivals in New South Wales when a large batch of the rebels of 1798 disembarked the following year—without a shipping list of any kind, and nor, in this instance, did one ever follow. Among the reluctant passengers on the very last transport ship, which docked in Fremantle, Western Australia on 9 January 1868, were 63 Fenians who had been arrested in the rising of the previous year (Rudé 1978).

On his visit to Australia in 1872 Anthony Trollope talked with several surviving transportees, the "old crawlers" as they were known. At the prison in Port Arthur, Tasmania, he encountered Dennis Doherty, an Irishman who thirty-nine years earlier, as an 18-year-old soldier, had been transported for desertion. He remarked that he had not since then enjoyed one hour of freedom. He had made several escape attempts, the most recent occasion being only the week before, he had lost an eye and was, he said, at last, a broken man. Trollope wrote: "The record of his prison life was frightful. He had always been escaping, always rebelling, always fighting against authority, and always being flogged . . . he stood there, speaking softly, arguing his case well and pleading while the tears ran down his face for some kindness, for some mercy in his old age. 'I have tried to escape; always to escape' he said, 'as a bird does out of a cage'." Trollope wrote that he would like to have taken him out of his cell and to have given him a month of freedom. And after he left, a confused and troubled Trollope wrote: "I was assured that he was thoroughly bad, irredeemable, not to be reached by any kindness, a beast of prey, and against whom it was necessary that every honest man should raise his hand. Yet, he talked so gently and so well, and argued his case with such winning words!" (Trollope 1968: 28–9)[5]

Transportation to Australia was, as a House of Common Select Committee concluded in 1837, "a strange lottery". There was a large element of chance both in the sentencing process itself and in the convict's eventual fate on the other side of the world. As noted above, the sentence covered an enormous range of offences, many of them quite trivial. As with capital punishment, which to some extent it served to replace, transportation was a public spectacle. People were taken in shackles by open carriage to Portsmouth and other ports, and as one contemporary account notes, exposed to "the gaze of the idle and the taunts and mockeries of the cruel" (Hughes 1988: 138).[6] Once at the docks they were for a while put to work in chain gangs, presenting for gawking tourists, as Robert Hughes remarks, a moral spectacle, good not only for adults but for naughty children as well. And with a new language of class taking hold in Britain and, in particular, notions of a criminal class, the dangerous mob was widely believed to contaminate the labouring poor. "Transportation sought to remove, once and for all", comments Hughes, "the source of contamination from the otherwise decent bosom of the lower working class . . . The main point was not what happened to it *there*, but that it would no longer be *here*" (Hughes 1988: 168). But by the mid-nineteenth century, the anxieties of the general public were easing, and to the degree that elimination remained on the agenda it was thereafter sought by other means.

India and the Andaman Islands

Although transportation to Australia was drawing to a close, Britain's involvement in this form of disposal was far from over. In India the courts, under the Bengal Regulation of 1797, had for some years sentenced persons to be transported "beyond the seas" to the Andaman Islands, as well as to Singapore, Penang and Mauritius. But transportation came into its own in 1857 when the British authorities responded to the Sepoy Rebellion by reopening the penal colony at Port Blair on the island of South Andaman in the Bay of Bengal, a thousand miles from the mainland. On 10 March 1858, under the command of Dr J. P. Walker, a prison official in the India Home Department, a thousand or so political prisoners were landed on the island. Within thirty years there were in excess of twelve and a half thousand persons held at Port Blair, mostly serving life sentences. They were confined under conditions which induced an annual death rate of 15 per cent. In exceedingly high temperatures, prisoners worked in solitary confinement on the *kolu*, a mill that was used to make oil by grinding coconuts. Given the quota of oil that had to be produced, they had virtually no opportunity to pause, even to take a meal. Vinajak Savarkar later wrote: "We got up, and began our work of pushing the handle and going round the mill like a yoked buffalo, with the perspiration dripping from our face, and its beads falling into the dish we were carrying in the other hand" (Savarkar 1950). Only one letter was permitted each year, with visits by friends or family a virtual impossibility. Eventually, after a series of strikes led by political detainees during the 1930s the penal colony on the Andamans was closed in 1938.

France, 1791–1949

The other European country with an extended involvement in transportation was France. Beginning in 1791, prisoners were shipped to Madagascar (Algeria was rejected as being too close to home) and, in the case of political offenders, to Guiana. There followed a period of disuse for white prisoners but not for non-whites who were thought better able to withstand the rampant diseases of Guiana. From 1864 and for the next thirty years or so, white prisoners only were transported to New Caledonia, an island in the South Pacific, not far from the recently abandoned penal colony on Norfolk Island. Michel Bourdet-Pleville has recorded that the "incorrigibles" of New Caledonia were buried with their chains. He added that the administration, deprived of some of its goods, sent the convict's family a bill for the chain and ankle-cuffs (Bourdet-Pleville 1960: 165). But for eighty years from 1858, it was to Cayenne in Guiana that some 80,000 French transportees would be dispatched and from which the great majority would not return, in part because they had to remain in Guiana for a period equivalent to their original sentence. The most feared part of the colony was the Iles du Salut—the Islands of Salvation—more generally known as Devil's Island where prisoners, held in solitary confinement, were chained to a wall. Few survived more than five years under these conditions. The entire colony was to be closed under a Parliamentary decree of June 1938, but this was overtaken by the war; and in 1945 there were still 1,100 convicts and 2,300 former convicts, serving out their *doublage* in Guiana. By 1949 all but a few who preferred to remain had been returned to France. Ten years earlier an English Prison Commissioner, Alexander Paterson, had visited Cayenne, which at that time still held 5,000 prisoners. He wrote privately to the French Government of "the spiritual despair of perpetual banishment among some thousands of them afflicted me more sorely than anything I have ever known . . . They look straight ahead with those staring eyes and see nothing. They move as men who have long been in Purgatory and know only Hell awaits them . . . It was but a procession among ghosts who are not allowed to die" (Ruck 1951: 157).

Russia from the 1750s

But the eliminative ideal, as pursued in the nineteenth century by Britain and France, pales in comparison with Russia in its use of Siberia. Although Russian penal exile to Siberia began in the sixteenth century, it was used most extensively from the 1750s. Between that time and the end of the nineteenth century some 1.2 million people were so transported. Because Siberia is not "beyond the seas" it would be regarded as internal exile but for its sheer size, twice that of Europe. Until 1860 prisoners had to march, usually from Moscow, to their final destination. In the case of Transbaikalia this was a distance of 4,700 miles, and 5,200 miles to Yakutsk, marches that took two and two and a half years respectively. From the 1860s the first part of the journey to Tomsk was covered by rail and steamer. As the Reverend Henry Lansdell, one of several English apologists for the Russian authorities, put it, this left to be walked "only the distance beyond Tomsk" (Kropotkin 1971: 143–4). This distance, however, was usually somewhere between 2,000 miles and 4,500 miles. The onward journey was even further in the case of the island of Sakhalin, in the north Pacific, which became a penal colony in 1869. For a few years, before use was made of the sea route via Odessa and the Suez Canal, prisoners were marched across Siberia and on to the ferry for Sakhalin.

There are many accounts of these marches to and through Siberia. Notable among these is the book, *In Russian and French Prisons* by Peter Kropotkin, an aristocrat with anarchist inclinations. Published in London in 1887, the entire stock of the first edition was bought and destroyed by the Russian secret police. The typical marching party consisted of 300 prisoners and 100 or so women and children. A row of soldiers led the march, and behind them came the hard labour convicts with their half-shaved heads. Each wore a chain, riveted to the ankles; the chain went up each leg and was suspended to a girdle. Another chain closely tied both hands, and a third chain bound together six or eight convicts. Next came the penal exiles, condemned to be settled in Siberia, followed by horse-drawn uncovered carriages which conveyed the baggage, the sick and the dying. The carriages were followed by family members who had decided to accompany the prisoners—usually wives and children. The rear of the march was brought up by soldiers who, under the law, had no authority over the families. However, a correspondent of the *Moscow Telegraph*, reporting on a marching party which set off from Tomsk on 14 September 1881, wrote that "the exhausted women and children literally stuck in the mud, and the soldiers dealt them blows to make them advance and keep pace with the party" (Kropotkin 1971: 145).

An especially acute observer was the American writer George Kennan, an uncle of the distinguished diplomat who bears the same name. On behalf of the *Century Magazine*, Kennan travelled across Russia and Siberia in 1885–6, accompanied by a Boston artist and photographer George Frost. On several occasions they witnessed marching parties and were also able to talk with prisoners in the desperately crowded forwarding prisons and as they assembled for the next stage of their journey. In his remarkable two-volume *Siberia and the Exile System*, Kennan describes how he encountered a marching party in the late summer, noting that "[t]he column moved at a rate of about two miles an hour; and before noon it was enveloped in a suffocating cloud of dust raised by the shuffling feet of the prisoners. In warm dry weather, when there is no wind, dust is a source of great misery to the prisoners, particularly to the sick, the women and the children . . . I have traced the progress of an invisible exile party more than a mile away by the cloud of dust that hung in the air" (Kennan 1891: i.378). On another occasion Kennan and Frost were sitting in a post-station waiting for fresh horses. "Suddenly my attention was attracted by a pecular, low pitched quavering sound which came to us from a distance, and which, although made up by human voices, did not resemble anything I had heard before. It was not a singing, nor a chanting, nor wailing for the dead, but a strange blending of all three. It suggested vaguely the confused and commingled sobs, moans and entreaties of human beings who were being subject to torture, but whose sufferings were not acute enough to seek expressions in shrieks or high pitched cries." This was the exiles' begging song which the marching party was permitted to sing as they passed through villages. It was, wrote Kennan, "half sung, half chanted, slowly in broken time and in a low key, by a hundred voices, to an accompaniment made by the jangling and clashing of chains . . . Rude, artless and inharmonious as the appeal for pity was, I have never in my life heard anything so mournful and depressing. It seemed to me to be the half-articulate expression of all the grief, the misery and the despair that had been felt by generations of human beings in the étapes, the forwarding prisons and the mines" (Kennan 1891: i.400–2). These long journeys had a high death rate, and Kennan and other observers described the desperate grief of parents as their children died on the marches and in the crowded barges and forwarding prisons. But the hard labour camps which awaited the prisoners offered no relief. In these silver and gold mines many were literally worked to death.

Who were the people who were marched to Siberia? While Kennan and other contemporary writers have provided vivid portraits, a more comprehensive answer emerges from a study of Russian criminal statistics, published in 1873 by the Russian Geographical Society, and which focused upon 160,000 people sent to Siberia between 1827 and 1846. Half of this total were sentenced by the courts and, of these, 18 per cent were convicted of murder and a further 18 per cent for other serious offences; but 51 per cent had been convicted of theft. The other half were not dealt with by the courts at all but were uprooted by "administrative exile". This group included political offenders, deserters from the military and escapees, but some 60 per cent had been dealt with for vagrancy, and of these two-thirds had simply failed to comply with passport requirements. Referring to these administrative exiles, the study's author remarked that, "we not only doubt their criminality, we simply doubt the very existence of such crimes as those imputed to them" (Kropotkin 1971: 134–5).

For the great majority of people transported to Siberia there was no record of their death. They simply disappeared without anyone knowing what had become of them. They vanished, wrote Peter Kropotkin, like a cloud in the sky on a hot summer day' (Kropotkin 1971: 175).

No more than a passing reference can be made to events which occurred after the Russian Revolutions of 1917 and 1918. There was a spontaneous amnesty of all political prisoners in the spring of 1917, but within a few years a new generation of camps was rapidly established. These included many of those long used in Tsarist times, including the Solovetsky Islands in the White Sea. Soon there followed the rapid expansion of the Gulag—that "sewerage disposal system" so minutely described by Aleksandr Solzhenitsyn: passengers leaving Moscow in closed railway compartments, desperately straining their ears to get a clue as to the train's destination. Robert Conquest has, for example, described Kolyma, one of the most remote of the Siberian camps. "When worn down, debilitated to the degree that no serious work could any longer be got out of them, prisoners were put on starvation rations and allowed to hang around the camp doing odd jobs until they died. Once sick, rations were cut and death followed. Of any batch of prisoners sent to Siberia in the years just prior to the Second World War, when the camps held an estimated five to seven million people, half would be dead within two to three years" (Conquest 1968: 325–6).

Germany, 1933–1938

A decree of September 1918 stated that in order to protect the Russian Soviet Republic, "class enemies" had to be isolated in "concentration camps". This term was to be used again in the very early days of the Third Reich. Indeed, precisely one month after Hitler was sworn in as German Chancellor, and the day after the Reichstag fire, the Emergency Decree of 28 February 1933 (Law for the Protection of the People and the State) extended protective custody. The authorities were quick to emphasize this was not intended as an instrument for dealing with punishable offences but as a "preventive" measure aimed at eliminating "threats from subversive elements" (Broszat 1968: 402).[7] On 20 March a press conference was called by Heinrich Himmler, appointed only weeks before as provisional president of the Munich police and shortly to become the "political police commander" of Bavaria, to announce the establishment of the first concentration camp in the grounds of a former munitions factory on the outskirts of Dachau, near Munich. To relieve the massive pressure of number in the prisons an order was issued the following month to remove protective custody cases to a hastily enlarged Dachau and to the other camps which had been created. There is agreement among historians that the years 1933–8 marked a first phase of the concentration camps. The next phase was the massive expansion of the camps between 1938 and 1941 and, finally, in the years after 1941, concentration camps became a key part of the overall apparatus of extermination. But during the first phase the focus was on elimination rather than extermination. This early period of the camps has been somewhat neglected by historians, overshadowed as it is by the enormity of the Holocaust. But it is because the first phase of the German concentration camps brings together many of the elements of the eliminative ideal that it merits a thorough reconsideration.[8]

By July 1933 some 27,000 people were held in protective custody. They were mostly Communist party officials, Social Democrats and trade unionists. One in every ten was Jewish, but this was not the primary reason for their detention. Until Kristallnacht on 9–10 November 1938, the crude social exclusion of Germany's Jewish population fell short of mass round-ups and placement in camps.

It was the role of Dachau and the other early camps, in the words of Eugen Kogon, to facilitate "the removal of every real or imaginary enemy of the Nationalist Socialist regime" (Weiss 1984: 117). As Werner Best, legal counsel to the Gestapo put it: "Any attempt to gain recognition for or even to uphold different political ideas will be ruthlessly dealt with, as the symptom of an illness which threatens the healthy unit of the indivisible national organism, regardless of the subjective wishes of its supporters . . ." (Broszat 1968: 427). From its inception, Dachau was the model for regulations, discipline, the allocation of formal inmate leadership positions, and the duties of personnel. Most of the rank and file guards, incidentally, were SS members in their mid-to-late teens. An early account of Dachau in a Munich newspaper stated that many of those detained would, after their "re-education", be released within months, but that this would not apply to "depraved, unreformable individuals" who have to be "kept away" from German society. Three years later the same paper referred to the inmates of Dachau, 80 per cent of whom at that time were political offenders, as "congenitally tainted individuals . . ." (Pingel 1984: 12).

But the role of protective custody extended far beyond persons who might be regarded as political offenders. In November 1933 the Law against Dangerous Habitual Criminals and Concerning Measures for Security and Correction had widened the scope of protective custody to include other "antisocial elements". Under this law persons with two convictions were to be regarded as "dangerous habitual criminals" and were to be sentenced by the courts not only to a limited prison sentence but to a period of unlimited protective custody. By early 1935 the police were using these powers to take petty habitual offenders into their custody and to transfer them to Dachau and other camps. The offence of many of these people was to have infringed conditions of police supervision, such as changing their place of residence. True to the spirit of the time Roland Freisler, then at the Ministry of Justice and later president of the People's Court, in February 1934 declared: "Our criminal friends have taken note that since 1933 a fresher and healthier wind has been blowing in Germany. There is no more sentimentality in our penitentiaries and prisons" (Muller 1991: 83). In February 1937 the police were ordered by Himmler to select and place in concentration camps 2,000 persons from their lists of "professional and habitual criminals or criminals who are a threat to public morality". There being no legal foundation for these arrests the emergency decree of 28 February 1933 was cited as the authority. This extension of police powers further erased what little remained of the legal limits of protective custody.

Because there had been some objections from the legal community, the Ministry of the Interior was prompted in May 1937 to issue a basic order on "preventive crime control by the police". Under this order, preventive detention was applicable in the case of:

- persons with not less than three previous sentences of imprisonment, or hard labour of at least six months, and "if they are likely to commit criminal acts in future";
- persons with previous sentences in which the seriousness of the offence and the possibility of repetition constituted "so great a danger to the community" that it was inadvisable to leave them at liberty;
- persons without a criminal record but who, by their "antisocial behaviour, endanger the community".

Once the individual was in custody, the period before any review could be made was extended from six months to two years. Far from restricting the net, this order envisaged an ever-widening range of "antisocial elements". Indeed, officially listed under this heading were: psychopaths and other mental cases, beggars, Jehovah's Witnesses, vagabonds, gypsies, vagrants, work-shy individuals, homosexuals, idlers, habitual drunkards, prostitutes and grumblers (Broszat 1968: 450).

Even before this order, and just prior to the Berlin Olympic Games, the so-called "work-shy" had been rounded up, and wearing a black triangle, occupied two of the ten blocks at Dachau. This was followed by a "single, comprehensive and surprise swoop" on the work-shy in January 1938, and after further action taken against other groups during that same year 11,000 "degenerate asocial elements" had been arrested and in most cases taken to the camp at Buchenwald. As the Law Leader, Hans Frank, declared in a speech that year: "The theory of congenital criminalty connotes a link between racial decadence and criminal manifestations. The complete degenerate lacks all racial sensitivity and sees it as his positive duty to harm the community . . ." (Noakes 1985: 19). From this time on, the concentration camp population began its inexorable rise. The twofold purpose of the camps was to supply the forced labour required to work in the SS-owned enterprises being constructed within or adjacent to the camps, and to eliminate persons who were "a burden to the community and thereby do it harm".

It was Himmler's intent to organize the concentration camps as legally administrative units, but *outside* the penal code and ordinary processes of law. In the early years, when there was still a debate within the various agencies about the future of the concentration camps, the authorities went to some effort to promote their legitimacy. As an internal Gestapo memo of December 1936 stated: "Excessive use of protective custody must discredit this strongest weapon of the Secret State police and give encouragement to efforts to abolish protective custody" (Broszat 1968: 444–5). Accordingly, the number of persons held in the camps was reduced, and maintained at around 7,000 to 10,000. Furthermore, the so-called "wild camps" were closed and the first commandant of Dachau, Hilmar Waeckerle, discovered that he did not enjoy complete legal immunity. In June 1933, together with the camp doctor, he was charged with aiding and abetting the murder of a prisoner. This decision, taken by the local prosecutor, forced Himmler to appoint a new commandant, Theodor Eike, who was soon to be transferred to Berlin to head the entire concentration camp system. In response to growing anxieties within the legal community about unnatural deaths in the concentration camps, commandants were ordered to report to the prosecutor's office any deaths not due to natural causes.

Limits of a sort were therefore in place during this first phase. Furthermore, for three years or so the government went to some trouble to counter what it described as "atrocity propaganda" in the foreign press. However, by 1936 the concentration camps had, in effect, become enclaves beyond the law, and over the next year there was a sevenfold increase in the death rate at Dachau. By the close of the first phase, as the German historian Martin Broszat has put it, "the attempt to make the concentration camps a firm and permanant institution [had] triumphed over the move towards ending the state of emergency" (Broszat 1968: 421). Furthermore, despite their close proximity to urban centres, the dissimilarities of the camps from the world outside, as Daniel Goldhagen remarks, were so pronounced and thoroughgoing that their inhabitants "might as well have been living on another planet" (Goldhagen 1996: 172).

The early period of the German concentration camps allows exploration of the question as to how, within a modern state, elimination might be achieved with at least some adherence to notions of legality. In the case of Nazi Germany, Shlomo Aronson has concluded that the task was accomplished in stages by using elements of the Prussian bureaucratic tradition of legal rule, by mobilizing widespread discontent with the Weimar democracy, and by cautious and well-planned manipulation of persons, power positions, pay-offs, terror and propaganda, to achieve seemingly limited objectives (Aronson 1984: 23). The concentration camps also need to be explored in terms of their impact upon German society as a whole. Daniel Goldhagen contends that the camp system was the "emblematic institution" of German society during its Nazi period "because it was within the camp system that many of Germany's most singular and essential practices were carried out and where the true nature of the evolving regime and society was, to a great extent, being forged and could be observed". Furthermore, he adds that "it was the main instrument for the Germans' fundamental reshaping of the social and human landscape of Europe . . . [standing] on its head the body of principles that had previously informed the public morality" (Goldhagen 1996: 458).

California in the 1990s

While the eliminative ideal is most completely realized within authoritarian societies such as the Third Reich it also finds expression within the legal framework of democratic systems of government. It is in this regard that certain contemporary developments of criminal policy in the United States and some other western democracies cause alarm. Nowhere is this more evident than in California where the prison population tripled during the single decade of the 1980s, and where a state once renowned for its provision of higher education now spends as much on its prison system. For the contemporary embodiment of the eliminative ideal, California is probably unsurpassed.[9] The Golden State is therefore an appropriate setting to conclude this paper by returning to the experience of "three strikes and you're out", and to the so-called "supermax" prison.

California's "three strikes and you're out" statute, which took effect in 1994, mandates that anyone with two earlier violent convictions be imprisoned for 25 years to life for *any* third conviction, no matter how minor unless the prosecutor approves a lesser sentence. The early and widely reported case of a man convicted under this provision for stealing a pizza was not out of line with a later study which found that 75 per cent of mandatory sentences under the "three strikes" law were for offences *not* involving violence. As might be expected, this blunt-edged approach in California towards sentencing has not been to the liking of the judiciary. On 20 June 1996 the State Supreme Court ruled that judges who believe a mandatory 25 years to life sentence is too harsh may ignore the rule and impose a less severe sentence. The Court ruled that as the statute did not specifically say that judges *could not* disregard a previous conviction they had the power to do so. This ruling poses a challenge to the State Assembly which had enacted "three strikes" with a two-thirds majority.[10] Although the legislature is expected to go some way to restrict the sweep of the statute, it is also likely to explicitly affirm the mandatory sentencing structure—in other words, sentencing will be little more than a rubber stamp exercise and the eliminative thrust of the "three strikes" law will thereby remain intact.

The deep end of California's sprawling penal system is its "supermax" prison at Pelican Bay, which is located in the remote north-western corner of the state, close to the Oregon border. Opened in December 1989 as a "prison of the future", Pelican Bay holds 3,700 inmates. Around a third of these people are held in a prison within the prison, in what is known as the "Special Housing Unit". Persons confined to this Unit have been identified by the authorities as being members of a prison gang, to have violated prison rules, or to be troublemakers. It is the opinion of the director of the California Department of Corrections that: "It's better to write off twelve hundred prisoners in return for the security of the rest of the prison population." Seen from the outside, the Special Housing Unit, to use the description of a federal judge, "resembles a massive concrete bunker; from the inside it is a windowless labyrinth of cells and halls, sealed off from the outside by walls, gates and guards. The physical environment thus reinforces a sense of isolation and detachment from the outside world, and helps create a palpable distance from ordinary compunctions, inhibitions and community norms." Painted white throughout and with virtually no natural light, a prisoner has described the Special Housing Unit as being "like a space capsule where one is shot into space and left in isolation".[11]

The Special Housing Unit consists of twelve hundred 80-square-foot windowless cells with two concrete beds and a toilet within which inmates, either in solitary confinement or with one other person, are locked for at least twenty-two and a half hours each day under the control of guards in a control booth with video cameras, rifles, gas guns and an assortment of other firearms. Meals are passed into the cell through a hatch and, in the words of a federal judge, the prisoners are "far removed from the usual sights and sounds of everyday life". Nor are they able to adjust the high temperature levels set by the authorities. They may exercise daily in a small, enclosed concrete space, but there is no mystery why so many prisoners prefer to remain in their cells. As one observer has noted with regard to the exercise facilities: "In the control booth, the televised images of several inmates, each in separate exercise cages, show them walking around the perimeter of their concrete yards, like laboratory animals engaged in mindless and repetitive activity" (Hentoff 1993: 3). After touring Pelican Bay in 1996, a prison governor from the United Kingdom observed that in terms of the regime, physical conditions and attitudes of staff, at all levels, it is the worst prison he had ever visited. In effect, he concluded that Pelican Bay is a prison without hope.[12]

Within two years of the Special Housing Unit taking its first prisoners some 300 law suits had been filed. These were eventually consolidated into a class action suit with the plaintiffs represented on a pro bono basis by a leading west coast law firm. In his judgement, delivered on 11 January 1995, Chief Judge Thelton E. Henderson of the US District Court, Northern District of California, ruled substantially in favour of the plaintiffs, finding that conditions at the Unit violated their constitutional rights, particularly those protected under the Eighth Amendment of the Constitution which provides protection against "cruel and unusual punishment". As the Chief Judge noted, the jurisprudence of the Eighth Amendment is clear: even prisoners at the "bottom of the heap" have, none the less, a human dignity. The judge went on to say that "dry words on paper cannot adequately capture the senseless suffering and sometimes wretched misery" caused by the prison authorities. Among the constitutional violations found by the Court was a "conspicuous pattern of excessive force", typified by the hogtying of prisoners—hands chained to feet—and by the forcible removal of prisoners from their cells with the use of gas guns and tasers, weapons which transmit an electric shock of 40 to 50 thousand volts resulting in temporary paralysis. The judge also discovered instances of prisoners being held naked in outdoor cages, a practice which he said exhibited "a callous and malicious intent to inflict gratuitous humiliation and punishment". More generally, the judge observed that "some of the defendants' comments, actions and policies show such disregard for inmates' pain and suffering that they shock the conscience."[13] The Court ordered the parties, under the supervision of a court-appointed Special Master, to develop a plan to make the prison meet constitutional standards. While this intervention by the Federal District Court is expected to bring some relief to the conditions of confinement, it will do little to diminish the eliminative reality of Pelican Bay and similar prisons.

Conclusions

Both these developments in California and the subsequent legal challenges have placed into sharp focus the complexities which arise in attempting to limit the pull towards elimination. This task is all the more daunting because the eliminative ideal as expressed in modern societies seeks legitimacy, and especially that afforded by the law. On one issue there can be no dispute: in setting limits of this sort, an independent judiciary has an absolutely crucial role to play. Moreover, to effectively challenge the eliminative ideal requires recognizing both its instrumental and expressive dimension. The case argued for elimination as an instrument for crime control needs to be, and I believe that it can be, fully countered. This task requires the sort of alternative perspective which has been developed by David Faulkner, partly in response to the eliminative tendencies inherent to the 1996 White Paper, *Protecting the Public* (Home Office 1996), and the subsequent Crime (Sentences) Act 1997 and its provisions for mandatory minimum sentences. In Faulkner's words: "Solutions to the problems of crime have to be sought by inclusion within the community itself—among parents, in schools, by providing opportunities and hope for young people and not by exclusion from it" (Faulkner 1996: 6).

But the challenge extends beyond instrumental rationales for elimination and must also address underlying expressive purposes. The eliminative ideal sits all too comfortably with contemporary pressures for social exclusion, with notions of a culture of contentment and of a functional underclass about which John Kenneth Galbraith has so eloquently written (Galbraith 1992). It is also facilitated by, to use Zygmunt Bauman's chilling phrases, the absence of any "uproar of emotions" and by the "dead silence of unconcern" (Bauman 1989). Criminal policy, of course, can never escape these issues of political economy and political philosophy which go to the heart of defining the sort of society which is sought. Elimination, as with punishment generally, is a social institution which, as David Garland argues, "helps define the nature of our society, the kinds of relationships which compose it, and the kinds of lives that it is possible and desirable to lead . . ." (Garland 1990: 287).

The various guises of the eliminative ideal in criminal policy need to be carefully remembered. As Ioan Davies has remarked, these episodes should be viewed not as "stops on a progressive evolutionary conveyer belt, but as dark moments of the human soul when the unspeakable happened, when men and women were treated, not as human, but as social pariahs . . ." (Davies 1990: 194–5). Some thirty years ago, Francis Allen, the American legal scholar, drew attention to what he described as the "rehabilitative ideal". While acknowledging that he had been a sharp critic of the exaggerated claims made for it and of the injustices resulting from its over-zealous application, he cautioned about abandoning the rehabilitative ideal. If this were to happen, he asked, from where would the impetus for compassion and decency come? We would, he warned, become apathetic about the individual human being caught up in the apparatus of criminal justice (Allen 1978). That Professor

Allen was justified in his caution there can be little doubt, and all the more so as this century draws to a close with the resurgence of elimination as an ideal of criminal policy.

Acknowledgements

Based on an inaugural lecture given at the University of Southampton on 8 October 1996. The event was much enhanced by the contributions of David Faulkner, who took the chair, and by the closing remarks of the Vice Chancellor, Professor Howard Newby. Grateful acknowledgement is due for assistance provided by Steven Curran, Aloma Hack and Careen Tompkins. As always, the article benefited from the keen eye and editorial guidance of Judith Rutherford.

Notes

1. See in particular Windlesham (1996) and Rutherford (1996).
2. DiIulio has stepped into the shoes of James Q. Wilson who has been a highly influential advocate of penal incapacitation since the early 1970s. For a critical appraisal of the impact of Wilson's writings, see Rutherford (1996).
3. When the second edition was published in 1994 the question mark at the end of the sub-title had been deleted. Among recent assessments of criminal policy developments in the United States see especially Miller (1996) and Currie (1996).
4. Personal communication, Professor Agnete Weis Bentzon of the University of Copenhagen, 20 June 1997.
5. For further information on Dennis Doherty, see Hughes (1988: 591–3).
6. On the public spectacle of transportation, see Weiner (1990: 98).
7. Robert Gellately has observed that "in the absence of legal recourse, and intimately linked to the formation of the burgeoning concentration camp system, this form of custody could easily be misused" (Gellately 1990: 28).
8. For detailed research on this period, in addition to the sources cited subsequently, see especially Browder (1990; 1996).
9. For an assessment of criminal policy developments in California, see Zimring and Hawkins (1995).
10. California Supreme Court, 20 June 1996. For an incisive critique of mandatory sentencing statutes in the United States, see Tonry (1996).
11. *Madrid v. Gomez* 889 F. Supp. 1146 US District Court for the Northern District of California (1995) 8.
12. Personal communication, Duncan McLaughlan, Northern Ireland Office, 17 April 1996.
13. *Madrid v. Gomez*, op. cit., 70.

References

Allen, Francis A. (1960), Raffaele Garofalo, in Hermann Mannheim (ed.), *Pioneers in Criminology*, pp. 254–76. London: Stevens.

Allen, Francis (1978), The decline of the rehabilitative ideal in American criminal justice, *Cleveland State Law Review*, 27: 147–56.

Aronson, Shlomo (1984), *The Nazi Concentration Camps, Proceedings of the Fourth Vad Vashem International Historical Conference—January 1980*, Jerusalem: Vad Vashem.

Bauman, Zygmunt (1989), *Modernity and the Holocaust*, Cambridge: Polity Press.

Beddoe, Deirdre (1979), *Welsh Convict Women: A Study of Women Transported from Wales to Australia, 1787–1852*, Barry: Stewart Williams.

Bourdet-Pleville, Michel (1960), *Justice in Chains, From the Galleys to Devil's Island*, London: Robert Hale.

Bowring, John (1843), editor, Bentham, *Works* i.

Broszat, Martin (1968), The Concentration Camps, 1933–45, in Helmut Krausnick *et al.* (eds), *Anatomy of the SS State*, pp. 397–504, London: Collins.

Browder, George C. (1990), *Foundations of the Nazi Police State*, Lexington, KY: University of Kentucky Press.

Browder, George C. (1996), *Hitler's Enforcers, The Gestapo and the SS Security Service in the Nazi Revolution*, New York: Oxford University Press.

Christie, Nils (1993), *Crime Control as Industry: Towards Gulags Western Style?*, London: Routledge.

Conquest, Robert (1968), *The Great Terror*, London: Macmillan.

Currie, Elliott (1996), *Is America Really Winning the War on Crime and Should Britain Follow its Example?*, London: NACRO.

Davies, Ioan (1990), *Writers in Prison*, Oxford: Blackwell.

DiIulio, John J. (1994), Let 'em rot, *Wall Street Journal*, 26 January.

Faulkner, David (1996), *Darkness and Light*, London: Howard League for Penal Reform.

Galbraith, John Kenneth (1992), *The Culture of Contentment*, London: Penguin.

Garland, David (1990), *Punishment and Modern Society*, Oxford: Oxford University Press.

Gellately, Robert (1990), *The Gestapo and German Society, Enforcing Racial Policy 1933–1945*, Oxford: Clarendon Press.

Goldhagen, Daniel Jonah (1996), *Hitler's Willing Executioners, Ordinary Germans and the Holocaust*, London: Little, Brown.

Hentoff, Nat (1993), Buried alive in Pelican Bay, *Prison Life*, 2: 3.

Home Office (1996), *Protecting the Public*, Cm 3190, London: HMSO.

Howard, John (1929), *The State of the Prisons*, London: Dent.

Hughes, Robert (1988), *The Fatal Shore. A History of the Transportation of Convicts to Australia, 1787–1868*, London: Pan.

Ignatieff, Michael (1989), *A Just Measure of Pain*, London: Penguin.

Kennan, George (1891), *Siberia and the Exile System*, 2 vols, London: James R. Osgood, McIlvaine and Co.

Koestler, Arthur (1991), *Scum of the Earth*, London: Eland.

Kogon, Eugen (1946), *Der SS Staat—Das System der deutschen Konzentrationslager*, Franfurt.

Krausnick, Helmut, *et al.* (eds) (1968), *Anatomy of the SS State*, London: Collins.

Kropotkin, Peter (1971), *In Russian and French Prisons*, New York: Schocken Books.

Miller, Jerome G. (1996), *Search and Destroy. African-American Males in the Criminal Justice System*, New York: Cambridge University Press.

Muller, Ingo (1991), *Hitler's Justice: The Courts of the Third Reich*, London: I. B. Tauris.

Noakes, Jeremy (1985), Social outcasts in Nazi Germany, *History Today*, December: 15–19.

Pingel, Falk (1984), The concentration camps as part of the National-Socialist system of domination, in *The Nazi Concentration Camps, Proceedings of the Fourth Vad Vashem International Historical Conference—January 1980*, Jerusalem: Vad Vashem.

Radzinowicz, Leon (1948), *A History of the English Criminal Law, Vol. 1. The Movement for · Reform*, London: Macmillan.

Radzinowicz, Leon (1991a), *The Roots of the International Association of Criminal Law and their Significance. A Tribute and a Re-assessment on the Centenary of the IKV*, Freiburg: Max-Planck Institut.

Radzinowicz, Leon (1991b) Penal regressions, *Cambridge Law Journal*, 50: 141–62.

Radzinowicz, Leon, and Hood, Roger (1986), *A History of English Criminal Law, v. The Emergence of Penal Policy*, London: Stevens.

Robson, L. L. (1965), *The Convict Settlers of Australia*, Melbourne: Melbourne University Press.

Ruck, S. K. (ed.) (1951), *Paterson on Prisons*, London: Frederick Muller.

Rudé, George (1978), *Protest and Punishment. The Story of the Social and Political Protestors Transported to Australia, 1788–1868*, Oxford: Clarendon Press.

Rusche, George and Kirchheimer, Otto (1939), *Punishment and Social Structure*, New York: Russell and Russell.

Rutherford, Andrew (1996), *Transforming Criminal Policy*, Winchester: Waterside Press.

Savarkar, V. D. (1950), *The Story of My Transportation for Life*, Bombay.

Sellin, J. Thorsten (1976), *Slavery and the Penal System*, New York: Elsevier.

Tonry, Michael (1996), *Sentencing Matters*, New York: Oxford University Press.

Trollope, Anthony (1968), *Australia and New Zealand. Vol. 2*, London: Dawsons of Pall Mall.

Weiner, Martin J. (1990), *Reconstructing the Criminal. Culture, Law and Policy in England, 1830–1914*, New York: Cambridge University Press.

Weiss, Aharon (1984), Catagories of camps—their character and role in the execution of the "Final Solution of the Jewish Question", in *The Nazi Concentration Camps, Proceedings of the Fourth Vad Vashem International Historical Conference—January 1980*, Jerusalem: Vad Vashem.

Windlesham, Lord (1996), *Responses to Crime, Vol. 3, Legislating with the Tide*, Oxford: Clarendon Press.

Zimring, Franklin E., and Hawkins, Gordon (1995), *Incapacitation. Penal Confinement and the Restraint of Crime*, New York: Oxford University Press.

Framing the Other: Criminality, Social Exclusion and Social Engineering in Developing Singapore

John Clammer

Abstract

This paper examines the issue of criminality as it is expressed in social policy in Singapore. This small South-east Asian country is characterized by great social and ethnic diversity, high rates of economic growth, but low crime rates. The relationship between these is pursued by examining the authoritarian political system and the social policies that have arisen from this to socialize and discipline the ethnically disparate and class-divided population. A brief survey of the social structure of Singapore, the role of colonialism in shaping the legal system, the legal measures introduced during the pre-independence anti-colonial and anti-communist struggles and the adoption of many of these by the new government of independent Singapore as weapons of social control introduces the paper. This is followed by an examination of the single-minded pursuit of developmentalism and security in the post-independence period and of the emergence of crime in political discourse as the paradigm of social disorder and self-exclusion from the developmental state, and the relationship of these to the dominant political problem of the management of ethnicity and social differences expressed as concern with classification, a commitment to socio-biology and the constant attempts to define a field of "Asian values" based on a local reading of Confucianism as the basis of social cohesion. The essay concludes with a discussion of the relationship between Singaporean images of social order and the pursuit of a distinctive form of positivist modernism and the question of whether a "Singapore model" is applicable elsewhere in the world.

Keywords:

Criminality; Singapore; Developmentalism; Multiethnicity; Orientalism

Introduction

The achievement of modernity, or even of postmodernity, in the advanced industrial nations has not brought with it an end to many forms of social

Address for Correspondence: *John Clammer, Department of Comparative Culture, Sophia University (Jochi Daigaku), 4 Youban-cho, Chiyoda-ku, Tokyo 102, Japan.*

exclusion, and has indeed bred new forms specific to modernity. The experience of many European countries for example (and Britain, Germany and France are conspiciuous in this respect) has been that the transition to late modernity, whatever its cultural achievements, has been accomplished at the expense of high rates of homelessness, poverty, single person and single parent households, unemployment and lack of full social or political participation on the part of the aged, migrant workers and ethnic minorities. Typically, the counter-modernity movements that have arisen as responses to these trends (neo-Nazism, New Age movements and religious fundamentalisms for instance), while possibly relieving the pressure on individual members, have done little to produce systemic social change and have in many cases rather contributed themselves to the growing sense of crisis and malaise.

The movement to the Right in many West European nations and the widespread abandonment of the socialist alternative has led to the depoliticization of large segments of the population, not least because of the widespread perception that politics can no longer manage precisely those areas that fall within its traditional mandate: the successful running of the economy and the maintenance of social order. Since the two are clearly intimately related, the sense of crisis and of things-being-out-of-control is deepened, particularly since the rhetoric, and to some extent the experience, of modern life is of one pervaded by insecurity arising not only from growing economic uncertainties, but very concretely from the presence of high levels of crime and from the growing legions of the socially excluded thought to be responsible for this crime. In such an environment a tempting political "solution" is to seek for social policy options that will provide publicly visible remedies and preventive measures, even if the root causes of this allegedly burgeoning criminality are not fully understood, or are explained in ways that legitimize certain politically-attractive options.

Criminality is indeed important for many contemporary governments, not only because of its potential scapegoat value, but also because it serves both to displace or disguise class, race and gender as the key issues in public discourse and to legitimize "solutions" by way of piecemeal social policy options rather than through wholesale political reform. But looked at in a comparative perspective this particular "language" of criminality by no means proves to be universal. There are societies outside Western Europe and North America that do not perceive themselves as having a major problem with crime, which have a fundamentally different approach to social policy as it applies to the management of crime, and which articulate the relationship between crime and social exclusion in ways distinctly their own. Two conspicuous examples that come to mind are Japan and Singapore. Here we have two Asian societies that have experienced high rates of economic growth and massive social changes in the last three decades, and which also have little in the way of crime by Western standards. While the case of Japan is well known and quite extensively documented (e.g. Eisenstadt and Ben-Ari 1990), Singapore is much less well known in this respect and it is on this latter example that this paper will concentrate.

Singapore is the smallest country in East Asia. Until 1963, a British colony mainly important for its role as a military base, and between 1963 and 1965 a constituent part of the Federation of Malaya, independent Singapore has experienced almost uninterrupted economic growth, intensive urbanization and massive expansion of the social infrastructure both in its institutional manifestations such as schools and medical facilities and in its physical ones such as roads, public utilities and airports. All this has taken place in a context marked by two key features: a society organized on the basis of a fundamental ethnic pluralism (a large Chinese majority and Malay, Indian and numerous smaller minorities) and one politically framed by the uninterrupted rule of an authoritarian government committed to the creation of a developmentalist state and an all-pervasive state apparatus influencing on a daily basis the life of every citizen (for historical, social and political background consult Rodan 1993; Chew and Lee 1991; Chen 1983; Clammer 1985). Singapore is always seen as one of the "little dragons" of Asia—a society that has achieved high levels of economic growth of a capitalist nature, but based on strong state direction and control and which has closely managed the social problems attendant on such growth while suppressing genuine democratization. "Growth with control" essentially sums up the Singapore experience (Deyo 1981; Rodan 1989).

The apparent calm of today's Singapore—its gleaming international airport, tree-lined roads, landscape of government-constructed high-rise apartment blocks in which the majority of the population of 3 million live, and downtown complexes of shopping centres, banks and boutiques—has not arisen naturally. Far from it; it has emerged from a turbulent history and is maintained today by draconian measures designed to ensure that the peace is indeed not disrupted and by a range of social policies designed to ensure the socialization and disciplining of the population in order to ensure that judicial measures are only invoked as a last (and very heavy-handed) resort. The origins of the criminal justice system itself, if not its present-day style of administration and application, lie in the colonial past. From this past and its legacy three main features emerged. The first of these was the adoption of British law, initially in in a fairly wholesale form, but with increasing adaptations after independence as Singapore sought to distance itself from its former colonial masters and as the operation of the law was increasingly shaped to political imperatives. Two examples of this were the early decision to abolish jury trials and to have, with the exception of High Court appeals, which are heard by a panel of three, cases heard by a single judge; and the more recent decision to abolish the right of appeal to the Privy Council in London as the pinnacle of the legal system. The former decision was based on an argument from the cultural, linguistic and ethnic diversity of Singapore, a feature which it was alleged would make it very difficult to regularly compose juries of unbiased individuals sufficiently educated to understand both the language of the courts (English) and the complexities of cases before those courts. Since capital punishment was and is a feature of the legal system, an argument could be made about the undesirability of a panel of randomly selected ordinary citizens deciding on the outcome of major criminal trials.

The second is the complexity and multiethnicity of Singapore society. Small the island may be (620 square kilometres), but it is of enormous cultural diversity with almost every major ethnic group and religion to be found in Asia represented on the island (Clammer 1977). This diversity was very directly the result of British colonial policy in encouraging the in-migration to Singapore and Malaysia of workers from China and India and of traders, entrepreneurs and craftsmen from the surrounding region, the Persian Gulf and the Middle East, and of bureaucrats and administrators from Britain and elsewhere throughout the Empire. Whatever its anthropological charms, this diversity had and continues to have enormous impact on the creation of social policy and the operation of the legal system. While historically this problem was dealt with by treating each ethnic community as a distinct administrative unit to be dealt with through its own headmen, such a solution could not survive into independence and the desire to create a strong, unified state. The resulting blanket application of British criminal law, the phasing out of the use of Chinese customary law and the retention of special privileges only for Muslim domestic cases unified the criminal justice system in theory, but not in practice. Often in the past and to this day judges and defendants, and even defendants and their lawyers, may not be able to speak the same languages and the role of court interpreters is still a critical one. Different cultural expectations and behavioural traits appear constantly in trials in Singapore courts. Ethnographically the legal scene is one of great diversity, even if a government bent on the very rapid achievement of modernity has submerged these differences beneath institutional unification.

The third consequence of colonialism was the anti-colonial struggle, and the fact, discomforting for the post-independence pro-capitalist and politically highly conservative ruling party (the People's Action Party or PAP) that this struggle was largely led by the Left. Indeed, the PAP itself during its quite short history has achieved the remarkable feat of transforming itself from a Left Leninist into a Right Leninist party. The rhetoric of the reformed PAP quickly became, and has remained, stridently anti-Left and particularly anti-communist. The historical origins of this shift lie partly in internal struggles within the PAP in the run-up to independence and partly in the genuinely destabilizing and dangerous circumstances of the Malayan Emergency—the period of armed communist struggle against the returned British colonial administration at the end of the war which lasted from the late 1940s until as late as the early 1960s until it was finally quashed. Legal measures against communism included the Internal Security Act (ISA) that allowed detention without trial for suspected communist party activists and sympathizers deemed to be a threat to the state. The new government of independent Singapore took over this legislation from the outgoing British and refurbished it as a frequently-used tool against their own internal opponents and a range of other elements seen as socially disruptive but not easily manageable under normal judicial procedures, such as members of Chinese Secret Societies and religious extremists, particularly those advocating social change of a form or by methods not approved by the government.

Secret societies had indeed long been a problem. Originating for the most part as resistance movements against the Manchu Qing dynasty and devoted at least officially to restoring the Han Chinese Ming dynasty, many secret societies rapidly degenerated into little more than criminal organizations. Many members of these societies moved abroad, particularly to Southeast

Asia, to seek economic opportunities or to escape Qing oppression as part of the huge Chinese diaspora of the late nineteenth and early twentieth centuries. Seeing them both as a threat to social order in Singapore and as involving the colony in the politics of a distant country, the British authorities actively attempted to suppress the secret societies. Their threat to social order came not only from their criminal activities (mainly extortion, opium trading and prostitution), but from their impenetrability on the part of the local law enforcement agencies and their links with many other associations around which overseas Chinese communities organized themselves—dialect, village, district, surname, occupational and religious associations. These associations, normally composed of members of a single linguistic group (Cantonese for example, or Hokkien), by their nature excluded outsiders, even other Chinese. They were for the most part opposed, often actively and even to the point of violence, to their rival counterparts or speakers of another southern Chinese language (Mak 1992). The overlaps between such legitimate associations (which largely ensured the peaceful self-governance of the local Chinese community) and secret societies made the latter very difficult to suppress or even to identify. This problem has come down to the present day and one rationale for retaining the ISA was precisely to use it against members of what are now purely criminal syndicates and gangs, but against whom normal evidence publicly sustainable in court is hard to obtain or to prove. Notwithstanding this rationale, one of the most frequent uses of the ISA has been to detain without due process political opponents and social activists whose activities could never be judged as criminal or subversive by normal legal standards (Seow 1994).

This sketch of the background to contemporary social policy developments suggests a number of interesting and significant factors from the point of view of a comparative analysis. Firstly, that social exclusion is seen in Singapore as directly related to crime and antisocial behaviour. Logically the solution to this is to ensure, by a range of means and by force if necessary, the integration of absolutely everyone into the modernist state system. These means, some of which I will discuss in detail below, include the compulsory registration of every member of the population all of whom are citizens or permanent residents and must carry at all times an identity card containing the name, address, race, bloodgroup and national registration number of its possessor together with their photograph and thumb print; compulsory military service for males; an active and pervasive internal security apparatus; a range of social policies designed to organize and monitor the population through control of public housing, a wide network of community centres and residents' committees; a strong belief in the efficacy of propaganda and exhortation in achieving social goals and a wide range of surveillance and policing activities, including introduction of a local variant, of the Japanese *koban* or neighbour-hood police box system (a network of local police posts scattered throughout residential areas and manned by police officers with an intimate knowledge of the locality and its residents); and, should all this fail, a punitive system of fines, punishments and mechanisms of public humiliation. The well-known taxi-driver's joke that "Singapore is a fine society! Don't flush the toilet-fine. Dog soil the sidewalk-fine. Litter-fine. Smoke in public place-fine. Eat chewing gum-fine!" has a sound basis in social reality, absurdly and perhaps pathetically underscored by a recent advertisement from a major local bank that its cash-card holders could now enjoy several important new services at the bank's ATMs: "Buy admission tickets to the Singapore Zoological Gardens, Night Safari and Jurong Bird Park; Pay parking offence tickets . . . and Pay traffic offence tickets and summons issued by the Traffic Police, Land Transport Authority and the Subordinate Courts." If nothing else, this remarkable document certainly indicates the extent to which major non-governmental institutions in Singapore and the public themselves have adapted to and aquiesced in a system of social control so pervasive that it has become invisible, even as it delivers the conditions suitable for the unfettered pursuit of material goods.

Social Policy and the Developmental State

The evolution of attitudes to crime in Singapore must be seen in the context of the pursuit of developmentalism. At the point of independence the Singapore economy was dominated by the presence of large British military bases, bases that were however just on the point of being wound down as British forces began their withdrawal from east of Suez. In addition to the economic crisis that this posed, made worse by Singapore's own separation in 1965 from Malaysia, the social infrastructure was bad, housing conditions were very poor ("worse than Bombay" according to a comment made to me by a foreign social scientist who had been there at the time), and the population consisted of an unintegrated mass of disparate ethnic communities with little or no sense of common purpose. This posed two initial problems for the new post-colonial administration: the creation of a viable economy and the welding of a population of (mostly) immigrants into some sort of cohesive whole. These were tackled by way of two main approaches: an economic one consisting of a mix of huge infrastructural projects designed to create employment and to produce the physical basis for foreign firms to invest in the country with its available pool of (as then) cheap labour; and a political one stressing "Nation Building" through the creation of common institutions (especially schools, the inculcation of loyalty to Singapore rather than to the country of ethnic origin and the vigorous suppression of any political alternatives (particularly as we have noted, Leftist ones) that might detract from this highly-managed policy of state capitalism (Drysdale 1984).

The two approaches were linked through the housing policy which neatly combined these objectives through the simultaneous stimulation of employ-ment and economic activity through its huge building programme, and the tying of the population to Singapore through home-ownership, a policy which it was rightly calculated would promote social stability, encourage embourgeoisification in a mostly working-class immigrant population and which would create strong political loyalties to the government which was providing this good life. One of the first acts of the new government was to create a massive statutory board—the Housing Development Board (HDB)—to oversee this construction programme and to manage it down to the finest detail (car parking, colour of doors, permissibility of certain kinds of air-conditioners and water heaters, ownership of pets, placement of pot plants, provision of playgrounds and latterly even the ethnic mix allowed in individual housing estates). Estates themselves were furthermore not only managed by direct bureaucratic means, but also through a set of politically-controlled institutions and networks, including community centres and residents' associations. A stake in the country through home-ownership, financed in most cases from use of the CPF or Central Provident Fund deductions from income and matching contributions from employers (there is no state-administered system of pensions or unemployment benefits in Singapore), close bureaucratic control of almost all of the population except the rich who live in private housing, and mutual surveillance on the part of neighbours who, if not technically responsible for each other's behaviour on the lines of the old Chinese or Japanese block systems, are certainly encouraged as "good citizens" to be aware of what is going on in their apartment complex, ostensibly to prevent or to detect crime.

There are three local rationales for this seemingly suffocating level of social control. The first is that of security, both economic and political. Singapore actually has, in proportion to its size, a strong and thriving economy, a strong currency, it is the beneficiary of heavy inward investment from major western and Japanese corporations, is a regional transport hub with a huge airline of its own and is itself an investor in numerous overseas markets including some rapidly growing ones like Vietnam and South China. The rhetoric however is that Singapore is small, vulnerable and subject to the machinations of enemies and envious rivals without and within. Consequently, to maintain economic growth and the high levels of consumption that Singaporeans now enjoy, constant vigilance, political and social stability, controlled media and the suppression of popular democracy are argued as being necessary. The strong state in other words recommends itself as the necessary condition of economic survival (and Britain, Australia and the Philippines are held up as examples of where too much democracy, a free press and a strong labour movement lead). Social control is thus linked in the minds of just about everybody with material success: one implies the other, and crime is not just an assault on private property or the person, but reflects something deeper—a pollution or cancer are terms often heard locally—which like a germ or a virus must be stamped out before it begins to infect even wider ranges of the social order. Crime is not just disorder in Singapore, it is paradigmatic of the dark forces of chaos lying just beyond the tightly-maintained boundaries of the state, psyche and society in this community that has been aptly described by one commentator as "a theme park with the death sentence".

This characterization is actually apt in a very telling way. Singapore does indeed have the death sentence applicable to murder, firearms offences and to drug trafficking. If crime in general is paradigmatic of social disorder in Singapore, drug offences are somehow the centre of that paradigm. While the death sentence does not apply to the consumption of drugs, it does apply to traffickers and is regularly applied. The significance of drugs is clearly signalled by this level of punishment. Apart from the clearly disruptive effects of drugs on societies like that of the US, drugs in Singapore are of profound concern to the political bosses because they trigger deep fears and provide the basis of sinister urban myths. Drugs are potent symbols firstly because they represent pollution (of the individual body and of society) and the dark forces waiting just outside the charmed circle of Singapore's boundaries. The strict policing of those boundaries and the control of those who may enter and those who may leave is indicative of this. Immigration is closely monitored, for example, and certain strict qualifications are demanded from those who would settle in Singapore, qualifications which include educational credentials, certain favoured ethnicities and a crime-free personal record. Singaporean males liable for military service may not leave at all without a special permit and those who go abroad for study are required to deposit large monetary bonds with the government to ensure their return. Social control, however, is not enough in Singapore. Wherever possible, psychic control is also attempted, through the rigid educational system, through control of the media, censorship of films and imported literature, through the banning of satellite dishes which enable the viewing of foreign television programmes and news, through consumption and material success as the main goals of life and through the encouragement of cultural patterns which create, especially in many Chinese Singaporeans, if not an authoritarian personality, at least a bureaucratic one—inflexible, rule-bound and subservient to authority.

These attempts at psychic management, however, are not uniformly successful precisely because of the ethnic and cultural diversity of Singapore. And it is the non-Chinese minorities who are particularly resistant to these blandishments and reflect this to the permanent chagrin of the PAP in their voting patterns. The major if unspoken reason for charging the HDB with the responsibility of ensuring that ethnic minorities do not congregate in particular housing estates is because such enclaves regularly vote against the government in elections. A large minority population in a given constituency would be sufficient to deliver that parliamentary seat to the opposition. The most problematic of these minorities from the point of view of the hegemony of the PAP is that of the Malays. Constituting 15 per cent of the population, closely linked culturally, linguistically and religiously with their co-ethnics in neighbouring Malaysia and Indonesia and with attitudes to life, money and social relationships very different from those of the majority Chinese, the Malays are the Other within. Worse, they are part of the international fellowship of Islam and as such have links around the globe. Given that "foreign influence" or "foreign interference" are themes constantly used by the government to whip up nationalistic feeling, a large group with universalist commitments outside of the country is very threatening. And to exacerbate matters, the Singapore Malay community now has a good model for Malay political and economic success right next door in Malaysia, one of the most successful and harmonious of the NICs in Asia and Malay-dominated to boot (Li 1989).

Malays are also generally poorer than Chinese or Indians, are less committed to education, are under-represented in the universities, in professional managerial or upper-level bureaucratic posts, and are regarded as much more religious, musical and sporty than the other communities. (Clammer 1981). Despite theoretically universal military service for men (itself a policy with rather more social than defence functions) many Malays are not in fact called up and as such languish in a kind of limbo as many employers will understandably not employ men who have not completed or been officially deferred from military service and who might at any moment be conscripted. Young Malays are consequently and with some empirical justification associated with "youth culture". They are bored, not well educated, an ethnic minority, excluded from the upper reaches of their own society and often employed in unskilled jobs. They also, and no doubt as a consequence of these social disadvantages, take drugs. The demonizing of drugs and their association with a particular minority culture (actually the most religious and law-abiding in Singapore) come to form a "natural" unity. What is fundamentally at stake here is not just the emergence of new forms of crime, but the association of those crimes both with a relatively excluded group and with the uncontrollable psychic energies of youth. Young people are liminal, even dangerous in Singapore (especially when they are minority youth) and as such must be heavily socialized through an over-heavy educational curriculum that creates little time for play or relaxation, collective socialization for (majority) males through military service, gender socialization for girls through the spread of Confucian values and the controlled encouragement of pietistic and non-socially critical forms of religion which are thought to encourage "correct" values such as honesty, hard work and submission to the political authorities. Singapore fits very well into the model of grid and group developed by the anthropologist Mary Douglas (Douglas 1973) in which she argues that there is a strong relationship between the control of bodily boundaries and social control. The Chinese in Singapore: short-haired, conventionally dressed, committed to careers in management, computers and engineering, are assimilated into the political structures; the Malays, long-haired, religious, non-materialistic, and interested primarily in social relationships, are not. A complex but discernible mapping of minority status, crime and culture on to one another lies behind many of the social policies which have emerged in Singapore since independence.

The paradox of developmentalism in Singapore is that it has set out to achieve modernity without inheriting the problems of that modernity. This has been done by a mixture of pre-emptive and adaptive policies. The first category includes the housing policy discussed above, deliberate economic "pump priming" to maintain high levels of employment and economic activity through massive public works projects: a network of new highways, the construction of a subway system, the development of the new Changi international airport and the creation of mass education at the lower levels and elite education at the higher (there are only two universities and far too few places for qualified applicants). The second includes modifying the ethnic mix in public housing estates, the progressive privatization of housing and hospitals to prevent rising levels of taxes to pay for social services and to prevent undue dependence on state-provided facilities (while of course maintaining strict regulatory control over such nominally privatized sectors) and constant interference in the family and reproductive lives of the citizenry—attempting to limit and then to expand the number of children per family, in encouraging graduate women to marry and to have more children while encouraging through tax incentives and grants less educated families (especially those of minorities) to limit their size. The result has been a state of remarkably Durkheimian characteristics—organized around a core of (state-generated) values enshrined in the recent attempt to encapsulate and institutionalize them in a "national ideology" (Clammer 1993) and deriving its legitimacy from a self-referential system of supportive mechanisms. This can be better understood through the examination of two elements in this totality; the nature of policy interventions and the underlying logic of the assumptions which have created these interventions.

Framing Exclusion and Situating Crime

Social policy rarely, if ever, exists in a vacuum, but rather is derivative from certain basic assumptions, the deep grammar of the society. It is consequently not only necessary to enumerate such policies, but also to attempt to relate them to that grammar. Crime, we have suggested, is not in fact so much a fact as a threat, the first sign of the unravelling of the carefully constructed and managed social fabric of Singapore. It is ingratitude, a perverse unwillingness to co-operate in bringing about the utopia that the government is so painstakingly building, it is the foolishness of refusing to accept a reality that everybody else can so clearly see. Worse, it suggests that the government's own social policies are not fully effective, and indeed when a policy does not seem to work in Singapore, it is rarely the policy that is blamed, but rather the recalcitrance of those who fail to submit fully to its demands. Consequently, people have to be monitored for their own good and crime has to be understood not as an outcome of objective social conditions, but as the chaos which breaks out if order is in the slightest relaxed. Crime, to use a Singapore metaphor, is like a virus in the bloodstream: it will break out if the immune system is weakened. It is perhaps not surprising that AIDS is talked about in much these terms: it is a foreign disease not least because homosexuality is not supposed to exist in Chinese societies, and will appear if moral vigilance is relaxed and westernized values are allowed to penetrate what is paradoxically probably the most westernized of all Asian societies.

The result is a concern not so much with content (for example exactly what "Asian values" are) as with borders—ensuring that certain things are contrastively excluded and thus demonstrating the rightness of that which is within the system. This logic can be seen operating through a set of concrete policies and control measures: surveillance, classification and close policing of the population in a postively Foucauldian way; the assumption that development and growth themselves provide the ultimate disincentives to social disruption—pure self-interest ensures conformity; a eugenics policy designed to promote the fertility of the highly educated and to depress that of the less educated; a profound belief in the power of exhortation—if you say it loud enough and often enough people will get the message; networks of informal social control and the encouragement of self-censorship in the belief that the surveillance apparatus is all-seeing; the organization of everyday life within a tight bureaucratic framework of institutions like the HDB and the Registrar of Societies from whom permission must be sought to do practically anything, to start any kind of organization, to run any kind of business, to keep a dog, own a bicycle or operate a TV set or radio, to marry, to choose particular kinds of names for one's children, and very much else; through punitive punishments for those who do break the law; and for a network of socializing agencies such as military service and the schools. In writing about the evolution of educational policy in Singapore, one scholar has indeed dubbed the system "social engineering", an apt term since it nicely captures the combination of constant tinkering and belief in technical and positivist solutions that characterizes the way in which social policy is formulated and applied.

The logic of this approach is also that people are not excluded, they exclude themselves. But the price of this is that one cannot select what one wants in Singapore and reject the rest, but to participate one must participate fully. Any eccentricity, criminal, political or cultural, is disloyalty. Singapore is thus "totalitarian" in the genuine sense of that word: it requires full commitment to what it is, and failure to do this excludes the deviant, upon whom the full wrath of the "system" unfailingly descends. The problem with this theory of self-exclusion and of criminality as wilful non-participation in the social good, is that it ignores objective exclusion based on objective factors (poverty, mental illness and age are three of the most conspicuous examples in Singapore), or resulting from the logic of the overall system itself. If, as it is, ethnicity is the primary means of social classification in Singapore, then minorities are almost by definition marginalized. People who cannot or will not participate in the society of consumption are deviant. This problem is managed by hiding such questions, conceptually by denying the applicability of class or gender analysis to Singapore, and empirically by denying that such problems exist. Poverty for instance, despite the evidence of large numbers of families who cannot pay their rent even for low-income HDB flats and the number of the indigent aged, is denied, or, when it must be admitted, is blamed on the fecklessness of the individual. The strong inclusionary logic of the Singapore state system ensures that those who cannot participate are excluded, but then blamed for their exclusion.

Modernity and Crime/The Modernity of Crime

But where do such theories come from? What are their intellectual roots? The argument from the fragility of Singapore, its tiny size and the coldness and hostility of the outside world, we have already noted. But there are other factors too. At the beginning of the history of independent Singapore a conscious decision was made to make race (in Singapore identified with ethnicity) the basis of social classification for two reasons: first that it defuses the possibility of classification based on class by locating identity in one's "vertical" biological lineage, rather than in the "horizontal" ties linking people by economic interest regardless of race, and second that it makes identity fundamentally biological and essentialist, rather than cultural and constructed. It is a short jump from a biological theory of race to a biological theory of criminality and indeed as far back as 1983 the then Prime Minister, Lee Kuan Yew, was arguing publicly for a policy to control the reproduction of "degenerates" and the "socially inadequate" and basing this on ill-digested ideas drawn from the murky waters of socio-biology (Chee and Chan 1984;

Clammer 1996). One intellectual source then lies in biological ideas which have been fiercely contested and criticized in the West, but which received little comment in Singapore largely because of the tame and co-opted nature of the local intellectuals.

Another lies in the uneasy co-existence in Singapore of belief in an amorphous complex of ideas called "Asian values" and supposed to define the distinctiveness of the somewhat complex cultural region that stretches from Rangoon to Tokyo, and an equally firm belief in capitalism. The problem is that despite constantly invoking Confucius as the source of East Asian economic growth, the fact is that commitment to a society based on consumption radically alters the basis of sociality, and a tension not surprisingly arises between the desire for political control and the demands for distributive justice. In a society based on distinctions, differences inevitably multiply, but must then be assimilated in some way into a system that is not only Durkheimian in form, but also functionalist in operation. The proliferation of the list of things that may not be done (as symbolized by the famous signboards within the Botanical Gardens: no ball games, no fishing, no running, no picking of plants, no skateboarding . . . requires that this be harmonized with the theory of the overall unity of the society as a totality: difference has to be made to serve holism, a holism defined in terms of the "needs" of a developing Singapore. The absence of any social movements in Singapore other than those sanctioned by the government itself means that there are no alternative outlets for energies than the official channels. Not to conform, even in ways that would not be considered criminal elsewhere, is to be deviant, and the line between non-conformity and criminality is a fuzzy one indeed in Singapore.

Over time indeed the groups most likely to be defined as criminal have shifted, from secret society members, to illegal street hawkers, to hawkers in general (allegedly notorious for not paying taxes and under-declaring incomes and a sociologically significant group given the Singaporean penchant for eating out at the many hawker stalls that occupy markets and eating halls throughout the island and for buying fresh food daily from petty traders), to migrant workers and more recently to rich brats (the bored children of the wealthy who take to vandalism and petty crime to spice up their jaded lives). Three of these groups are significant in the light of the foregoing analysis: they are mobile, fluid in social organization, often poor and in many respects beyond the reach of the state and its monitoring organizations, and as such are both marginal and threatening.

Two observations might be made on this. The first is that in much of the literature on social exclusion in the West (e.g. Sibley 1995) such exclusion is *spatially* defined. Certain groups are not only marginalized, but that marginalization is reflected in place of residence, type of housing and absence from centres of social activity such as shopping malls or parks, which are policed to ensure that "undesirables" do not congregate there. The urban geography of Singapore, however, imposes a different pattern. There the excluded are not spatially separated, but are spatially insulated or encapsulated within the shared landscape: hawkers in markets, poor families in rent-arrears in older blocks of flats in the midst of regular housing estates,

migrant workers gather in the atria of certain downtown shopping centres
—the Filipinas in Lucky Plaza on the up-market but universally utilized (at
least for window-shopping and promenading) Orchard Road, the Thais in the
shopping centres of Beach Road, Malay youth in the fast-food outlets of
fashionable Scotts Road. While the mental hospital is significantly inconveni-
ently located in a semi-rural area some distance from the city, in Singapore
even the prisons are in or adjacent to residential areas.

But if physical separation is not a viable option, psychic distance is, and for
all its formal multiracialism, Singapore is still a society in which relatively
little actual social mixing or intermarriage between ethnic groups takes place.
People eat in their own ethnic restaurants (the fast food places are the major
exception), if possible sit next to people of the same ethnicity on public
transport, do not know their neighbours of a different race in their HDB block,
but have close social contact with co-ethnics on a different floor or in another
block. Whereas an essentialist notion of a bounded self is widely challenged
and criticized in the West, such a notion is actively encouraged in Singapore,
despite the Buddhism of much of its population. And this bounded self is seen
as having a biological basis and as being defined not by its protean nature and
constant remarking of itself as in postmodernist discourse, but by the close
guarding of its boundaries, the externalizing of inner fears on to external
threats and an association of otherness with dirt and pollution, either of a
physical nature or of a moral one (hence the fact that the words "decadent"
and "western" regularly occur together in Singapore). Puritanical concern
with bodily boundaries and with the perception of otherness as pollution and
its projection on to ideas of racial difference is not a uniquely western
phenomenon, but has occurred on a wide scale in Singapore as a result of the
peculiar mixing of essentialist and biologistic Chinese notions of identity with
a control-obsessed and deeply pollution-fearing political order. A seriously
neglected and under-researched aspect of life in Singapore is that of
psychiatric practice and the way in which it very directly contributes to the
construction of the bounded self along these lines.

Modernity in Singapore has meant in effect the imposition of what
Durkheim would have called mechanical solidarity on a society which,
because of its intrinsic diversity, lacks organic solidarity. The widespread
existence of racial stereotypes, despite many years of living side-by-side on the
part of different ethnic groups, indicates how unformed organic solidarity is,
despite attempts by the state to create it through a national ideology and
through the invention of national symbols (of which the annual National Day
parade is the most conspicuous). The quite deliberate use by the authorities of
"moral panics"—a "Marxist plot", AIDS, foreign interference in Singapore's
internal affairs, the irresponsibility of foreign news media in reporting
Singapore (and the frequent banning and/or suing of such media), the crisis
facing the country because educated women are not marrying or having
sufficient numbers of children—suggests that the maintenance of rigid
boundaries requires the constant invention of crises in which the self and the
state are threatened. The example of AIDS is very telling in this respect, it
being seen (totally inaccurately) as a "western" disease and furthermore as a
product of homosexuality, something, despite all the evidence to the contrary,

not supposed to occur in Singapore, or indeed even in Asia. As the Singapore foreign minister Wong Kan Seng stated at the UN Human Rights Conference in Vienna in 1993, "Homosexual rights are a Western issue, and are not relevant to this conference." As Chris Berry points out (Berry 1996) this attitude (quite apart from its empirical absurdity) in making homosexuality paradigmatic of otherness, does so in terms of geography and cultural difference. The logic of Orientalism reappears, paradoxically in the Orient itself: East and West are fundamentally divided from each other and the line of division proves again to be an eroticized one, generated this time not out of a clash between western colonialism and the indigenous societies of the East, but between a deeply modernist view and an emerging postmodernism, or between the pressures of globalism upon bounded localisms. In commenting on Wong's remarkable assertion Berry observes that "Indeed, I would argue that the remark is part of a Singaporean government response to the emergent postmodern world order that attempts to resolve its contradictions between localization and globalization by asserting a new and coherent regional identity. This region is referred to as East Asia, and it consists of those areas that share an at least relatively buoyant economy and a Confucian heritage, including such countries as Japan, Taiwan, Hong Kong and South Korea" (Berry 1996: 163). This argument provides both the framework for the reappearance of discussion of "Asian values", moribund since the 1970s, and for claims about the non-universality of human rights. By rooting human rights in particular cultural traditions (in this case "Confucianism") two things occur: a far-reaching cultural relativism is introduced into the discussion of rights, and a rhetoric of communal rather than individual rights emerges linked to an idea of "Asian democracy" (Hsiung 1985) which turns out on closer inspection to be exactly the kinds of "guided" or authoritarian "democracy" advocated by the Singaporean government and other less-than-liberal regimes in the region.

Of course the ideological effect of this is to deny personal responsibility. While there is little sympathy in Singapore with the idea of "decriminalizing" crime by psychologizing it (Singapore indeed is not a society friendly to psychologists of any stripe, except for Behaviourist ones), the "communalizing" of responsibility, very compatible though it is with the Durkheimian project of establishing mechanical solidarity ("in which there is little scope for differentiation between individuals and each individual is a microcosm of the whole")—in a moral sense, that is, not an ethnic or cultural one—removes the autonomy of the subject. While the ideology of the subject and the psychologizing of crime has led Western criminology in one distinct direction, no doubt with its own shortcomings, the ideology of holism (disguised as Confucianism) and the suppression of psychology has led Singaporean criminology in quite other and rather more positivist directions. Logically, the denial of individual autonomy of course reduces the moral status of the average citizen, something that has indeed happened in Singapore, but in so doing it also reduces the responsibility of the criminal. But illogically, while the first conclusion has been drawn, Singapore's political and legal elite have been quite unwilling to draw the second.

What Zygmunt Bauman calls the "legislative obsession" characteristic of modernity (Bauman 1995: 34) is an apt characterization of the Singapore approach to crime and social disorder. A society of anxiety, seeking indeed in Benthamite fashion to achieve the happiness of the gretest number, but seeking it not through the advancement of individual freedom, but also in Benthamite fashion through the Panopticon: surveillance and technical solutions to human problems. The curiously nineteenth-century, Victorian atmosphere of public culture in Singapore comes from this strange paradox of a group of technocrats attempting to achieve an organic society: to plan the spontaneous, to co-opt the different, to take credit for every innovation. A society which put engineers in charge of the Ministry of Education has clearly not transcended positivism. The desire to root identity in biology, to normalize the exuberant, to fear "decadence" as the hothouse growth that will choke civilization and to guard against it with a regime of discipline and order, to create moral panics and scapegoats where there are none is the Singaporean elaboration on the theme of modernity. "From the start modernity meant an excess of means over ends, abilities and resources always rushing ahead of objectives and feverishly seeking their own uses" (Bauman 1995: 175). The fear of proteophobia: "the apprehension aroused by the presence of multiform, allotropic phenomena which stubbornly elude assignment and sap the familiar classificatory grids" (1995: 181) lies at the base of the Singapore political cosmology in general, and of its views of deviance and criminality in particular. Singapore is in many ways a fossil, despite, or disguised by, its economic dynamism and constant state of physical reconstruction: it is, strangely in the middle of Southeast Asia, the quintessentially modernist society. And its social policies can only be fully understood in this light.

In broad theoretical terms two concluding points can be made. The first is that in the modernist sense Singapore is a "society of fear", fearful of the outside world and its contaminations, fearful of the stranger within and of the state itself and its pervasive apparatus of surveillance. As such it fits very interestingly into Ulrich Beck's discussion of the "risk society" (Beck 1994). Externally Singapore is a society in which the rhetoric of risk dominates political language; internally it is a society dedicated to the suppression of that risk by making itself a society of order, classification and one set firmly against transgression, whether that transgression be criminal, political, sexual or cultural. Singapore has become very literally a "defensible space": "a place with secure and efficiently guarded borders, a territory semantically transparent and semiotically legible, a site cleansed of risk, and particularly of the incalculable risks—which transforms merely 'unfamiliar people' . . . into downright enemies" (Baumann: 135). The second point is that whereas many modern industrial societies have succeeded in institutionalizing large sectors of the excluded population by keeping them in prisons or in mental hospitals (Christie 1993), Singapore has in a sense institutionalized the whole population, if not in a prison then certainly in a gigantic school: medicalized, sanitized and warned constantly of the degeneracy flourishing outside the walls and symbolized by the deviants within, those who will not "play the game" and who consequently must be exposed, shamed and punished, but certainly not understood, for to do that would immediately open the floodgates

150

and allow in the psychologizing of crime and the breakdown of the binary oppositions on which the logic of the system depends.

A Singapore Model?

It has become fashionable in some quarters to see Singapore as a model: of economic growth in particular, but also of social harmony. Clean streets, greenery, forests of high-rise apartments and little crime are indeed attractive features to the non-streetwise Japanese tourist or to the all-too-streetwise denizen of many North American or even European cities. Singapore stands as a model because it proves that high growth can be achieved without the massive problems that plague many of the older developed industrial economies. What this paper has attempted to demonstrate is that such solutions are possible—Japan and the other Asian "tigers" have also proved this—but that there are preconditions and costs. The essential precondition is probably that of cultural predisposition, reinforced by centuries of folk memories of lack of political freedoms. Neither of these are available to much of the West. Which still leaves the policy options and the social planning which Singapore as our case in point has so "successfully" undertaken to invent and apply. Can these be taken from their context and applied elsewhere, say to contemporary Britain? Probably not, for several major reasons. The first is that the politics of identity in Singapore has, post-independence, taken a distinctive form: highly nationalistic, formally based on a rigid ethnic classification and with a distinctive balance between the particularistic claims of one's cultural group and the absolute claims of the state, and closely structured through a near-universal system of socialization based on schooling (Singaporean children may not attend any of the international schools in the country), military service and incorporation into the socio-political community of the housing estate.

The second is that the approach to crime control and prevention is heavily based on the developmental model or "economic" solution. This is to some extent possible in a rapidly-expanding economy, but is of course dependent both on that expansion and on a population willing to sacrifice political freedoms for material security. The third is that when crime does occur, its conceptualization takes place only from an elite perspective—the people's voice is rarely heard in Singapore except in the coffee houses and private homes—and the solutions to it consist of a mix of moral exhortation and technical devices. Debate about the electronic tagging of offenders in Singapore has not focused on the ethical questions raised, but on the purely technical issues of the reliability of the devices, and how offenders might attempt to avoid surveillance and how this drawback might be overcome.

If social and economic development is the key to crime prevention, and obviously it does reduce the possibility of crimes originating from absolute deprivation, it does not, as the Singapore experience also demonstrates, actually abolish crime. What it does is to displace it. While street crime is very low, white-collar crime is on the increase. In creating a culture of what a former foreign minister dubbed "moneytheism", the government has built its own Trojan Horse in which crimes motivated by relative rather than absolute deprivation expand and where sheer boredom rather than real need (or even real creativity) triggers deviant behaviour, in a society in which the band of approved behaviour is very narrow indeed. Singapore perhaps exists as a warning in two directions: that crime can indeed be minimized, but in this model at the cost of excessive control and the suppression of non-criminal deviance; but also that there are alternative routes to modernity. Singapore has chosen one such route and it too, like the societies that have chosen the alternatives, must live with the very specific consequences of the road taken.

References

Bauman, Z. (1995), *Life in Fragments: Essays in Postmodern Morality*, Oxford: Blackwell.

Beck, U. (1994), *Risk Society*, London: Sage.

Berry, C. (1996), Sexual DisOrientations: homosexual rights, East Asian films, and postmodern postnationalism, in Xiaobing Tang and S. Snyder (eds), *In Pursuit of Contemporary East Asian Culture*, Boulder, CO: Westview Press.

Chee, H. L., and Chan, C. K. (eds) (1984), *Designer Genes*, Petaling Jaya: Insan.

Chen, P. S. J. (ed.) (1983), *Singapore: Development Policies and Trends*, Singapore: Oxford University Press.

Chew, E. C. T., and Lee, E. (eds) (1991), *A History of Singapore*, Singapore: Oxford University Press.

Christie, N. (1993), *Crime Control as Industry: Towards Gulags, Western Style?*, London: Routledge.

Clammer, J. (1977), *The Ethnographic Survey of Singapore*, Singapore: Department of Sociology, University of Singapore.

Clammer, J. (1981), Malay society in Singapore: a preliminary analysis, *Southeast Asian Journal of Social Science*, vol. 9: 1–2.

Clammer, J. (1985), *Singapore: Ideology, Society and Culture*, Singapore: Chopmen Publishers.

Clammer, J. (1993), Deconstructing values: the establishment of a national ideology and its implications for Singapore's political future, in G. Rodan (ed.), *Singapore Changes Guard: Social, Political and Economic Directions in the 1990s*, Melbourne: Longmans Cheshire; and New York: St Martin's Press.

Clammer, J. (1996), Sociobiology and the politics of race: "scientific" knowledge, theories of Chineseness and the management of pluralism in contemporary Singapore, in D. Sautman (ed.), *Ethnic Relations in East Asia*, Hong Kong: Hong Kong University of Science and Technology Press.

Deyo, F. C. (1981), *Dependent Development and Industrial Order: An Asian Case Study*, New York: Praeger.

Douglas, M. (1973), *Natural Symbols*, Harmondsworth: Penguin.

Drysdale, J. (1984), *Singapore: The Struggle for Success*, Singapore: Times Books International.

Eisenstadt, S. N., and Ben-Ari, E. (eds) (1990), *Japanese Models of Conflict Resolution*, London: Kegan Paul International.

Hsiung, J. C. (ed.) (1995), *Human Rights in East Asia: A Cultural Pespective*, New York: Paragon House.

Li, Tania (1989), *Malays in Singapore*, Kuala Lumpur: Oxford University Press.

Mak, L. F. (1992), Convergence and divergence: traditional voluntary associations in Singapore, in M. C. Yong (ed), *Asian Traditions and Modernization: Perspectives from Singapore*, Singapore: Times Academic Press.

Rodan, G. (1989), *The Political Economy of Singapore's Industrialization: Nation, State and International Capital*, London: Macmillan.

Rodan, G. (ed.) (1993), *Singapore Changes Guard: Social, Political and Economic Directions in the 1990s*, Melbourne: Longmans Cheshire; and New York: St Martin's Press.

Seow, F. T. (1994), *To Catch a Tartar*, New Haven: Yale Centre for International and Area Studies, Monograph 42.

Sibley, D. (1995), *Geographies of Exclusion: Society and Difference in the West*, London: Routledge.

Tu, W. M. (ed.) (1996), *Confucian Traditions in East Asian Modernity*, Cambridge, MA: Harvard University Press.

The New Social Policy in Britain

Catherine Jones Finer

Abstract

This paper starts from the proposition that approaches to crime and penal policy in contemporary Britain are of a piece with approaches to social policy across a number of fronts. "The New Social Policy" is examined in terms of "the stakeholder idea", its implications for how people are meant to behave, and the distance between this and socio-economic realities. The paper then explores various sectors of stakeholder social policy in their new order of importance—employment and training, education, health care, social care, housing, social security—before commenting on policies in respect of crime and crime prevention, in the light of the foregoing observations and with particular reference to the "lock-'em-up" tendency. The paper concludes that stakeholdership is no recipe for crime prevention

Keywords

Social Policy; Stakeholder; Crime; Britain

Introduction

Not all crime is the product of social exclusion and not all social exclusion leads to crime. However, to the extent crime is perceived as being a product of social exclusion over and above individual delinquency, the incidence of such crime will be taken as a comment on structural, material conditions in society. By the same token, to the extent crime is perceived as being primarily the work of individual delinquents, the incidence of such crime will be taken as comment on the people concerned, along with their families, their teachers, perhaps their social workers—and anyone else who can be blamed for failing to prevent them going wrong. This paper starts from the idea that a society's "positioning on crime" in this respect is likely to be in tune with its positioning across a range of social policy fronts. Certainly this is a case worth arguing with reference to contemporary Britain.

Ever since Margaret Thatcher's "departure", the leaderships of both main

Address for Correspondence: *Catherine Jones Finer, Department of Social Policy and Social Work, School of Social Sciences, University of Birmingham, Edgbaston, Birmingham, B15 2TT*

political parties have been competing for a new centre ground they have in effect been mapping out between them, in her wake. Naturally, politicians on both "left" and "right" have been vehement in their denials that this is the case. Equally naturally, it is difficult to sum up the substance of their agreement in social policy respects under a single snappy title. If we choose below to utilize Tony Blair's notion of "stakeholdership" for an exposition of the new social policy, this is not—in fairness to Mr Major—because stakeholdership is a bright new crystal-clear idea; but because it is sufficiently *im*precise to encompass what needs to be encompassed. In other words it is consensual.

The Stakeholder Idea

Stakeholder implies shareholder, which in turn implies a view of society as a form of joint stock undertaking on behalf and in the interests of all its "paying" or "paid up" members. Irrespective of how unequal the "stakes" or "shares" may be, no bona fide member or family should on balance fail to *gain something* as a result of membership, to the extent that they make or are deemed to have made an honest effort to play by the rules. Interestingly, this is as reminiscent of Rawlsian notions of the good (fair) society by US standards, as it is supposed to be reflective of the "Asian values" permeating today's self-styled "national corporations" of such as Singapore,[1] South Korea, Taiwan and (so far) Hong Kong, not to mention Japan *Inc* (cf. Jones 1993). The one phenomenon it does not accord with well is European-style social corporatism. Stakeholdership is about empowerment and responsibility rather than collective security.

Champions of the postwar British welfare state used to proclaim the virtues of social solidarity and the pooling of risks, precisely because these were seen as being under threat once the unifying force of war had been removed (e.g. Titmuss 1950). Present-day Britain is being exhorted to go back to even more basic values in respect of individual, family and community responsibilities, which allegedly we once lived by but have, since the welfare state, too much forgotten. Everyone is entitled to a fair chance in life but, by the same token, they are expected to make the most of such opportunities as lawfully come their way, as well as to look after their own and make such contribution as they can to the life of their community. Crimes and misdemeanours should be properly punished and victims recompensed, ideally at the wrongdoer's expense. Families should be responsible for their dependants, young and old. "Communities" should strive to be self-sustaining both morally and materially.

The difficulty with this—much as it might appeal to alleged generations of voters and politicians, disillusioned and morally shaken by the extravagances of the welfare state—is that the Britain of near 2000 is not the same as the Britain of before the beginnings of the welfare state. There are key differences in point. Women count as relevant individuals to an extent not true of a hundred years ago. Concepts of the family have to acknowledge and take account of varieties of structure and relationship inconceivable for policy purposes a hundred years ago. Today's urban "communities" are a far cry from the needs-be-life-long street solidarities of a hundred years ago. Multi-ethnicity and multi-culturalism are no longer confined to the backstreets of a few city ports of entry. People are living longer and no one nowadays is supposed to starve or to die from an "everyday" disease or to be executed for committing an offence, however heinous. Life has become altogether more expensive and expansive and less susceptible to being run in accordance with a single, clear, uncompromising set of rules. So, for all the efforts of leading politicians to compete with one another on the morality stakes, former Prime Minister John Major's "back to basics" formulation could only ever give a moralistic gloss to Tony Blair's idea of the stakeholder society. It could not and cannot make it behave.

It is this atomized reality which separates stakeholdership, British-style, not merely from the in-built conformities of Japan or the engineered inclusivenesses of Singapore, but from continental European (e.g. French) notions of how to build social inclusion as a key to social cohesion. No matter how much "communitarianism" might appeal to Blair, for instance, as an ideal complement to the forces of stakeholdership, the makings for it—in the sense of interlocking, self-sustaining and self-policing social networks encompassing virtually the entire population and thus capable of providing that "normative foundation . . . culture and tradition, fellowship, and place for moral dialogue" prerequisite to the communitarian paradigm (Etzioni 1997: 257)—are patently missing from the scene.

British stakeholdership itself may *sound* inclusive and indeed be meant to be inclusive—to the extent governments can succeed in motivating every adult member of the population *to include themselves* in the national project. Nevertheless, the needs-be ideal is one of diversity in participation. Different sorts of people have different sorts of stakes in different sorts of ventures, with presumably differential prospects, different orders of risk and different rates of return attached to them. The underlying project has been to break down the "big battalions" of government, organized labour, owners and employers, not to build them up.

Hence the real revolution that has been taking place in the public sector of the one-time welfare state. Whether one dubs this "postmodern", "post-Fordist" or simply "post-big-government", the *new public management* of social policy has been hailed as one of the outstanding legacies of Thatcherism. In place of the monopolistic, professions-led, open-ended, "jobs for life" welfare state industry of the past has come the pluralistic, to an extent *anti* -professional, competitive, short-term contract and target-led managerialism of the present. So runs the rhetoric. Understandably, this was a harder pill for the Labour party to swallow than for post-Thatcherite Conservatism, but the signs are that the world of quasi-markets in a swirl of welfare pluralism has come to stay.

The object has been to make "stakeholders" of everyone involved in the delivery of social policy. In the language of the quasi-marketplace, they must be functioning either as competitive providers of services or else as dis-criminating purchasers; despite the fact that certain key staff will still have to be functioning as both. At the level of central government this has involved the "farming out" of what had hitherto been direct service responsibilities to "free-standing agencies" contracted to deliver services within specified

156

frameworks to specified target populations.[2] By the same token, local government—so comprehensively written off by Thatcherism as much for party-political as for any other sorts of reason (e.g. Kavanagh 1990: 286–8)—is increasingly being expected to commission agents to take on what had previously been its own work. For old-style statutory social services, read new-style *statutorily commissioned* social services; which by the same token require to be regulated, measured, inspected and "league-tabled" as never before.

Two points stand out from this scenario. First, it raises questions as to the role and status of professionals in the new order. Accountants might be in the ascendant, but the situation of "social professionals" such as teachers, social workers and to some extent doctors is looking increasingly exposed. More accountability to managers; more performance monitoring; more practice guidelines to be adhered to; more checks on "consumer satisfaction"; more league tables of "results": it is hard to see much of a future for professional autonomy here. How far are the likes of hospital consultants or head teachers or chief probation officers supposed also to be able to manage their respective "enterprises" to order—and what will it cost them if they can't? How far are they to be expected to serve both as expert providers and evaluators of their own and each others' performances? How far, in the case of GPs, probation officers and social workers, are they to be expected to operate as both providers and purchasers of treatment, and how might they be enabled or required to cover themselves against risks of failure on each or every count?

Second, the scenario raises questions as to the identity and status of social policy's recipients. Manifestly the "purchasers" of the new-public-management-speak are not always the end *users* of a particular service, any more than are the other interested parties likely to be consulted. There can be some distance between a policy/service decision, the form or extent of its implementation, and the final recipient. Both professionals and carers/minders tend to intervene. The implications of such potential triangular relationships have been best illustrated to date in respect of the elderly and disabled (Wilson 1994; Ungerson 1997; Morris 1997). Yet the message holds good for *any* recipient (voluntary or no) not deemed to be sufficiently informed, equipped, capable or willing to decide for themselves. Thus it is not just schoolchildren being decided for by their parents in consultation (it is to be hoped) with teachers, but "ordinary" patients being decided for by their GP's choice of hospital consultant, let alone "common criminals" being decided for by their probation officer's capabilities in court. Whereas, at the other end of the spectrum, market-led "reform" has seemingly left some of the most vulnerable in society to sort out such crucial items as "their own best personal pension" entirely for themselves (Klein and Millar 1995; Waine 1995). The language of empowerment raises questions as to who is being empowered, at whose expense; just as the language of purchasers and providers can leave ordinary people feeling out of the count.

Stakeholder Social Policies

Since these now consist as much of exhortations, regulations and prohibitions as of benefits in cash or kind, they are not best subsumed under the traditional banner heading of "social services". Not that the traditional *big five* policy sectors of social security, health care, education, housing and social care have gone away. Rather they have been repositioned and reinterpreted in accordance with a different set of priorities.

Employment and training

The postwar British welfare state was based on a presumption of full employment, which seemed for the first near twenty years of its existence to be well founded. So, unlike the high-profile social service sectors of health, education and social security, there was no serious attempt to refurbish employment and training services after the war and indeed, student textbooks on social policy scarcely made reference to employment or labour market issues or even to the state of the economy at all, before the end of the 1960s. Today the emphasis is quite reversed, with considerations as to the state and requirements of the economy prefacing virtually every social policy debate. Nevertheless, paradoxically or no, the provision of employment and training services has remained one of the least developed and least coherent policy sectors in Britain. Mrs Thatcher's great achievement in this sphere, it should be remembered, was not *what she did* for the unemployed, but rather that she convinced sufficient of the unemployed themselves that the assurance of full employment was no longer to be considered a responsibility or indeed capability of government.

True, there has been a series of shifts and stratagems continued by governments since the 1970s, in an effort to be seen to be doing something, notably for the young and for the long-term unemployed. But these have been efforts targeted more at the people concerned than at the state of the labour market. The adult unemployed may be eligible for a six-month Job Seeker's Allowance (in place of the hitherto *twelve-month* NI unemployment benefit or eligibility for Income Support), provided s/he can demonstrate at Interview that s/he is actively seeking and available for work and has signed an Agreement specifying the sorts of work being looked for and the steps to be taken (by both the individual and the Employment Service) to find it. The Labour government's "welfare to work" programme aims to target the under-25s with a choice of work (commercial), work (non-profit), education or training, "without a fifth option of life on full benefit"; whilst offering lone mothers whose youngest child has reached the second term of fulltime school, a proactive employment service "to develop a package of job search, training and after-school care to help them" (Department of Social Security 1997: 8). The stratagems are becoming ever more demanding.

Manifestly, these are policies more social than economic. It is the behaviour of categories of the non-employed which are implicitly being held up as the problem, rather than any underlying reasons for their predicament. Unemployed young people deprived of a chance to acquire habits of industry constitute not merely an expense but a moral hazard to society; as do the long-term unemployed whose families (where they have any) have perforce been learning to get by without "proper" support. The present penchant for varieties of "workfare" on both sides of the political divide rests not so much on its faint chances of saving money on the social security bill by obliging recipients to work for their money, as on the perceived consensual appeal of the idea that work *per se* is good for people, just as "getting something for nothing" is bad.

Education

This is mainstream social policy territory redefined. Education in the age of the postwar welfare state had notionally been about social reconstruction in the cause of a more egalitarian society, at the same time as about national manpower investment, at the same time as about equality of opportunity for all to make the most of their various talents. If the message had been a "best of all worlds" pot-pourri, no less confusing and patchwork had been the manner of its delivery; as "autonomous" LEAs of all shades of political affiliation strove to keep their own stamp on local school arrangements, despite such central initiatives as the attempt (the famous Circular 10/65) to impose comprehensive secondary education.

The 1988 Education Act reordered the education universe. It undermined the ability of LEAs to control the activities of what had hitherto been "their own" schools. It attempted to convince school managements and local parents (stakeholders all) that the future of *their* schools lay with them. Yet at the same time it reasserted the right of central government in principle to dictate not merely curriculum content but forms of assessment and even styles of teaching. In the drive to force an open, competitive and accountable system on what were seen to be recalcitrant professional and other vested interests, all were to be subjected to fresh mechanisms of inspection and control—in other words, cut down to market size.

When first introduced, these were radical moves indeed—the very stuff of Thatcherite confrontation. Whereas now, virtually the same agenda (plus a few additions and refinements) is being pursued along increasingly and unmistakeably "consensual" lines. Witness the 1997 election contest, as party leaderships vied with one another to demonstrate who could further the same transformation processes most efficiently, effectively and economically. Apart from in the most diehard of teaching and LEA circles, there is less and less objection to be heard to such ideas as budget management by schools, the retention of self-governing grant-maintained status for those schools which have opted for it, streaming children by ability, standardized pupil testing leading to published "league tables" of exam results school by school, or even standardized teacher assessment and retraining requirements capable of removing unsatisfactory teachers from post more "efficiently" (and speedily) than ever before. (See Stationery Office 1997, *Excellence in Schools*, for a comprehensive exposition of the latest thinking.)

Today's concerns centre more on the adequacy of the measures being taken than on the principles behind them. Witness Labour-inspired moves to refine the tables of exam results (hitherto such a Labour *bête noire*) by incorporating information about the "intake quality" of the children being recruited to the different types and locations of school, so as to give an indication of the value being added on, in order, ostensibly, to enable parents to make a more informed choice. If, after all this, the promise of parental choice of school remains more honoured in the breach than the observance for those unrealistic enough to dream of placing their child in an "impossibly popular" establishment, then at least the imposition of market and marketable values on the schools system as a whole, should ensure that all children benefit from the competition in the long run. Or rather it would, were it not for the fact that, since virtually all children have to attend school somewhere rather than nowhere, and since it takes time for even the most willing of schools to be able to respond to surges in demand, the sink schools of the system (those not actually taken out of it or taken over altogether by central government) will always be able to recruit. Poor people in poor neighbourhoods continue to end up poor "choosers" from sheer lack of choice.

Meanwhile, a further ground of debate continues around the question of how sufficient and appropriate is what is being taught and examined in state schools in any case. At one end of the scale, too many school-leavers are still exiting the system possessed of no formal qualifications whatsover. At the other end of the scale, seemingly unstoppable rates of improvement in GCSE, A level, university entrance and for that matter university degree results, continue to provoke suspicion as to the validity and reliability of the standards being applied over time. Yet finding answers in place of scapegoats remains difficult. Whatever the international evidence seeming to link levels of labour-force educational achievement to "ensuing" levels of economic performance, the British—certainly the English—have never seemed much good at transforming education/training into employability *per se*. Recent moves to devise ever more serious and relevant National Vocational Qualifications as a credible alternative to A Levels for the "vocationally minded", seem to have been more productive of jobs in the education/training industry than of so-called real jobs outside of it.

So what else might be hoped for? If the schools system is not to be looked on as a guaranteed route to employment or even employability, the least it should be doing, according to one prominent cross-party band of critics, is turning out decent law-abiding citizens. We may not all be successful but we can at least be good. Understandably, teachers tend to dispute the leading role assigned to them (as against "family" or "community") in this scenario, just as members of minority ethnic groups and/or religious persuasions object to the prospect of "majority values" being thrust upon them. The vacuousness of the National Forum for Values' first attempts (Autumn 1996) to distil "the prevailing consensus" into a single *Moral Code for Schools* (commissioned for government via the Schools Curriculum and Assessment Authority) is proof, if proof were needed, of the impracticability of this particular communitarian project.

Health care

Once again, this is traditional social policy with a difference. The National Health Service of Aneurin Bevan's dream was about affording everyone the care they needed, without question of payment at point of contact, to the very best standard the country could afford. Practical limitations apart, the actual NHS emerged as *the* flagship programme, symbolic to many of the spirit of the postwar welfare state: "socialized medicine" as American commentators were wont to describe it; simply the most popular social service ever, as British opinion polls were wont to confirm it.

Yet organizationally the NHS was makeshift from the start. Its so-called tripartite structure (hospitals administration; independent practitioners administration; municipal health services administration, in descending order of cost priority) was indicative of nothing so much as differences of status within the medical profession (from senior salaried hospital consultant via "freely contracting" general practitioner right down to local authority medical officer of health), as well as the fact that hitherto separate, albeit overlapping, systems of health care delivery had had to be slotted together at short notice on terms doctors could accept—which had meant largely at the expense of the municipal authorities.

The great and glorious goals of the NHS were to prove incapable of realization. Optimum health care according to need, without payment at point of contact, was doomed to be an escaping target in an age of conspicuously advancing medical science, not to mention of a conspicuously ageing and increasingly health-conscious population. Yet attempts to "reform" the NHS from the 1960s invariably focused on its organizational shortcomings as if, being so obvious (and attackable), these were somehow at the root of all its trouble.

Paradoxically, however, it was this same makeshift NHS which by way of consequence was possessed of the supreme attribute of being subject to central government budgetary control. Hence the NHS was eventually to prove not merely the battered darling of the British people, but the envy of cost-conscious governments panicked by "runaway" health care expenditures elsewhere. In short, the one attribute of the NHS of which its champions in Britain had been most resentful—the ability of any government of the day simply to resist demands for "sufficient" additional funding—had emerged in the eyes of others by the 1980s (not least in the British Treasury) as being its single greatest strength. Hence, even had public opinion permitted it, this biggest single public sector employer in Europe could not be scheduled for out-and-out privatization nor even for "demotion" to the form and status of a system of socialized health insurance. Instead, the object, as from 1990, has been to render this vast agglomeration of public sector activity into as-near-as-maybe a market unto itself, run by and for stakeholders in the guise of "purchasers" and "providers" in the service of patients who have formally been assured of their rights.

This then has been the project: one for which the organizational pluralisms of the NHS might have been thought well suited from the start. Hospitals have been prodded into forming themselves into self-governing trusts for the purpose of competing for business (as "providers") from the likes of "purchasers" such as GP group practices (to the extent these have opted for fundholding status) or local health authorities (in respect of everyone and everything else). The money is supposed to follow the patient, at any rate in the case of fundholding GPs, who are notionally supposed to ascertain the patient's preferences and/or act on the patient's best behalf, in exploring all the possibilities for treatment prior to recommending a particular "purchase" or choice of purchases. Meanwhile, GP practices themselves are supposed to be free to compete for patients; not least by advertising for them (albeit discreetly) and by offering additional services, such as minor routine surgery, over and above those that all practices are nowadays obliged to provide under the terms of the Patients' Charter.

The year 1990 had thus inaugurated not one great "reform" so much as a conglomeration of would-be reform processes, each capable of developing its own momentum and of impinging on other aspects or areas of the NHS in ways quite impossible even now to predict or fully measure. From the perspective of stakeholdership, however, two lines of development—or arguably *non*-development—stand out.

First, there are the ramifications of the alleged shift of power away from the one-time omnipotent consultant to today's "play-making" GP. Much has been remarked about the inequities which it was presumed must result from the introduction of even a *quasi*-market into what had hitherto been the "cost-disregarding" culture of the NHS. If the introduction of GP fundholding meant that some practices were liable to be more successful than others in purchasing best possible treatment for their patients, then other GPs' patients (especially those in non-fundholding practices) must, by implication, lose out. There was even fear that the introduction of budget-holding responsibility would "force" competitive practices into turning away potentially expensive (e.g. already elderly) new patients; just as there was also fear that the vagaries of GP preference, once untrammelled by district health authority block bookings, could place entire hospital specialisms at risk, in favour of more attractive deals to be obtained elsewhere.

Results to date would seem to have been less dire than at first predicted by those, not least in the Labour party, gut-conditioned to leap to the NHS's defence. Certainly there have been outrages over hospital and ward closures, underfunding in general and the denial of expensive treatments to hard cases in particular. But these are hardly matters new to the history of the NHS and, short of dreams of unlimited funding all round, it is hard to estimate just how many of them might have been avoided (as against conceivably rendered less visible) had the NHS not had an internal market thrust upon it. Inequities of treatment (certainly of waiting times) as between patients of more—as against less—"successful" GP practices may be little more than an open version of inequities taken for granted hitherto, courtesy of the old-boy network and the fact that some GPs were and remain smarter operators with better contact networks than others. Certainly, aside from the fabled class of grey-suited hospital managers, the chief gainers in all of this have been the GPs—no longer mere gatekeepers but veritable linchpins of the revamped system—at the notable expense of the consultants. Indeed, it was the growing satisfaction expressed by fundholding GPs which seemingly obliged not merely the BMA but the leadership of the Labour party and hence the present government, to tone down their hitherto out-and-out opposition to the changes. But it remains to be seen how far the promised drive to cut down on "excessive paperwork" might alter the workings of the system yet again, "once pound notes cease to be attached to individual transactions".[3]

Second, and much harder to estimate, is the balance of benefit or otherwise to the proverbial patient consumer, in the light of whose preferences treatments are now supposed to be negotiated, and in the path of whose footprints the money is supposed to flow. The literature on British doctor –patient relationships is replete with information to the effect that a patient's ability (or wish) to communicate with a doctor (let alone that of a doctor to communicate with a patient) on anything approaching a quasi-market business basis, will be conditioned both ways by such factors as age, sex, level of education, social class and family status, quite apart from any particularities or special considerations arising from the patient's actual medical condition.

On balance, latest evidence would seem to suggest, unsurprisingly, that most patients still do not see themselves as anywhere near on a par with their GP and are just as reluctant, therefore, to take responsibility for mapping the course of their own treatment as is their GP to encourage them to do so. Nevertheless, a minority of patients will presumably be doing better for themselves and their families, if not by actually shopping around, then at least by reading the small print of the Patients' Charter and insisting on value for their (taxpayer's) money. Furthermore, the same sorts of people are likely to have access to private medical insurance cover and so to be in a position to take advantage of the very best mix of services the current "cash-starved" NHS, working in conjunction with the private sector (in respect of "two-way" consultancy arrangements as well as of the positioning of private beds in NHS hospitals), may be able to offer. The possibility of charges being introduced for certain services within the NHS itself adds further to the prospect of there being a widening gap between the more successful and the less successful categories of patient; which persistent regional and district inequalities in standards of provision will continue to reinforce.

Social care

Where medical needs overlap with social care requirements—as is so often the case—families constitute the first resort; as they always have, with or without insistence from the state. The tradition of regarding social work as essentially a supplement to or substitute for family care in times of stress, dates back to the Charity Organization Society's first essays of a hundred years ago. Social work has come a long way since then, whereas the family has arguably been on the retreat. *Every* venture in collective social provision can be portrayed as having subtracted from family responsibilities; for all that few would nowadays wish to see the likes of education, health care, housing and social security reduced entirely to whatever families could fix up for themselves. However, the current emphasis on "back to the family" in respect of social care, would seem to be focused on the very sorts of families whose predicaments and prospects render them least liable to be able to cope.

This is not simply a case of assuming that households resident in deprived areas—and especially in "sink" housing estates—will consist disproportionately of lone-parent families and/or families "on benefit". Modern varieties of family tend to look less functional, from a social caring point of view, right across the socio-economic spectrum. The vulnerabilities of the elongated family (fewer children and longer-lived elderly) have been compounded as much by geographic mobility and the movement of women into the labour market as by the consequences of higher rates of divorced, remarried and unmarried—to say nothing of unemployed—parenthood. Nevertheless, the sorry saga of the Child Support Agency constitutes a lesson not merely in how *not* to implement a novel and contentious piece of legislation but in how difficult and morally questionable it can be to try to impose "family responsibilities" on families who don't fit the bill (see e.g. Clark *et al.* 1995).

Nor does the next line of social care resort, voluntary action, necessarily offer much of an answer. "Traditional" voluntary action (e.g. of the Victorian great name variety) took time, money, commitment, social confidence (on the one side) and social acceptance (on the other) based notionally on a shared set of norms and values. Today's society is ostensibly much less hierarchical, less deferential, certainly less "mono-cultural" and above all less possessed of a reserve army of well-brought-up potential volunteers (women especially) with time on their hands and the acquired social conscience once so characteristic of their social position. Today's voluntary action, furthermore, has to operate not merely in the wake of such momentous (and ongoing) social upheavals, but in the wake also of a welfare state which had been committed, precisely, to promoting the role and responsibilities of the state on the grounds of its superiority—both moral and practical—to whatever voluntary action could effect.

It was not until the welfare state unease of the 1970s that the voluntary sector was again to command serious social policy attention (see e.g. Wolfenden 1978); and it was only from the 1980s that the language of voluntary-statutory "partnership" was to come back into fashion. Since then, however, and especially since the passage of the 1990 Health Service and Community Care Act (implemented from 1993 in respect of community care), the object has been to tap much more systematically into voluntary and volunteer "sectors", together with other private and commercial care sectors, in an effort to obtain not merely better value for money on the state's behalf but ostensibly a better range and variety of services for the user and/or his/her advisers to choose from. But, if it was the imposition of an internal market on the NHS which made headline news, the repercussions of this further venture into marketization have been no less far-reaching.

The idea of public authorities subsidizing the activities of voluntary groups was hardly new. Very few voluntary organizations had proved capable of functioning entirely independently of the public sector in the welfare state, however uneasy they might have been about accepting its "money with strings". But today's "contracts culture" is of a different order. In place of the annual local authority block grant in support of its activities (however implicitly conditional on "good performance"), service-delivering organ-izations—whether of the *non*-profit or *for*-profit variety—are now supposed to compete for contracts specifying precisely what is to be provided, to what standard, for how many, at what cost, over what period; and thence, if selected, to deliver accordingly.

To many, the very prospect seemed to spell the end of the voluntary sector as they had known it. Less formal groups wondered how they were to continue to attract volunteers once job descriptions were so firmly laid down and the scope for experiment reduced to the status of an un-paid-for activity. Larger organizations expected (accurately as it now seems) that they would have increasingly to ape the private (for-profit) sector in the competition for business and thus to become ever less distinguishable from it. Taken in conjunction with the equally novel prospect of having to compete before a committee of the great-and-good for a share of the take from the National Lottery at the literal expense of raising their own gifted money from the public, this was a new world order indeed.

Yet earliest evidence suggests that the sky has not so far fallen in (see e.g. Deakin 1996). Local markets in care do not materialize from nowhere, so it is scarcely surprising to find that care purchasers have tended more often than not to turn to those with whom they have had dealings before. Equally, it is not surprising to find that most voluntary organizations hitherto in receipt of some form of public funding tend, if only from want of competition, to be in receipt of it still, albeit on ostensibly different terms. Even so, it would be unnatural if some organizations were not inclined to play more safely than before, now that they are expected to account so much more specifically for what they have and have not achieved.

No less dramatic, meanwhile, has been the transformation effected with regard to local authority departments of social service. The only terms on which an originally Thatcherite administration could be persuaded to channel money for community social care via local authorities had been to make it clear that their function was henceforth to be primarily one of *enablement* via the commissioning and purchasing of care from *other* providers of services. The most conspicuous losers in this context have thus been local authority-employed social workers.

Of all the welfare state's professions, social work has been the one most firmly associated in the public mind with the worst excesses and shortcomings of statutory welfare as was. This is ironic, since at the institution of the postwar welfare state there was doubt over how far such a brave universalistic system could or should be in need of something so demeaning as personalized social work, save in respect of particular vulnerable groups (notably children at risk). Thereafter, however, it was the very shortcomings of mainstream statutory welfare which ensured an increasing demand for social work, if only to help pick up the casualties and keep the welfare state show on the road.

Unsurprisingly, this proved a thankless task. The efforts of the 1960s through the 1970s to build "generic" social work into a single recognized profession served if anything to concentrate its unpopularity. The scandal-ridden years of the 1970s and 1980s showed social workers being blamed both for failures to intervene *and* for officious excesses of intervention. Systems of social worker education/training have accordingly been subjected to perennial demands (and programmes) for review in the cause of "practical common sense" and in repudiation of "excessive theorizing". At the last, social workers employed by local authorities have been instructed that they are no longer to engage in caring themselves, to the extent they can commission others to do it on a more cost/care-effective basis.

So where does this leave their would-be clientele? Whoever else "markets in community care" are supposed to serve the interests of, they cannot at present, save by patronizing presumption, be deemed first and foremost to be serving the interests of the end user. This is not to attribute fresh shades of unfeeling to service "purchasers" or "providers". It is merely to note that those on the receiving end may already have been conditioned into not expecting too much—and into not making too much fuss for those they have to rely on for such help as they can get. If, in such circumstances, harassed social workers tend to prescribe care packages more attuned to the availability of commissionable resources than to the supposed needs, let alone stated preferences, of the "consumer" ("*Have* I been assessed? *When* was I assessed?"), this can be difficult to prove and even more difficult to protest about without some fear of repercussion. Notions of stakeholdership can seem of little relevance here.

Housing

Possession of a stake in the form of a vote used to depend on the possession of a form of property, most obviously (in the case of the urban classes) a house. Subsequent extensions to the franchise whittled away at this qualification at the same time as path-breaking public health legislation sought—in the interests of all—to mitigate the worst of popular housing conditions. The year 1919 saw the famous "homes fit for heroes" promise heralding the introduction of council housing as a central government-subsidized, local authority-run form of tenure for working-class people capable of paying a reasonable non-profit rent. Yet, for all the advances made in quality and quantity of council housing erected from the 1920s through to the 1960s (apart from the horrors of the worst tower blocks), the provision of housing *per se* was never recognized as a unquestioned core function of the welfare state.

On the contrary, it was the very institution of council housing which enabled Margaret Thatcher to kick-start her campaign for a "property-owning democracy" by the simple but winning expedient of selling off the best of the existing council stock at knock-down prices to its eager sitting tenants. It was a masterly achievement. At one stroke the Labour party was wrong-footed, entire ward voting patterns were set at risk and the race to convert as high a proportion of the population as possible to the virtues of home ownership was on. Not until the end of the 1980s and the collapse of the house-price boom did the limitations of this pursuit begin to make themselves felt, not least in the figures for mortgage default and property repossession. Today's apparent recovery in the housing market is not, we are assured by experts of every shade of political and propertied opinion, to be regarded as *in any way* a return to the nirvana of the 1980s.

Meanwhile, council housing has not gone away. Too much of it had proved unsaleable, on the one hand; and too many people were continuing to report as being in need of council accommodation, on the other. So the situation within England and Wales has been coming to seem ever closer to that of the USA; whereby council housing, far from being the mainstream equivalent of continental European social housing it once was, now represents a last-resort provision for poor people with problems. Attempts in the meantime to invigorate independent non-profit forms of provision, via existing and new housing associations, under the auspices of the Housing Corporation (another free-standing public agency contracted to deliver results), seem destined to achieve at best a modest outcome; for the same reason that attempts to invigorate the commercial private rental sector at this end of the market have tended to fall by the wayside. The provision of accommodation of an acceptable modern standard costs more for builders to build (or to renovate) and property owners to operate, than many households can afford to pay for without help. A cash-starved, tax-frozen public sector can thus, in this context, spell at best a proliferation of housing ghettoes (public, semi-public, private) for the poor.

Not that this constitutes the whole of the "housing problem". Just as housing conditions can feed into all manner of other societal concerns, so can all manner of societal concerns end up looking like a housing—or in this case a *lack* of housing—problem. Today's homeless, however defined, are not simply or even primarily to be supposed a "housing" category. Rather they are an assemblage, more visible if not more numerous than ever before, of today's losers. Their problem is not typically lack of accommodation *per se*, since there is usually *some form* of accommodation notionally on offer. Rather their predicaments range right across the spectrum of needs already discussed, compounded by the fact that without a bona fide address it can be hard to lay claim to anything else. In a society of stakeholders they have no stake.

Social security

So we come last to what would typically have ranked first in any social policy review of ten years ago. To be sure, the size of the social security *bill* continues to rank first in social spending terms; yet its significance for policy purposes seems now as much to do with how to cope with the legacy of the past as how to handle the needs of the present. Which is in itself a portent for the future. Stakeholders are going more and more to have to provide for themselves.

Short-term benefits, whether means-tested or contributions-based, have never represented the same order of hazard for governments as benefits of a longer-term pensions variety, simply because it is easier to change the rules and get away with it in the case of the former than in the case of entitlements "deservingly" built up for the future over a protracted period (no matter how unmanageable the latter may seem to have become). The unemployed have seen their entitlements pruned with seeming impunity by successive administrations to an extent the present beneficiaries of the still youthful but potentially far more "burdensome" State Earnings Related Pension Scheme (SERPS) have not and will not. Instead we can expect a determination on both sides of the party-political divide to ensure that, from now on, in the context not merely of an ageing population but an increasing "very elderly" population, more and more people will not merely be encouraged but expected to take out long-term cover for themselves.

Meanwhile, the intermediate problem is essentially simple, but nevertheless intractable. People who are or have been employed in mainstream, quality, opt-out occupations may rest assured of their income-related disability/ pensions cover, over and above their entitlement to base-level benefits from

167

the state. People not so employed in quality opt-out occupations and hitherto reliant on SERPS have been encourged, in the wake of efforts (1986) to downgrade SERPS itself, to take out private pension plans of their own. Many of them have done so to ill-effect, given that these have tended to be precisely the sorts of people with earnings patterns private pensions providers could least satisfactorily provide for (Waine 1995). Yet aside from requiring pensions contractors to compensate those worst offended against, this has not and will not be seen as a direct responsibility of government, for all the arguable culpability of the original advice.

Meanwhile the interest in social security's "shortest-term consumers" continues more moral than economic. In the words of Frank Field, minister of state for social security and welfare reform:

> Welfare does not operate in a social vacuum. It influences character for good or ill. Because of the growing dominance of means tests, welfare increasingly acts destructively, penalizing effort, attacking savings and taxing honesty. The traditional cry that means tests stigmatize is now a minor issue . . . Means tests are steadily recruiting a nation of cheats and liars. (Field 1996: 11).

So much for the efficacy of targeting. In future, *everyone* is going to be expected to pay up and play the game—in so far as they can be made to.

Crime and crime prevention

In the light of the above, we arrive at the question of what a stakeholder society can hope to do about its *non-* and *anti-*stakeholders. Keep them out (in the case of economic migrants and suspect asylum seekers), police-cordon them in (in the case of problem housing estates) and/or lock them up (in the case of persistent malingerers, burglars and muggers)? This may seem a parody of the most extreme expressions of right-wing authoritarianism, yet it points the direction in which policy has been moving, not merely as championed by one combative former Home Secretary (Michael Howard), but as implicitly endorsed by the needs-be law-and-order aspirations of both party leaderships. No one with claims to political seriousness can nowadays afford to look soft on crime, no matter how many reservations they may entertain about the causes of it—or indeed about the efficacy of locking up so many varieties of criminal (from debt defaulters to drug-addicted petty thieves) for so much time at the public's expense.

Probation looks out of fashion, save maybe to the extent it can be rendered more militaristic, simplistic and punitive in style. Community security orders are likewise out of fashion if only because they *seem* soft, irrespective of content or even proven results. By contrast, the promise of "fast track punishment" for young offenders (cf. the "short sharp shocks" of yore) and of mandatory (i.e. longer) prison sentences for specified adult offenders look distinctly *in* fashion, irrespective of their respective chances of delivering "results". Bona-fide stakeholders are not expected to be much interested in results, beyond seeing to it that stake robbers and snatchers are put out of harm's way for as long as possible, as punishment to them and deterrence to others.

Nevertheless, a major practical problem for the new order has arisen from the shortage of sufficient suitable (e.g. not in police cells) prison space. With the best will in the world, it has proved impossible to construct new prisons—even private or privatizable prisons—fast enough to keep up with escalating demand. Witness therefore Michael Howard's enterprising plan, since taken over by Labour's Jack Straw, to commission a prison ship for Portland harbour in an effort to ease the shortfall for the time being. Naturally this has not gone down well with the local tourist industry any more than with local residents. But it is hard to see how any British administration is going to find it worthwhile even to try to "roll back" the lock-em-up tendency in the short to medium term. Stakeholders want to feel safe with their stakes.

So, for the sake of completeness and consistency, we may look forward to a further milestone in the history of stakeholdership: the dawn of the fully-privatized, competitive, pluralistic prison service, whereby prisoners mandatorily sentenced to specified categories or periods of incarceration might be expected, encouraged and up to a point *enabled*, to seek it out and pay for it themselves, either at the time or even in advance, by way of an investment.

Conclusion

If Thatcherism was about dismantling the culture of the welfare state, stakeholdership is about trying to put something in its place: a culture of incentives and disincentives capable of shaping behaviour in ways to benefit each and everyone together: social policy for profit and profitability. It is almost uilitarianism rediscovered.

Unfortunately, just as utilitarianism turned out to be less practical than its proponents had presumed, so too might stakeholdership. It also makes little allowance for the implications of, in modern parlance, social exclusion.[4] Nor, for all the post-1970s nostrums about the burdens of welfare on the economy, and for all the wealth of related literature since about the apparent relationships between types of welfare spending and economic performance (notably Pfaller *et al.* 1991), has there emerged any surefire formulation for making social policy programmes self-financing let alone mutually profitable at a national level. The language of stakeholdership has thus to be a language of winners and losers, not just winners. So how many losers might there be, and who is to be held accountable for their losses?

For that matter, how many *winners* are there likely to be? This remains unknown territory, which is why, in political terms, stakeholder social policy is as much about covering for the retreat as preparing for an advance. To the extent we are all deemed responsible for the state we are in, we cannot be blaming politicians too much for the mess. Only politicians who make rash promises (as against threats of maybe worse to come) are liable to be called to account; as Labour's Blair/Brown partnership has been quick to appreciate.

The gift relationship is gone. Stakeholders want bargains not presents; freehold rather than leasehold) as proof against theft, fraud and assault as can possibly be contrived. This may be a recipe for prosperity for some, even most.

What it cannot be is a recipe for crime prevention. Those without stakes or *sufficient* stakes in a world where stakes are everything will not simply go away.

Notes

1. It was in a speech to the Singapore Business Community (8 January 1996) that Blair first used the expression "stakeholder" with reference to the economy (Blair 1996).
2. An idea which could all too easily backfire when coupled with the introduction of a radical new policy also: witness the wretched record of the Child Support Agency (see p. 164, below).
3. Personal communication.
4. Cf. Karl Marx on Jeremy Bentham: "Bentham is a purely English phenomenon . . . With the dryest naivete he takes the modern shopkeeper, especially the English shopkeeper, as the normal man. Whatever is useful to this queer normal man, and to his world, is absolutely useful . . . Had I the courage of my friend Heinrich Heine, I should call Mr Jeremy a genius in the way of bourgeois stupidity" (Marx 1952: 301).

References

Blair, A. (1996), *New Britain: My Vision of a Young Country* (special selection from *New Statesman*), Fourth Estate: London.

Clarke, K., Craig, G., and Glendinning C. (1995), Money isn't everything: fiscal policy and family policy in the Child Support Act, *Social Policy & Administration*, 29.I: 26–39.

Deakin, N. (1996), *Meeting the Challenge of Change*, Report of the Independent Commission on the Future of the Voluntary Sector in England, NCVO: London.

Department of Social Security (1997), *The Quarterly*, issue no. 23, DSS: London.

Etzioni, A. (1997);, *The New Golden Rule: Community and Morality in a Democratic Society*, Profile Books: London.

Field, F. (1996), *Stakeholder Welfare*, Institute of Economic Affairs: London.

Jones, C. (1993), The Pacific challenge: Confucian welfare states, in *New Perspectives on the Welfare State in Europe*, ed. C. Jones, Routledge: London; pp. 198–217.

Kavanagh, D. (1990), *Thatcherism and British Politics: The End of Consensus?*, 2nd edn, Oxford University Press: Oxford.

Klein, R., and Millar, J. (1995), Do-it-yourself social policy: searching for a new paradigm?, *Social Policy & Administration*, 29.4: 303–16.

Marx, K. (1952), *Capital*, republished in the series "Great Books of the Western World" ed. Robert Maynard Hutchins for Encyclopaedia Britannica Inc., William Benton: Chicago, London, Toronto.

Morris, J. (1997), Care or empowerment: a disability rights perspective, *Social Policy & Administration*, 31.1: 54–60.

Pfaller, A., Gough, I., and Therborn, G. (1991), *Can the Welfare State Compete?*, Macmillan: Basingstoke.

Stationery Office (1997), *Excellence in Schools*, Cm. 3681, Stationery Office: London.

Titmuss, R. M. (1950), *Problems of Social Policy*, Stationery Office: London.

Ungerson, C. (1997), Give them the money: is cash a route to empowerment?, *Social Policy & Adminstration*, 31.1: 45–53.

Waine, B. (1995), A disaster foretold? the case of the personal pension, *Social Policy & Administration*, 29.4: 317–34.

Wilson, G. (1994), Co-production and self-care: new approaches to managing community care services for older people, *Social Policy & Administration*, 28.3: 236–50.

Wolfenden, J. (1978), *The Future of Voluntary Organizations*, Croom Helm: London.

Index

declining role of 65–6
equal opportunities and 84
Stewart, G. 101, 102
Stewart, J. 101, 102
surveillance 150

Tawney, R. H. 83
Taylor, M. 30–1
training, policies for in UK 158
transportation 118, 119–20
    to Andaman Islands 123
    to Australia 120–3
    of children and women 121
    from France 123–4
    to Siberia 124–6
Treadway Commission 11
Trollope, Anthony 122

unemployment 30
    linked with crime 17–18
    and social exclusion 100–1
United Kingdom, youth justice and
    crime prevention in 42–3, 45–6,
    47
United States of America 4–7
    criminal policy in 118–19, 130–2
    institutional infrastructure 41, 42
    social isolation in 53
urban regeneration 18

Vanstone, M. 105

victimization 24, 39, 70
victims, support for 19
violent crime 18
voluntary action, in social care 164–5

Wacquart, L. 42
Wagner, P. 65
Walmsley, R. 25
Webb, S. 89
welfare to work 158–9
Wilding, P. 91
Wilson, W. J. 40, 41
women
    discrimination against in criminal
        justice system 93n1
    transportation of 121
Women's College 15

young people 38, 39, 42, 63, 70
    and citizenship 61, 62, 66–7
    detached work with 73–4
    in labour market 38, 67–8
    in Singapore 144
youth justice, crime prevention and
    42–4, 48–9
youth market 63
Youth Service 63, 64, 71, 72–3, 74–5
youth work
    in late modernity 71–5
    in modernity 61–4

zero tolerance 109